Feb

Gary,

Enjoy

Doc was a great

supporter of the game

from GrassRoots to NHL.

Best Regards

STAYING IN THE GAME

STAYING IN THE GAME

~

The Remarkable Story of Doc Seaman

By Sydney Sharpe

Foreword by the Honourable Peter Lougheed

DUNDURN PRESS
TORONTO

Copy-editor: Barry Jowett
Design: Jennifer Scott
Jacket Layout: Erin Mallory

Library and Archives Canada Cataloguing in Publication

Sharpe, Sydney
      Staying in the game : the remarkable story of Doc Seaman / by Sydney Sharpe.

Includes bibliographical references and index.
ISBN 978-1-55002-881-2

1. Seaman, Daryl K. 2. Bow Valley Industries Limited--Biography. 3. Calgary Flames (Hockey team)--Biography. 4. Canada. Royal Canadian Air Force--Biography. 5. Businessmen--Canada--Biography. 6. Industrialists--Canada--Biography. 7. Calgary (Alta.)--Biography. I. Title.

HC112.5.S38S46 2008   338.092   C2008-904873-3

1   2   3   4   5   12   11   10   09   08

Conseil des Arts
du Canada

Canada Council
for the Arts

ONTARIO ARTS COUNCIL
CONSEIL DES ARTS DE L'ONTARIO

We acknowledge the support of the **Canada Council for the Arts** and the **Ontario Arts Council** for our publishing program. We also acknowledge the financial support of the **Government of Canada** through the **Book Publishing Industry Development Program** and **The Association for the Export of Canadian Books**, and the **Government of Ontario** through the **Ontario Book Publishers Tax Credit** program and the **Ontario Media Development Corporation**.

Care has been taken to trace the ownership of copyright material used in this book. The author and the publisher welcome any information enabling them to rectify any references or credits in subsequent editions.

J. Kirk Howard, President

Unless otherwise noted, all images are courtesy of Doc Seaman's personal collection.

Printed and bound in Canada by Friesens.
www.dundurn.com

Dundurn Press
3 Church Street, Suite 500
Toronto, Ontario, Canada
M5E 1M2

Gazelle Book Services Limited
White Cross Mills
High Town, Lancaster, England
LA1 4XS

Dundurn Press
2250 Military Road
Tonawanda, NY U.S.A.
14150

Contents

FOREWORD

by The Honourable Peter Lougheed

Although I already had worked with Doc Seaman, I had no idea why he wanted to see me at the Premier's Office in Edmonton one day in 1980. He brought the most brilliant idea for gathering up into one package: the 1988 Olympic Winter Games, an NHL team, a hockey arena for both, and long-term funding for amateur sports. This was a remarkable initiative. Like all of Doc's community ideas, this one wasn't designed to make him any money. Rather, it was just another way he'd found to donate his own.

I was delighted because the plan made such elegant sense. We wanted to help the 1988 Winter Olympics by building a coliseum, and here was the best reason of all walking though my door. Still, I wasn't surprised. Doc's elaborate, ingenious plan was typical of his business life. For decades he built companies through sound but creative planning; so often, and so successfully, that over the years I've come to believe Doc is a kind of organizational and motivational genius. Luckily for Canada, though, he was always interested in much more than making money for himself. Indeed, I don't think that was ever his motivation at all. For decades he has also worked outside the business sphere, using his remarkable talents to better his community and his country. Yet he has done this so quietly that his name is relatively unknown to the general public.

Doc was one of the major creators of the oil and gas industry in Canada. As this book vividly shows, that was never as easy as many Canadians believe. Early Canadian companies were often stymied by the dominance of the international oil giants, the reluctance of Canadian banks to lend them money, and regulations that favoured the big players. My government removed some of these barriers in Alberta after we took office in 1971. But without players like Doc, who took enormous calculated risks, a strong Canadian industry would not have emerged. And he was behind one of the greatest of all the success stories, the creation of Bow Valley Industries, a legendary company propelled onto the international stage by the force of Doc Seaman's will and talent.

I admire Doc for all this; most of all, though, I admire his values. A child of the prairie Depression, he grew up with poverty all around him. In some this bred contempt for the poor; but in Doc, the dreadful slow march of the unemployed created a powerful desire to help. What people needed most was work, so Doc dreamed of creating jobs. He took his dream through World War II, where he served with great distinction, and brought it back whole to Alberta's oil patch. He created dignified work for thousands. Before long he was involved in many philanthropic ventures, from medical research to the economic betterment of aboriginal people.

It's no accident, perhaps, that Doc was raised in Saskatchewan and moved to Alberta. Something remarkable happens when the energy and values of the two provinces meet and merge. The combination often produces an outpouring of creativity unique in Canada. This ethic of self-reliance, combined with selfless giving, must not be lost to the country. Perhaps Doc's story will help encourage it in others.

I'm very fortunate, more than two decades after leaving government, to lead a very active life of travel and work. But one of the highlights is the annual trip my wife Jeanne and I take to Doc's remarkable OH Ranch, where I ride and enjoy a world so pure and beautiful that it's impossible to describe without emotion.

Doc plans to preserve it in its original working state, with native grasses and water sources intact, for the enjoyment of the people of Canada. That is entirely typical of Doc Seaman, thank heavens. His story, well told here, should make its way proudly across the country.

INTRODUCTION

Nation Builder

American author and broadcaster Tom Brokaw called the American veterans of the Second World War "The Greatest Generation." They sacrificed in war and won the freedom the next generation too soon took for granted. They were a generation that loved deeply and gave generously, but as individuals, they often kept their emotions embedded within.

Canadian authors have perhaps not spent enough time and words on our own greatest generation who endured the Great Depression, courageously fought in the Second World War and emerged to build modern Canada. The story of one of them, Daryl Kenneth "Doc" Seaman, illuminates all the best qualities of the veterans who became nation builders: generosity, love of country, and self-reliance. These men and women wanted to do things, not have things done for them. They exemplified the virtues that shaped modern Canada.

Born in Rouleau, Saskatchewan, now best known as the scene of television's *Corner Gas*, Doc Seaman grew up in hardscrabble times. He knew risk from his early years riding a steel-tracked Caterpillar alone in the darkness of the prairie with lightning snapping across the horizon. After the Second World War broke out, a teenaged Doc joined the Royal Canadian Air Force (RCAF), piloting a Hudson bomber, ducking German Junkers and Messerschmitts, and climbing to the clouds to stay alive. He flew an extremely rare total of eighty-two sorties, once limping back to base with a dead radioman behind him, his own shattered leg tied to the rudder, his crew's lives riding on his uncertain ability to stay conscious.

Having witnessed the devastation of the Depression, Doc's main goal was to create jobs for other people. Seeing the horror of war, he vowed to make a difference in honour of all those who didn't return.

Doc and his brothers, B.J. and Don, made their mark in Alberta's burgeoning oil and gas industry, where Doc turned his meagre war savings into a tiny drilling company. His $6,000 investment grew into Bow Valley Industries, a global energy powerhouse that, at its height, was the top trader on the American Stock Exchange. Doc risked his very existence on frontiers within and beyond Canada, discovering huge reserves off Newfoundland's Grand Banks, in Europe's North Sea, and on Indonesia's island of Sumatra.

Against many odds (some imposed by his own country), Doc became one of the creators of a great Canadian industry. His perseverance and adaptability were astonishing. Peter C. Newman, in his book *Titans*, called Doc "The Totem of the Titans."[1] In 1994, Talisman Energy bought Bow Valley's oil and gas assets and continues to exploit those discoveries.

Doc's interests are extremely varied. He became a member of the Macdonald Commission, which recommended the North American Free Trade Agreement, and was one of those who urged Finance Minister Michael Wilson to adopt free trade.

Doc is a mentor to a legion of Canadian entrepreneurs who respect his integrity and his ability to drive a hard but fair bargain. Over time Doc built companies that produced thousands of jobs and provided funds for his many philanthropies, from medical science to social well-being to community sports. He also champions aboriginal economic development through First Nations' training programs and partnerships in the oil and gas drilling business.

Doc was the key player in bringing the Flames to Calgary. With a National Hockey League franchise, Calgary was able to build the Saddledome, a centrepiece of the city's successful bid for the 1988 Winter Olympics.

He played a large role in rescuing Canadian amateur hockey from growing mediocrity, sending Canadian teams back to medal podiums at the Olympics and World Championships. Canada's world junior hockey wins have their roots in Project 75, now called the Seaman-Hotchkiss Hockey Foundation.

Doc also saved a huge chunk of southern Alberta ranching land from environmental ruin when the Canadian military wanted it for training operations. The historic OH Ranch spans the foothills nestled just below the eastern slopes of the Alberta Rockies, some of the most beautiful country on earth. Doc intends to conserve the working ranch for the people of Alberta and all of Canada as a living example of our national heritage.

There was a rare moment in Doc's life when he thought he might retire. Yet he became busier than ever, fuelled by the conviction that boredom kills. His current mission is to convince Canadians to stay active, to never quit, and to give back to the community. New research shows he's right: active, useful people really do live longer and enjoy themselves more.

Doc Seaman is one of the last of the breed of post-war entrepreneurs who make deals on a handshake. The integrity of these Depression-bred leaders is deep and powerful. Sadly, it is sometimes lacking in their modern successors.

This is Doc Seaman's story, a remarkable saga of courage, resolve, struggle, disappointment, and success. It leads down surprising and fascinating roads, and ultimately leaves us with a deeper understanding not just of one iconic figure but of the country itself.

PART ONE

~

The Early Years

CHAPTER ONE

The Rouleau Kid

"ACT AS IF WHAT YOU DO MAKES A DIFFERENCE. IT DOES."
— WILLIAM JAMES

M any people drift through life; others are purposeful from youth, often because an early experience suddenly illuminates the path before them. Those people — whether more insightful or simply more fortunate — often go on to achieve great things.

Daryl Kenneth "Doc" Seaman remembers his moment, the sight that began to fix his life's work in his mind. It would forever shape his view of the world and the goals he set for himself and others.

Doc was a boy of fourteen in his hometown of Rouleau, Saskatchewan, a tiny community between Moose Jaw and Regina, when the Depression reached its bleak nadir in the mid-1930s. On his rounds about the town after school, he could hardly miss one of the saddest sights in Canadian history, a pageant of misery spreading like slow poison along rail lines across the Prairies.

"We had men come through Rouleau on freight cars, looking for work," Doc recalls. "Some hung out around the tracks for weeks. We got to know them. They had finished high school or university and hit the rails looking for jobs, only to find no work. You could see the desperation of those young guys. No matter how ambitious they were, there were just no opportunities for them."

Things weren't much better for the Seaman family, but they were a tight-knit southern Saskatchewan crew that survived difficult times through hard work and unity. And they had food on the table, at least.

So the boy went home and raided the pantry.

"I felt sorry for them, I guess," Doc remembers, peering more than seventy years into the past. "We had a big garden, and my mother always canned a lot — vegetables and fruit, and also chicken and beef. I would take the odd one of those from the pantry and give it to the young guys down by the tracks."

Among Canadians who still enjoyed some security, the Depression spawned two main types: the scornful, spiteful hoarders and the big-hearted givers. Doc showed in those days that he was part of the admirable second group. So were his parents, Byron Luther and Letha Mae Seaman, who surely knew about his "thefts" but never said a word.

The boy's thoughts were already taking him far beyond simple charity. He could see that even though the rail-riders desperately needed food and were grateful to get it, they were also shamed to be on the receiving end of generosity, especially from a much younger boy. They did not want handouts; they craved independence and self-respect. They needed jobs.

"It impressed me … how meaningful it was to have a job," Doc says. He began to feel "a moral responsibility" to use whatever talent he had to create jobs for others.

"It's hard to believe the level of destruction brought on by the Depression — it was particularly tough on parents who were trying to get their kids through school and feed them," he says. "It was a very difficult time. The value of having a job is taken for granted today because finding one is so easy. But there were times when people were desperate just to have employment. A high percentage of people rely on another organization or companies or governments to create employment for them. Very few people actually use their own capital and go out and create jobs. I feel that job creation is so important. If you have the ability to be of some good to society, it is your responsibility to do that."

Doc would go on to create thousands of jobs in his own companies, and he still pursues the same goal less directly by financing new ventures.

"I've put money behind some of them and been successful in creating a lot of new jobs," he says. "That's kind of a second-generation effort." His focus is "placing venture capital with young people I trust who have good business instincts."

While creating employment for nearly sixty years, Doc Seaman has also created a great deal of wealth, for both himself and others. But his primary motive has never been money. Like many entrepreneurs who seem to spin personal wealth out of thin air, he focuses passionately on his goal, and if he succeeds the money is merely a welcome by-product, like confetti at a wedding. Business people whose sole goal is to get rich are seldom happy, even when they accumulate vast fortunes. Those who have a wider purpose, especially a social one like Doc's, are often content and fulfilled and rarely stop working. At age eighty-six, as this is written, Doc still goes to his downtown office in Calgary every business day. "Never quit, never retire," he says. He knows how to relax on a golf course or during a vacation, but after a lifetime of toil and a wartime of danger, the thought of ceasing to strive appalls him. He will not retire and recommends it to no one else.

Daryl Seaman's character was moulded in some of the most beautiful prairie country on earth, the belt of subtly changeable flatlands carved by coulees and streams in southwestern Saskatchewan. Prairie boys, it is often said, make great sailors and superb fliers, because the grasses constantly roiling in the winds strangely resemble the sea, and the sky is so overwhelmingly vast that a child is almost raised within it. The sky smiles and nourishes, scowls and deprives, grants plenty in times of rainfall and spreads poverty in years of drought. The sky is visually larger than the land and in some ways more important. As a typical prairie boy who played and worked outdoors for his entire youth, Doc was sharply attuned to the sky's shapes, moods, and dangers.

In the summer of 1939, Doc finished Grade 12 at age seventeen. He immediately went to work for his father operating heavy road-building equipment on the graveyard shift from six o'clock in the evening to six o'clock in the morning.

"Those were long, lonely nights out there on the vast prairie," he says, recalling the awe and insignificance he felt in the face of nature's ferocity. "During the thirties, summer storms brought little or no rain, but the booming thunder drowned out the sound of my engine. Lightning bounced all over the place, and there I was sitting atop steel. We had one young guy killed on a steel-wheeled tractor when he was struck by lightning. So when I saw those thunderstorms rolling in, I was always a bit apprehensive."

Doc learned early how to cope with both isolation and the heavy responsibility of operating machinery in a dangerous environment. The lessons he took from those vast nights later helped him excel at one of the loneliest jobs on earth, flying a plane under enemy fire with no co-pilot on hand.

Before he turned nineteen, Doc joined the Royal Canadian Air Force. He trained as a bomber pilot in Canada and England and went on to fly an astonishing total of eighty-two sorties in North Africa. "Eighty-plus missions is simply unbelievable," says Dr. David Bercuson, distinguished military historian at the University of Calgary. "The odds went up drastically with every sortie." But the sky the young man had studied so closely never betrayed him, even as comrades fell all around him — and, one horrible day in the cockpit, right behind him. Doc Seaman did not fly fighters, so he never became a famous pilot back home, but he was arguably one of the great Canadian fliers of the Second World War, a prairie boy truly at home in the sky.

Daryl K. Seaman was born on April 28, 1922, in Rouleau, the town now known to millions of Canadians as Dog River, the scene of the TV comedy show *Corner Gas*. He isn't sure if he came into the world at the local hospital or the family home. His sister, Dorothy Verna, arrived first, on October 12, 1920, and two brothers came afterward, Byron James, known as B.J., on September 7, 1923, and Donald Roy on July 26, 1925. Much later, Daryl would be tagged by his teammates with the nickname "Doc" because he carried his baseball gear around in his dad's old black leather suitcase, which looked like a doctor's bag. "Remember what Yogi Berra said about a suitcase," laughs Doc. "Why buy a good one — you only use it for travel." For nearly sixty-five years, family, friends, and business associates have known Doc by that name.

The parents of these rambunctious children hailed from tough, talented cross-border stock in an era when the American-Canadian border was much more fluid, a guide rather than a divide. They arrived from the United States along with thousands of other immigrants who settled in southern Saskatchewan and Alberta, giving a distinctly American flavour to a long stretch of prairie. The self-reliance so precious to Americans lived on in the children. Years later, Doc would refuse to accept a Canadian government pension for his war wounds on the grounds that he did not want to feel dependent. It was another early sign that the young man cared more about character and conviction than he did about money.

Descended from United Empire Loyalists in New York State, Byron Luther Seaman came up to Saskatchewan from Wisconsin during the First World War to help Canadians with the harvest. At a dance in the town of Avonlea he met Letha Mae Patton (always known as Mae), who had been born in Unadilla, Nebraska, in 1899 and moved to Traux, Saskatchewan, with her family at age thirteen.

When the Americans joined the war effort in 1917, Byron returned to the United States to train and then fight in the last stages of the war as a machine-gunner in the American Expeditionary Force. There wasn't much talk about his service in the Seaman household, but Doc learned that his father had seen action in several battles near the end of that cataclysmic four-year conflict. He was involved in trench warfare and survived a mustard gas attack. Byron then served with the occupation army in Germany before returning to Saskatchewan in January 1920 and marrying Mae the same month.

At first Byron and Mae both worked on a farm, but Byron, eager to be self-sufficient, used the money he saved to buy road-building equipment. In 1928, he started constructing municipal roads in the Rouleau area, but the onset of the Depression and the Dust Bowl almost eliminated construction by the early 1930s. Conditions improved somewhat by the mid-1930s, however, and the family struggled through. "When I was thirteen and big enough to contribute to the family livelihood by handling a Caterpillar tractor," Doc wrote in *Oilweek Magazine*, "we were able to go back to building roads in the district. Revenues were meagre. But our father-and-son team made ends meet because we had no wages to pay, worked ten- to twelve-hour shifts, and did our own cooking and camp chores."[2]

While driving the Cat, Doc usually got up at 5:00 a.m. and ran the machine until dusk. "When we were on projects some distance from home, we 'bached' in a cook car and bunk house," he recalls. "Mother would prepare food for us for the week."

Once Doc started building roads with his dad, he learned his first hard lessons about patronage politics. His father was Conservative, but governments in those days were mainly Liberal, and Liberal friends usually won the contracts.

"There was a job to build the road from Maple Creek to Cyprus Hills," he recalls. "We bid, and so did a farmer who only had an old D4 Caterpillar that was too small for the job. But he voted right — he was a Liberal and we weren't. So he got the contract, but then he subcontracted to us because he didn't have either the equipment or the know-how."

Money was hard to come by even before the Depression, and Byron Seaman learned a deep respect for both the land and the people needed to keep a family moving toward some kind of security. Doc remembers him fondly as "quite an easygoing person, but a hard worker and ambitious. He had little or no money, but when he got his first tractor he decided he could build roads. He couldn't have had much experience at that. He had to work long hours in the summertime. For a while, until I was old enough to work, his brothers and half-brothers used to come up from Wisconsin as part of his crew."

Mae became a classic prairie housewife, working longer hours than most of the men; yet she had artistic yearnings, too, and always longed for a piano. Once she managed to buy one with her few savings but she and Byron were forced to part with it when the family needed money. Dreams fell hard in the Depression Prairies.

"Mother had to leave school after Grade 8, and it was a big disappointment to her," says Don Seaman, Doc's youngest brother. "She was determined to play the piano and have us do it, too. One by one we failed her, I'm afraid. I can't remember playing piano, but I sure remember practising. It took time out of sports."

Today the boys remember their mother with deep affection and admiration. "She looked after us young kids and cooked for the men. She did it all. She was absolutely amazing, our mother," says Doc. "I think she had the toughest assignment, even tougher than the men, because she'd be up at four in the morning to cook breakfast, with us kids still to look after. The men worked twelve-hour days or longer. They worked all the daylight hours they could. So Mom cooked three meals a day, as well as washing clothes by hand with a little scrub board and a tub. The men stopped in for lunch for a half hour, and they'd be back at it again. Then they'd come in for dinner late in the evening, and Mom looked after that too."

During the busiest seasons, there was no full day off; the crews worked six days and used the seventh to buy supplies and maintain equipment. The only break for the men came when hard rains hit and all work stopped. Like many women of the era, though, Mae rarely had a day without caring for everyone: men, workers, and children.

Despite the hardships of the Dirty Thirties, she was positive and optimistic; like her clergyman father, she had a resolute faith forged by life on the Prairies. Doc does not remember his mother complaining even once, but he still vividly recalls the day she cried.

"My mother was a very good housekeeper, and everything was always spotless," he says. "The homes weren't as well constructed in those days, and the window and door casings certainly weren't airtight. I remember one day a fierce dust storm blew in, and even though it was around noontime, we had to turn the lights on because there was so much dirt in the air. My mother had just cleaned the house, and suddenly the inside was covered with a layer of black topsoil from the fields. I guess her disappointments had piled up and were just too heavy that day. That was the only time I saw my mother cry."

Out on the prairie farms, dust storms and drought caused much more misery than undoing a day's cleaning. They ruined and even ended lives, as desperate farmers sometimes saw no hope and killed themselves.

"There were several local farmers who committed suicide because of the bleakness of the situation," Doc says. "They had planted crops and waited for some reward, but after the grain had begun to grow, the sand would just carve the stalks right off. They were done for another year. Most of these people were hard workers. It was a pretty heartbreaking time."

Byron Seaman struggled against the dire economy as best he could, showing independence and adaptability that helped bring the family through. "Our dad was a bit of an innovator," says Doc's brother Don. "He had the first gas-driven Caterpillar in the area."

Byron's skills and drive made a deep impression on both Doc's later business methods and his view of life. "Seeing how hard he and my mother worked just to keep us kids in school and clothes on our backs with enough food to eat," Doc recalls. "It was fundamentally the family unit that made things work. We used all our own resources to do what had to be done."

The family moved only once, says Doc, "from the east side of Rouleau to the west side of Rouleau" — a distance of a few blocks. "We had a typical house at the time. There was no central heating. We had a hard coal stove with a magazine on top that we filled up with golf ball–sized pieces of anthracite coal. It would burn nicely all through the night." By age fourteen, one of Doc's many chores was the annual fall trek to the coal merchant, thirty miles down Highway 39 to Milestone. Doc would drive the three-ton truck, shovel on enough coal to last the entire winter, and then shovel it off again when he got home.

There was no indoor plumbing — hardly anybody had that — but the little town did have a good well to supply water, even though the pipes weren't buried deeply enough and kept bursting in winter. The family had no phone, either; anybody who wanted to reach Byron on business had to drop over or send a messenger.

Despite hard times, there was plenty of fun at home, in school, during community events, at holiday festivals, and in sports — the social glue that binds rural communities to this day. Byron and Mae were active in the United Church, where Byron was an elder. The boys served as ushers. When Doc reached high school, he would be called out of classes to usher at community funerals. "In those days, funerals were conducted with open caskets," Doc recalls. "It was a duty I didn't like much."

All the Seaman kids knew their roles both in town and at home. Chores brought them closer together. "We learned the value of care, of working with each other," says Doc's brother B.J. "We all had things to do at home." B.J. and Doc, being close in age, were inseparable. The younger Don had his own crowd, but both brothers recognized Doc's seniority. Don says, "He was somebody to look up to: he was the best athlete; he was the leader of the gang; he was the best in school." The brothers are over eighty now, but they still see Doc — and he sees himself — as the family leader, although he says his sister always had the better school marks.

The kids had their mischievous moments, and their pranks sometimes got them in trouble both at school and at home. After all, their dad also sat on the school board. "I'd often play tricks on my sister, who was a grade ahead of me," Doc recalls and then laughs. "Well, it wasn't only my sister. I had some other favourite targets as well."

At lunchtime, the kids headed home for the noon break. "My mom always had a nice lunch for us. I was the one who got to go into class ahead of the others to make sure their books were in place. So one day, when I was at home for lunch, I went out to the shed and saw a woodpecker there. I caught it, brought it in a bag to school, and went in early and put it in Dorothy's desk," Doc recalls.

"As soon as she opened her desk to get her books, the woodpecker flew out, she screamed, and the bird dashed from one wall of the room to the other. Mr. Jones, the teacher, went after it, rushing and jumping and grabbing away until he finally caught it. Then he took it outside and let it go. He came back in and said in his booming voice, 'Seaman, did you do that?' 'Yes, sir, I did,'" Doc confessed. "He always asked me first because he knew that 90 percent of the time I was the one responsible."

Those were the days when tricks and transgressions were penalized with the strap. "There were a number of incidents like that, but it didn't deter me much," Doc recalls.

But George Jones was no persecutor or sadist. As both the principal and a teacher, he emerges in Doc's stories as one of a legendary breed, the wholly original character who ran a prairie school. Certainly George Jones became an important model in the boy's life.

"He seemed to see something in me — I don't know what it was. He had a mink farm, and I'd go out on Saturdays and shoot rabbits with my .22 rifle to feed the mink. He paid me ten cents for a jackrabbit and five cents for a small bush rabbit," Doc says.

"The school skipped me past Grade 8 into Grade 9, and by the time I reached high school I was more serious about my classes. I'd become a pretty good student and took both Latin and French, as my sister, Dorothy, did. It turned out that George Jones was the only Latin teacher, and by Grade 12 I was the only Latin student," Doc recalls. "One day, Mr. Jones was immersed in reading Homer's great epic, *The Odyssey*, and suddenly he was standing on the chair behind his desk, calling out to the whole wide prairie, looking for Ulysses. Can you imagine that?"

Most likely, this gifted teacher was trying to encourage exactly that — imagination — in his promising student.

All the Seaman kids did real adult work from the moment they were physically able. By the time Doc turned ten in 1932, the Depression was entrenched, and even children knew that only unstinting toil could keep families strong and united. There was little tolerance for shirkers, either child or adult. Kids learned not only to work hard — often in conditions that would be technically illegal for children today — but also to see a job through to the finish because it was vital and others were simply too busy to do it. Early on, Doc was charged with looking after the crucially important family garden.

"My mother kept a large garden, and I dug it all myself," he says. "A neighbour, Scotty Bob, did have a horse and plow but he kind of slowly poked around and he charged two dollars for the job which I thought was pretty expensive. So I took a spade and just did it by hand."

The prairie garden in the Depression was a very different thing from today's little hobby patch of flowers or vegetables. The garden fed the family when there was little or no money to buy food. Vegetables could be traded for meat as housewives struggled to keep their children on a balanced diet. Junk food and the fad diet industry hadn't been invented. Obesity was almost unknown in working families. Nobody obsessed over eating too much; they were too busy finding enough. And yet, if children avoided diseases that were often fatal in the days before antibiotics, they grew strong, fit, and energetic. They worked and played with vigour sadly unknown to many sedentary children today. Adults, too, were less likely to suffer from obesity, high blood pressure, and heart disease.

The garden produced food that was fresh, natural, and delicious. Berries went into pies and other desserts. Doc, exercising the rights of the biggest sibling, often marked the territory by sticking his finger in the largest piece at lunch. "No way I was going to argue with that," laughs Don, the youngest.

As often happened in rural families, the eldest siblings became surrogate adults, expected to tend to everything and everyone. "As the oldest boy in the family, I was given quite a lot of responsibility to look after things, especially when my parents were away. I was in my early teens, and I had to keep the house warm, shovel snow away from the doors and driveway, get the coal and wood in," Doc says.

"Sometimes my dad was away hunting so we'd have enough meat," he adds. "I'd have to fill up the woodshed. Ever try splitting wood? It's hard work." Some of the jobs Doc did were unhealthy and dangerous, but he was surrounded by other children doing the same things.

"Before I was old enough to run the earth-moving machines I hired on with local farmers to help with harvesting in late August, about three weeks before school started," says Doc. "I had to harness a team of draft horses and hook them up to a grain wagon and drive a couple of miles to the pool elevator. The stalls were narrow, and the horses were massive. They weighed at least two thousand pounds, and I was just a kid so I had to get in tight to put on the harness. Sometimes those huge horses would shift sideways as I was struggling with the harness, and I worried they would squeeze me against the stall or step on my feet."

Harvesting grain was gruelling work. Once the ripened fields of grain were cut and bound into sheaves, crews gathered and stacked the sheaves on end, forming stooks (small stacks) so the grain could dry. Then they were thrown onto a stook-loader, which elevated them into a horse-drawn hayrack.

"The first year I worked in harvesting, I was the youngest guy on the crew so I was given a job as the 'hound.' I followed the stook-loader and recovered any sheaves that fell off the conveyer or the hayrack. I was glad for the work and wanted to make sure I kept up with the men.

"So I started out on my first day picking up missed sheaves, running them up to the loader, and then rushing back to retrieve others. The crew let me do this for a while before one of the older guys saw that I was getting tired. 'Hey, kid,' he said. 'You don't have to run like that. Just take them over to the closest stook and we'll pick them up on the next round!'

"I still remember that," Doc says, laughing. "It was a good lesson in working smart while working hard."

Once the hayrack was full, sheaves were pitched onto the conveyer belt of the threshing machine, which separated the wheat from the straw. The grain was taken in horse-drawn wagons or trucks to the elevators in town or stored in granaries on the farm. During the Depression, there were neither hydraulic hoists on the trucks nor power augurs to help handle the grain.

"I spent lots of hours inside granaries, shovelling wheat from the entrance to the back wall," Doc recalls. "It was hard, physical work, and the dust was really miserable."

Doc's sister handled the female side of the chores. He adored Dorothy even though, as family friend and NHL star Bill Hay says, "she was the only one he couldn't control — Dorothy was a pistol." Doc was grief-stricken the day Dorothy was killed when hit by a vehicle in 2006. Only a month later, his mother died in Calgary at the remarkable age of 107, a rare Canadian who lived in three centuries. She and Byron had been married for fifty-nine years when he died in 1979, yet she would survive him by nearly three decades.

Sport was always pure fun to Byron and his boys. Byron was a good athlete who became a top Saskatchewan curler. He also enjoyed hunting. Doc inherited both loves, along with high athletic ability. He would be a gifted athlete in every age group, in both hockey and baseball. Brothers B.J. and Don were crazy for sports too, and B.J. was just as keen for hunting as his older brother. Don, the youngest, never took to it; he stuck with fishing.

Doc played senior baseball when he was only sixteen and always enjoyed the game, but hockey was his first love. Little Rouleau claimed a treasure rare in rural Saskatchewan: a covered hockey rink. All the boys played, and Doc became a standout. At the age of seventeen, he was invited to play for the Moose Jaw Canucks, one of the country's leading junior hockey teams. He was also asked to sign a "protection card" with the New York Americans of the NHL, committing himself to play for them if he turned professional.

"We had teams that went to sports days, and not just in our town, but in all the small towns around," he says. Both in baseball and hockey, the Rouleau teams sometimes played against Notre

Dame College, just a few miles down the road in Wilcox. And that's how Doc, like many other lucky prairie kids, met a founding father of Canadian hockey, Monsignor Athol Murray — creator of the college, mentor to generations of athletes, and now a posthumous member of the Hockey Hall of Fame.

Père Murray had been raised in a well-to-do family in Toronto but studied for the priesthood and was sent to Regina in 1922. There he formed a sports club of boys — Protestant boys — who'd been caught stealing candy from a church. In return for joining the club, called the Argos, they wouldn't be charged. That episode set the direction of Père Murray's life: he would develop character through sports. When he was assigned to the village of Wilcox, south of Regina, some of his Regina Argos came with him. Notre Dame College, founded in 1933, was well established by the time Doc started playing hockey against the Notre Dame Hounds, and sometimes for them.

"I got to know Père Murray pretty well," Doc says proudly. "He called me 'the kid from Rouleau.' When our team got knocked out of the playoffs, I was picked up by the Hounds and travelled with them to the south Saskatchewan midget-level playoffs."

Doc hasn't forgotten how Père Murray, operating a school with little money in the Depression, made sure his charges got what they needed.

"On this trip he picked me up in Rouleau, and we were travelling in the back of a grain truck with a canvas over it and a little heater stove. We stopped in Moose Jaw because the truck needed some repairs. Père Murray walked in to the Modern Café there and said to the proprietor, 'These boys are hungry and you have to give them something to eat because we don't have enough money.' So he got us all a free meal. Then we went to a movie theatre next door. He said, 'We have to put in some time and we don't have enough money to see the show.' So we all sat in and saw a free show."

When they reached Shaunavon, where they were playing, Père Murray told the opposing coach the same thing — there was no money for a hotel. So the players lined up opposite each other, goalie to goalie, forward to forward, defenceman to defenceman, and the Hounds went to stay with their opponents' families for several days.

"I really remember how persuasive Père Murray could be on anything. How he kept that school going through those years was a real marvel, actually. He was a person I greatly admired."

Many years later, Doc Seaman would pay for a new men's and boy's residence at the college to show his gratitude. He still skates at age eighty-six and didn't stop playing hockey until he was over seventy. He and his brother B.J. are part owners of the Calgary Flames, and their passion for the game is undimmed, partly because of their boyhood brush with the inspirational leader who touched so many lives.

A former Hound and colleague of Doc's, Bill Mooney, wrote the foreword to Jack Gorman's *Père Murray and the Hounds*, starting with this remembrance from Père Murray: "Ideas are not initiated by Industry, Governments, Organizations or Associations, they come from individual human beings."

In 1939, Doc graduated from high school with excellent marks, including 90 in geometry and 91 in chemistry. He thought briefly about becoming a pharmacist. Dorothy was already at the University of Saskatchewan, and Doc rather reluctantly signed up in engineering. But the young man wasn't sure about any of it yet.

Far away, in Europe, his future was already being decided for him, as it was for many other Canadian boys. Britain declared war on Germany on September 3, 1939. Doc recalls the moment clearly: "I remember being in a Chinese café in Maple Creek on a Sunday with my dad when it was announced on the radio that

Britain declared war." Canada's declaration would come a week later, on September 10.

"I didn't fully appreciate the gravity of this development, but my dad sure did," Doc recalls. "I was still only seventeen, not old enough yet to go into the services. It was a year and a half later that I signed up, and before I turned nineteen, I was in the air force."

Doc and thousands like him were still boys, but in a purely coincidental way they were finely tuned for war. These prairie kids were tough, fit, and hard-working. They were at ease outdoors, they knew how to shoot, and childhood had taught them sharp lessons in risk and danger. Hitler's Nazi forces would have a fight on their hands with these kids from Canada. But Doc would need every fibre of his ability and willpower, along with a large measure of luck, to come home alive.

Chapter Two

The Defender

"Never never never never surrender."
— Winston Churchill

Perhaps mercifully, time has robbed Canadians of their personal understanding of total war: the family devastation as thousands of sons and daughters are slaughtered, the economic wreckage from turning a country on its head to support battle alone, the daily dread that the struggle might be lost and the country pillaged and ruined. Canadians lived in such fear for nearly a full decade during two world wars, from 1914 to 1918 and again from 1939 to 1945.

All Canadians know this, or should. But as veterans grow old and pass on, we gradually lose the true memories of ground quaking from shellfire, of cities burning, of planes tumbling from the sky, of friends falling dead at one's side. We begin to rely on facts and figures that perversely dull the sense of individual suffering. If we allow a moment for imagination, though, those brutal numbers show that modern Canada was forged in war by people who knew everything about risk, sacrifice, and heroism.

Canada had a population of only 7,879,000 in 1914, when the First World War broke out. By the time the conflict ended, 67,000 Canadians had been killed and 173,000 wounded, many in futile trench battles for tiny scraps of ground that lacked any strategic value. At the Battle of Passchendaele alone, between October 26 and November 15, 1917, 16,000 Canadians were lost in a struggle so savage and senseless that a German general, Erich Ludendorff, later described the human landscape as "no longer life at all — it was mere unspeakable suffering."

The population of Canada totalled 11,267,000 when the Second World War began in 1939. By 1945, more than 42,000 Canadian military personnel had died, 37,000 in battle, the rest from accident or illness. Another 55,000 were wounded. Canadian casualties were somewhat lighter in this more mobile and technological war, but the human cost ran deep in nearly every village, town, and city. For almost six years, war was the national obsession and loss the common condition.

Militarily, Canada's modern engagement in Afghanistan is small by comparison. And yet, as the number of Canadian troops killed in action since 2001 climbed above eighty-two by mid-2008, the nation was engrossed in debate about the mission. This distant echo of the great wars gives some idea of how stricken the country felt when an entire generation of young men shipped out to fight. "In those days the whole country was at war," says military historian David Bercuson. "Schoolchildren were at war. Homemakers were at war. Everyone was at war. It was a wartime psychology, an extension of the national will. It was very different than our situation today."

On September 10, 1939, when Canada declared war on the Axis powers, Daryl Seaman was still only seventeen, a prairie boy who had never been east of Regina, west of Maple Creek, or north of Saskatoon. "I'd never been out of Saskatchewan and only a few times away from home," Doc recalls.

He had less direct knowledge of the planet than many modern kids who might at least expect a family driving trip out of province or even a flight to Disneyland. There was no television, newspaper photos were all black and white, and popular magazines such as *Time* and *Life* arrived a week or more behind the news. The outside world filtered in mainly through the radio, carried primarily by American voices in news broadcasts, dramas, comedy shows, and live coverage of sporting events. Radio was a great trigger to the imagination — nobody who heard those programs forgets the thrill and mystery — but it was no substitute for experience. Prairie youths were little different from young soldiers of earlier centuries, as far back as Roman times, who lived isolated rural lives until war suddenly scooped them up and scattered them like leaves.

And yet, being teenagers, most of Doc's contemporaries worried less about death and injury than about status, competition, and reputation. Could they measure up to an enemy already engraved on their minds as evil and ruthless? Would they prove to be brave or cowardly in battle? Would they be popular, find friends (and girlfriends), and maybe even have some fun? Those were their concerns as manhood gathered to rush at them with brutal force. Doc was no different — but like many of his peers, and rather to his own surprise, he would prove to be an exceptional warrior.

In the fall of 1939, Doc enrolled as planned in a technical school in Moose Jaw and signed up for hockey with the Canucks. He soon came down with jaundice, however, and went home to Rouleau to recover. In the spring, he operated a Caterpillar for his father on a Prairie Farm Rehabilitation Administration irrigation project in Maple Creek, drawing the twelve-hour midnight shift. When the job was finished in September, Doc enrolled in engineering at the University of Saskatchewan in Saskatoon.

But the call of war was growing louder. By Christmas 1940, many of his old schoolmates and pals from Rouleau were joining the South Saskatchewan Regiment. "When a recruiting team came to Rouleau in February of 1941, I went to the municipal office to join up," Doc says. He had every intention of signing on for infantry duty, but a recruiter spotted his high marks in math and science.

"He suggested I should enlist for air crew in the Royal Canadian Air Force (RCAF)," Doc says. "This was the first intervention by a kind fate in my military career. The SSR became the principal attack force for the Dieppe raid in August of 1942, when nearly half of the men in the assault were lost, largely as prisoners."

But he was not really so lucky as he'd have us believe, to be heading for the air war rather than the infantry. Eventually Doc ended up with the Mediterranean bomber command, which had extremely high casualties from enemy fire.

First there was the training — the endless, tedious training. Pilots were prepared for every emergency imaginable, even for blind landings (by practising with hoods over their heads). Examining Doc's official Pilot's Flying Logbook, yellowed but still legible after sixty years, it is apparent that training was everything. Despite a severe shortage of combat pilots, the government wisely did not rush them overseas. There was no point in training a man insufficiently, only to lose him, his crew, and his equally precious machine on the first sortie.

After enlisting, Doc was sent to Brandon, Manitoba, west of Winnipeg, where he and hundreds of other recruits were issued their first uniforms and military numbers. Doc became R-102355. Here they also got their initial taste of the key to all military operations — discipline. Sleeping in double bunks in the commandeered hockey rink, grandly called Manning Depot, several hundred men adapted to the regimented chaos of military life. "It was hard to get to sleep," Doc says. "Somebody would call out, 'Anybody here from Saskatchewan?' and others would swiftly reply, 'Shut the hell up and go to sleep!'" During training, they all spent shifts on guard duty to learn to stay alert even while exhausted and deeply bored, no small feat for young men.

From Brandon he was transferred to Regina for more basic work at an Initial Training School. During this period, men were carefully observed for a sense of their aptitudes. Doc was singled out as a potential pilot, and by fall he was shifted eastward once more, to a base near Virden, Manitoba, where the RCAF had established an Elementary Flight Training School. The instructors were all civilians, members of the Brandon-Virden Flying Club and the Moose Jaw Flying Club. Throughout the war, such civilian experts would be crucial to training men for air battles few people had even imagined to this point in history.

However, this was no amateur effort. The Virden base was part of a vast international program called the British Commonwealth Air Training Plan, set up by the British Air Ministry. Britain was unsuitable for training because of enemy attacks, strain on existing airfields, and uncertain weather. The Dominion countries — mainly Canada, Australia, and New Zealand — agreed in 1939 to train 50,000 crews a year for as long as necessary. Those would include 22,000 from Britain, 13,000 from Canada, 11,000 from Australia, and 3,000 from New Zealand. Many aircrews got initial training in their home countries and then came to Canada for advanced courses. Doc had become part of a huge international effort — still the largest in the history of aviation — that was crucial to the war effort. Without this program, which became known simply as "The Scheme" or "The Plan," the struggle might well have been lost.

Doc's first logbook entry appeared on September 26, 1941, when he flew for fifty-five minutes in a Tiger Moth trainer with his instructor, Mr. Stevens. Within three days he had recorded three and a half hours in the air; training at that early stage was intense but not exhausting. Student pilots also had a great deal of book learning to absorb, along with complex safety and signal systems.

On October 15, Doc went up for a fifteen-minute solo check with Stevens still in the pilot's seat. This was a crucial moment, because the logbook showed exactly ten hours of training time. Doc says, "Beginners had to learn fast enough to solo in ten hours of training or wash out of flight school." After the preliminary solo check, Stevens shook Doc's hand, sent him up alone, and

watched him return safely fifteen minutes later. Doc had qualified in a fashion that made the enterprise look safer than it actually was. He recalls sadly, "One of the boys from Rouleau, Bobby
Greer, was killed on a routine training flight in a class that followed mine at Virden."

Doc still remembers the first solo as a bit surreal. "You're not
quite expecting it," he says. "You kind of know, and you follow
the drills with the instructor. Then, at the end of the runway, he
says, 'You're on your own and let's see you go.' There's a little rush
of exhilaration." He realized that he loved to fly. "I felt at home,
somehow. I can't remember an incident at all in elementary
training school. There didn't seem to be any difficulty, whether it
was a stall exercise or loops."

There was still plenty of training to do at Virden, including
twenty-eight solo flights and another twenty-one with instructors
at the controls. All Doc's flying to this point was in the venerable
Tiger Moth, a single-engine biplane first used as a trainer by the
Royal Air Force in 1932. In photos today it looks like something
out of the late stages of the First World War, but the Tiger Moth
inspired great affection as a nimble trainer that gave students a
sublime sense of the sky.

By November 25, Doc was reassigned to Number 12 Service
Flight Training School at Brandon. Here he moved up to twin-
engine Cessna Cranes, training aircraft that had been introduced
in 1939. "This step up the air force ladder involved more intensive
training, with numerous cross-country trips, including night
flying," he says. That winter was bitterly cold, but the training
went on with temperature extremes harsher than any he would
encounter in Europe or Africa.

There was also plenty of ground school training to go along with
the flights almost every day. By the time Doc completed training,
he had logged a total of 126 hours, 45 minutes of service flying.
Wings were presented at Brandon on March 12, 1942, and Doc

was delighted that his mother and father were there, surely feeling the mixed pride and dread that all wartime parents experience on such occasions.

Throughout his career, Doc would be assessed mostly as an "above average" pilot, significant praise in an era where the goal was to record achievement, not boost self-esteem. Yet the technical designation doesn't record his larger virtues as a flyer — his readiness to take responsibility, both for himself and his crew, and his ability to select solid, trustworthy comrades who would bring out the best in everyone. Those qualities would be essential to success, and survival, over the next three years.

After a few days' leave, Doc and his classmates were sent to Halifax, where he spent his twentieth birthday, April 28, 1942. It was no party. "We had only a short stay in Halifax and we were often CB — confined to barracks — for security reasons," he says. "This was the time when German U-boat activity and notorious submarine wolf packs made the North Atlantic extremely hazardous. The security seemed ineffective, though, at least for keeping our movements secret from any German intelligence operations."

On May 1, soldiers and airmen marched through the streets of Halifax to board the HMS *Batory*, a Polish vessel built in 1936 and mobilized into service as a troop ship at the outbreak of war. Her sister ship, the *Pilsudski*, far less lucky, had been sunk in 1939.

Any pre-war luxury had been stripped from the *Batory* to make room in the holds for as many men as possible. Soldiers were ordered to stay below deck to discourage enemy attacks. Even for Doc, no stranger to roughing it, the conditions were appalling.

"The accommodations were extremely crowded," he says. "Instead of double-decker bunks, we had five-deckers. You could not sit up in one and had to crawl in sideways. Once we left port and hit rough water, there was a good deal of seasickness. Even apart from the stench, it was a tough place to be for anyone from open country or who had a trace of claustrophobia." Doc decided to sleep on deck. He and Pete Hamill, who'd grown up in Whitewood, Saskatchewan, grabbed adjacent lifeboats as sleeping quarters.

"We didn't realize at the time that a lot of the army guys on the lower decks were told they couldn't go on the deck at all," recalls Hamill, who met Doc on the trip. They've been friends ever since, for more than sixty-five years. "For the whole trip, Doc and I slept in lifeboats on the deck using the jackets for pillows. Below deck was pretty foul, with guys getting sick."

The convoy was under constant enemy attack. "The *Batory* sailed in the middle of the convoy, within a ring of smaller transport ships that were in turn surrounded by patrolling destroyers and other escort vessels," Doc says. "The trip was our first taste of real war. There was continuous activity, with depth charges going off around the clock." Hamill recalls flashes of gunfire all during the night; but fortunately the *Batory* came through without being hit and docked in Glasgow May 12.

Doc had no time to sample Glasgow's charms. Within hours of disembarking, many fliers were heading for their first deadly taste of the Nazi air threat to Britain. "We took a train down to Bournemouth, where a lot of the aircrew were stationed prior to being assigned to the advanced flying units," he says. "After a few days they had us down on the beach doing exercises — to keep us out of trouble, I guess."

Three Luftwaffe Messerschmitt 109 fighter-bombers suddenly appeared over the sea. The fighters were flying "on the deck" — as close to the water as possible — to avoid detection. "They pulled up as they got to shore and started firing," Doc says. "The three of them dropped their bombs and turned around and went back out to sea. One of them was either hit by anti-aircraft fire or misjudged. He flew right into the water." With his waterside view, Doc knew he was extraordinarily lucky not to be in his quarters at that moment.

"Obviously they had intelligence as to where the aircrew were stationed and they hit our barracks. Several died when bombs hit a nearby billet."

Realizing that the large group of fliers was highly vulnerable at Bournemouth, the commanders immediately dispersed the men to various bases. Doc went to the 11th Devons, a British infantry unit training in Cornwall. Flyers weren't allowed to be idle, though; they had to join army maneuvers with everyone else. Doc's diary for May 16 says: "Army maneuvers and mock air raid — myself participating as casualty."

After a short time with the army, he was transferred back to Bournemouth and then posted to Number 15 Advanced Flying Unit in Kirmington, Lincolnshire. There, Doc spent many hours flying twin-engine Oxford planes with crews practising navigation. It was during this extended training period, on August 19, that Canadian troops landed at Dieppe across the Channel, along with Doc's pals from the South Saskatchewan Regiment. In the nightmare that followed, about four thousand Canadian and British troops were killed, wounded, or taken prisoner. More than nine hundred Canadians died either in the battle or afterward from their wounds.

The South Saskatchewan Regiment left eighty-four dead on Green Beach. Another eighty-nine, including Lieutenant-Colonel Cecil Merritt, the regiment's commander, were taken prisoner. Merritt was later awarded the Victoria Cross for high courage. Everyone knew that many of his troops were just as deserving.

"The badly wounded there included Murray Greer, who had been our catcher on our Rouleau ball team, and whose brother, Bobby, had already died in RCAF pilot training," Doc says. "Dieppe was a horrific slaughter for those guys. I could well have been a casualty too, since the South Saskatchewan Regiment was exactly where I had been heading before the recruiters asked me to try for the air force."

On August 19, 1942, Doc flew his last training run in an Oxford, a quick forty-five-minute flight at the base. He was marked down as a proficient flyer with no weaknesses that needed observation or action. The terse designation "average" became a wry joke among the pilots. No matter how brilliant a flyer was, no matter what heroics he performed, he would still, at the end of the day, almost certainly be marked "average" by the British officers. In their eyes, these were kids from "the colonies." It was a testament to Doc's abilities that he would several times be graded "above average" in flying, navigation, and bombing.

From Kirmington, Doc transferred to Harrogate, North Yorkshire, for the crucial General Reconnaissance course. "This training concentrated on astral navigation, or fixing positions by taking star shots with sextants," he says. "Learning the ancient methods of mariners was critical for flyers in the Second World War. We did not have the navigational aids taken for granted today. Yet we had to be precise. Our airfields were blacked out against enemy bombers at night. To get even minimal guidance from a landing light, we had to come close enough to the runways to identify ourselves. Sometimes this had to be done visually with a flare pistol fired out the side of the airplane." Such identification codes constantly changed. "Between 1:00 a.m. and 3:00 a.m., say, the signal might be a cartridge that burned green, then red." Only after all the security conditions were met would controllers briefly illuminate part of the scene. Even in training, such flying required nerve and coolness. Pilots who lacked those qualities were quickly transferred to other duties.

Today, Dr. Bercuson describes these challenges to give his students a sense of the incredible hardships fliers faced at a moment in history when military machinery could operate over long distances but electronic and guidance systems were still primitive. "Every fall in my military history class, I say, 'Okay, GPS [global positioning system] is still far in the future. Yes, there are radar beams, but those are over land and very rare. Imagine you have to go on a long flight over water — it's like putting a hood over your head and walking around a room. On top of that, you have an enemy that wants to kill you.' Students today are not very often aware of the difficulty presented to the people who fought that war."

But life for a flier in training wasn't all war, work, and worry. The trainees were also lively young men with as much interest in personal affairs as military ones. Doc's personal diary shows a discerning eye for the ladies, including Jean Boyd, whom he met at a dance in Grimsby. "A very nice girl," he recorded. Two weeks later he was at a dance at Bath — "a good time" — but a week after that, on September 11, he reported, "nothing ever happens — a very dull existence."

Things began looking up rather quickly, however. On September 15, he met Rene Hook from Harrogate, another "very nice girl — best treatment yet in England," he wrote. Doc had dinner twice in following weeks with Rene and her parents.

"Those meals were such a welcome change from the service grub that was almost inedible. I'll never forget breakfasts. We would get in the lineup and grab a plate. As we filed past the counter, the mess staff would give us a piece of bread drenched in grease and lightly cooked to make the crusts crispy. Then a ladle of liver and kidneys was slapped on the toast. Plus a mug of tea — tough going to start the day," says Doc with a grimace and then a laugh. "That's why it was so nice to get out. Of course the English were on rations, but Rene's family still managed to serve a nice meal."

Britain had been at war for more than three years and almost every British family knew of a serviceman who had gone to the front and not returned. "At dinner, Rene told us that one of her girlfriends had given a silk scarf to a Spitfire pilot to wear as a good luck charm," Doc recalls. "She said it seemed to work. We all laughed, but as I was leaving their home, Rene opened her purse and slipped me one of her silk stockings. I wore it around my neck

for eighty-two consecutive sorties." Many such friendships led in
later years to cross-Atlantic marriages, although Doc's lingered
only as fond memories. Two years later, as he sailed home on the
Aquitaine, he would again meet Jean Boyd, now pregnant and
married to an American officer.

By October 1942, Doc's time in the General Reconnaissance
course was ending. He passed the exams and was given seven days'
leave, beginning October 13. Doc went to sightsee in Aberdeen
and Edinburgh, then returned to Harrogate. On October 26 he
was posted to Number One Operational Training Unit, on the
northwest coast of England at Silloth, Cumberland.

"The barracks were tin Nissan huts," says Doc. "It was damp
and cold, so we often went to bed in our flying clothes. We were
rationed only one pail of coal each day, so a few of the guys would
sometimes sneak out and grab a bit more."

At Silloth, Doc would meet his companions for the next two
years — his fighting airplane and his crew. He was assigned to
pilot the Lockheed Hudson, the first American-built aircraft to be
used in operations by the Royal Air Force during the Second World
War. In various configurations, this sturdy workhorse could serve
as a troop transport, photo-reconnaissance platform, bomber crew
trainer, target tug, or anti-submarine patroller. The Hudson could
carry five machine guns and sixteen hundred pounds of bombs or
depth charges. The plane was usually assigned to maritime patrol,
and Doc's mission would often be the most dangerous job of all —
hunting German U-boats.

It's tempting to wonder why Doc, with his natural talent for
flying, wasn't assigned to fighters. The most admired servicemen
in Britain were Spitfire pilots, who played a crucial role in holding
off the Nazis in the desperate months before the war began to run
in the Allies' favour. But fighter pilots, although they had to obey
orders from their squadron commanders and were wise to get along
with their ground crews, essentially fought alone in their single-seat

machines. They needed incredible talent and courage; team building, however, was not a vital part of the job description.

Larger aircraft, on the other hand, needed tight-knit crews whose members obeyed orders without hesitation and trusted each other absolutely. In Doc's case, his military mentors undoubtedly saw early on that forming groups based on mutual trust and respect was almost instinctive to him. "Doc was a natural-born leader," says his friend Pete Hamill. "I realized it pretty quick — in the U.K. he was the one to organize golf and we'd go scrounge around and play. He was always the leader." It's the same quality his brothers and friends had seen back in Rouleau. Doc might well have become an excellent fighter pilot, but his larger talents would have been wasted.

Describing his training at Silloth, Doc says, "The most important event was crewing-up, or forming the four-man units needed to fly and fight in a Hudson. It was a somewhat haphazard process, a little like choosing up sides for baseball or hockey matches, except we did not know one another and the consequences of mistakes could be much worse than losing a Sunday afternoon pick-up game."

The commanders obviously knew how to deal with a generation of young men who'd grown up on the playing fields of Britain, Canada, Australia, and New Zealand. Choosing sides is a natural way for fliers to assess each other and decide whom they like and might be able to trust. Men with the potential to be friends seem to recognize each other instinctively. Doc had that feeling almost at once as he strolled in the crowd for companions who might someday save his life.

"We were in a hangar with pilots in one group, navigators in another, and a third group made up of the WAGS [Wireless Air Gunners, who alternated as radio-radar operators and machine gunners]. We milled around, eyeing each other and trying to guess who would be compatible," Doc recalls. "After a short while, Tom McGlade approached me to see if I would crew up with him. We had never met, but I was fortunate. It turned out that he was not only an excellent navigator, but we were especially compatible, and he became my best long-term friend." McGlade's brilliant navigation and Doc's canny flying would get the crew out of many a scrape.

"The commonality was they were both incredibly bright," says Thomas McGlade Jr., who has been very close to Doc's family since his father passed away in 1971. "These were two individuals whose minds and ambitions were unusual, and they were both small-town kids — my dad was from Smiths Falls, Ontario. So it was a fateful meeting. My dad's math skills were among the things that got them through the war."

After deciding to pair up, Doc and Tom found their WAGS: Eddie Thorpe, from Yorkshire, who was about twenty-six years old, and a nineteen-year-old Londoner named Will Fletcher.

"Eddie and Will were both solid guys and good at their work. Will generally operated our radar and radio equipment, and Eddie manned our turret gun," Doc says. "Eddie was older by wartime standards and already married, and he was more cautious than the other three of us. When we started flying bombing sorties on naval targets, we would go in at low altitudes to drop our payload. We referred to these passes as flying 'mast-high.' Eddie hated that part. During one of our sorties, he made the mistake of suggesting to Tom and me that we should drop our bombs from a higher altitude. We never let him live it down. We took to calling him 'Mast-High Thorpe.' It added humour to our stories when we got back to base after bombing runs, and we all had a bit of fun with it."

Once the foursome came together, all training was done as a crew. So was most of the celebrating. Doc briefly wondered about McGlade's navigating skills one night after visiting a London pub. "The city was blacked out, and Tom wasn't doing too badly himself — then he bumped into a lamppost and broke a front tooth," he laughs.

This final training at Silloth continued from November 1, 1942, to January 24, 1943. "We did cross-country navigational trips, including night flights and both high- and low-level bombing practice," Doc says. As both pilot and bomber, Doc now scored above average. Fifteen months after his first solo flight in the little Tiger Moth, he was truly ready for the fight. And the most crucial thing he learned through the whole process, he says, was discipline.

"Crew discipline was very important. After takeoff from base, we had to maintain radio silence. Communicating was a no-no. Whatever wavelength we were on, if there was yakking all the time, the Germans could track us." Each crew member had to be trusted to do the job on his own, often silently, for the good of all.

Doc recalls one example of lax discipline that could have cost lives. "At Advanced Flying Unit, I saw one plane land right on top of another one. The top one cut through the other just as he was landing. Incredibly, no one was killed. The pilot was looking ahead down the runway, but not below, even though the control tower would have been shooting off red flares. The pilot didn't pay any attention. Now, that's poor discipline."

Near the end of their training regimen, in January 1943, Doc and McGlade took in a movie, as they often did when they were given time off. Just before the feature show, the theatre screened a newsreel of Prime Minister Winston Churchill meeting in Casablanca with American President Franklin Delano Roosevelt. Remarkably, the impression it made would soon lead to a decision that saved their lives and that of their aircrew.

On February 20, 1943, Doc flew his bomber, Hudson FK 640, to Portreath in Cornwall. There he got his first operational orders: deliver the aircraft to Gibraltar. As the details of the mission became clear, it must have seemed like a strange way to enter a war.

"To make the long transit to our operations base, our plane was crammed with fuel," Doc says. "Wing tanks were added, to use first and then jettison over the Bay of Biscay. A special tank filled the bomb bay, and all the armament was stripped off the aircraft to lighten it." In other words, Doc was expected to fly around and over enemy territory with no way to defend the airplane. He was also told flatly at the briefing that if for some reason he couldn't land at Gibraltar, there would not be enough fuel for a diversion.

"The briefing officers were pretty casual about it. They told us we'd only have enough fuel to get into Gibraltar, and if we didn't make it there, that was that. When I asked one briefing officer whether he had an alternate plan, the reply was a terse 'No.' We also learned that the Germans were taking accurate fixes on aircraft ferrying to North Africa and there was a very high rate of them being shot down."

With Flying Officer Seaman in the cockpit, the crew lifted off from Portreath just after midnight on February 28. Very quickly, two of Doc's qualities as a flier became apparent: his foresight and his good fortune — the kind of inexplicable fate, or divine intervention, that allows a man to make the most of talent, skill, and preparation.

With just enough fuel to reach Gibraltar, some pilots might simply have flown on with only that destination in mind. But Canadian boys from the Prairies who had worked magic on broken machines and stretched fuel further than the last mile knew how to get the best out of their aircraft. And despite his briefing officer's gloomy projections, Doc was determined to put in place his own contingency plan.

"Once we got on course, I held FK 640 at a constant altitude and started trimming back my fuel mixture. Then, by fine-tuning the throttles and carefully monitoring my temperature gauges, I found an optimum cruising speed to match the lean fuel mixture.

As events played out, this bought us an extra hour and a half of flying time."

The crew had its first close brush with disaster just after dawn over the Bay of Biscay, when Doc suddenly sighted a flight of three Messerschmitt 109s cross directly in front of the Hudson at the same altitude. They were only a thousand yards apart.

"Luckily, we were coming out of darkness and the German pilots did not see us," he says. "If they had, we would have been shot down in short order, particularly since we had no armament aboard to protect ourselves. Our bomb bay was full of fuel tanks. We were sitting ducks" — exploding ducks, in the event of a hit.

As usual, Doc recounts the incident in matter-of-fact tones. The reality was more dramatic — the Luftwaffe would have picked off his plane with the ease of hawks swarming a defenceless sparrow. Doc and his crew came within a whisker of dying in the early hours of their first operation.

As the flight went on, Doc says, "Tom McGlade's dead-reckoning navigation was bang on. After making landfall at Cape Finisterre, and following the west coast of Portugal, we entered the Strait of Gibraltar precisely as planned."

The Rock of Gibraltar is a magnificent sight, a massive limestone sentinel rising almost fourteen hundred feet out of the water to stand guard over the entrance to the Mediterranean Sea. On this day, however, the crew aboard FK 640 had no opportunity to enjoy the view.

"When we arrived, there was a severe thunderstorm in the strait," Doc vividly recalls, "and I had almost zero visibility. The Rock of Gibraltar rises steeply, and the aerodrome was right behind the north side of the rock. I made a number of passes, flying just above sea level between fifty and one hundred feet, trying desperately to get a glimpse of the runway. There was no room for error."

The tension aboard FK 640 ratcheted up with each attempted approach. There were no electronic navigation aids, and Gibraltar was socked in. The rain was thumping hard against the cockpit window, and the plane was flying so low that Doc could see the whitecaps off the strait. There had been no mention of North Africa in their mission briefing; they were in unknown territory, and their fuel was alarmingly low. All the while, they were trying to contact Gibraltar by radio, to no avail.

"As I pulled up after the last pass, I looked over at McGlade. We knew that further attempts to land would border on suicidal, and we both remembered the newsreel we had seen a few weeks earlier at the movie theatre in England. From this news footage, we'd learned that Prime Minister Winston Churchill and U.S. President Franklin Roosevelt had held a ten-day conference just a month before in Casablanca, Morocco. Casablanca had been chosen to highlight the Allies' success in ousting the Germans from Morocco the previous November, so we knew the airfield there would be secure. I talked it over briefly with McGlade, and we decided to make a last-ditch run for North Africa, all the while hoping that our fuel supply would hold out."

Doc and his crew hadn't yet seen the famous movie starring Humphrey Bogart and Ingrid Bergman. Neither had anyone else in Europe. Although *Casablanca* was first screened in Los Angeles and New York on November 26, 1942, it didn't go into general release until January 23, 1943, during the Casablanca Conference. A print of the movie was rushed to American troops in North Africa, but never shown because of French fears that the movie would create resentment among Moroccans.

"We decided to try for Casablanca," Doc recalls, "reasoning that if we ran out of fuel it still might be possible to ditch the airplane near a beach on the west coast of Morocco and then, hopefully, swim to shore."

Once they cleared the Strait of Gibraltar and turned south into the Atlantic, the weather improved dramatically. And after reaching the coast of North Africa, they spotted the Rabat aerodrome.

"It had been bombed out by the Germans, and planes were strewn all over. There was no way to land, so we pressed on to Casablanca," Doc recalls. "Fortunately, the fuel we saved early in the trip and McGlade's pinpoint navigation paid off. When we finally made it to Casablanca, we had been in the air ten hours and forty-five minutes. Our flight plan to Gibraltar was supposed to take nine hours, and that was considered a stretch. By the time we landed, we could only have had but a few gallons of fuel in our reserve tank."

From Casablanca, they radioed back to Gibraltar, where the reaction was pure delight. "They thought we'd been lost," Doc says. No wonder. Twenty of twenty-six aircraft that had set out from England to Gibraltar never made it. Doc and his crew, ordered to return from North Africa, reached the British possession two days late, but alive and very welcome.

After refuelling, they were promptly sent back to North Africa. The very next day, the crew was posted to RAF 500 Squadron, which had taken over a French air station at Blida, south of Algiers at the base of the Atlas Mountains.

At Blida, Doc's crew met a rich mix of Commonwealth service-men, including commanding officer D.G. Keddie, a Canadian in the Royal Air Force. The two flight commanders were a New Zealander and an Irishman. "There were many Canadian, Australian, and New Zealand flight crews. The administration and all ground crew were British," Doc says.

"General Charles de Gaulle was around northern Algeria quite a lot in those days," remembers Doc. It was only a few months later, in May 1943, that de Gaulle moved his Free French Government headquarters from London to Algiers.

After a few days of orientation, Doc and his crew began to fly in combat. "They're called 'operational sorties' — 'mission' was the American term," explains Doc, "Ops mainly consisted of convoy escort, U-boat searches and strikes, and general reconnaissance. Our squadron was armed with bombs and depth charges depending on our targets. Some of our aircraft were also fitted with eight rockets, four under each wing."

The early operations were routine, but that changed quickly after a number of crews, including theirs, were transferred to Tafaroui, a small air base near Oran in northwestern Algeria, where they slept in tents.

Doc's logbook entry for March 29, 1943, records six hours and forty minutes of flying time on an op summarized as: "U-boat strike. Att. Ju 88." That was terse shorthand indeed for a mission at once tragic and heroic — the toughest day of Doc Seaman's war.

"McGlade, Fletcher, Thorpe, and I were sent to finish off a damaged U-boat said to be somewhere between the Balearic Islands and Corsica," he says. "We went up in Hudson FK 440, loaded for action to finish off the submarine. We took off from Tafaroui in rotten weather at about 4:00 a.m. so we would reach our target area at first light."

They scoured the area, searching for the sub. Time became the enemy, as the target was proving too elusive. Then they were sure they saw it — a submarine periscope or conning tower.

"We banked sharply and opened the bomb bays to attack," continues Doc. "As we zeroed in, the sub was nowhere in sight. So we climbed steeply to two thousand feet to take another look. Just as I tipped the nose down to level off, we spotted a Messerschmitt 210 — he was coming straight towards us at two hundred knots, machine guns blazing and cannon shells firing.

"By the time we saw him, he was only a thousand yards away, and closing so fast we didn't have time to use our nose-mounted .303. Eddie Thorpe in the turret started burning machine gun shells. Suddenly, a German cannon shell blasted right through the front end of my plane on the right-hand side. It was followed quickly by a burst of machine gun fire, and I felt a bullet slam against my right thigh.

"McGlade's voice reverberated in my headset: 'Fletcher's been hit, dammit.' Tom scrambled back to try to help, but the cannon shell had gone right through Will Fletcher's heart, killing him instantly. Will, operating the radio, had been sitting right behind me. The difference between Will and me getting killed was milliseconds.

"There was no time to think, just react. I had to get us out of trouble. I knew the enemy would be turning around fast and coming at us hard. Our bomber would be mismatched in a dogfight with the quicker, more agile German fighter. There was a layer of thin cloud dead ahead and about a thousand feet above us — it wasn't ideal cover, but I said to myself, 'I've got to get in there.' I jammed the throttles forward, getting everything I could out of both engines. Incredibly, with all the fire we had taken, no damage was done to the two engines, the propellers, or any of the fuel and electrical lines.

"I was aware of a searing pain in my left calf as we headed for the clouds. I had difficulty working my left rudder pedal, but we managed to make it to cover ahead of the German fighter. Once inside, I banked hard right. It was a good guess. We never saw the Messerschmitt again.

"As soon as I felt confident we had eluded the enemy, I reached down and tried to assess the damage to my legs. I could see that I was bleeding quite badly. A machine gun bullet had hit my right thigh and lodged itself in the bone. A second bullet had sliced through my left calf, severing some tendons. No bones seemed broken, but I had pretty much lost control of my left leg."

Even after they evaded the German plane, the surviving crew had no time to succumb to the shock of the attack. Will Fletcher was dead, and the only way for the rest to stay alive was to stabilize and protect their pilot, who was seriously injured and heavily bleeding. The muscles of his left leg had gone into spasm, making it almost impossible to work his left rudder.

"After McGlade and Thorpe laid Fletcher's body over the bomb bays, I called them to patch me up. They dressed my wounds as best they could and tried to stem the bleeding. Then I had them tie my left foot to the rudder pedal, and we were ready to leave our cloud cover and make a run for base.

"It was a bit painful, but I could now operate both rudders again. I felt I could manage as long as I didn't lose too much blood. And in any case, we had no other recourse. I was the only pilot on board.

"I don't remember panic at all, actually. You don't have time to think about how you're feeling. That sounds strange, but it all depended on skill, training, and the will to preserve the crew and yourself — the will to live. That's a big part of the discipline that was ingrained from early training.

"Thorpe took Fletcher's post at the radio and sent an emergency message. There was no confirmation. The German had shot out our IFF [identification-friend-or-foe device] and radio receiver. We had no idea whether we had gotten our message out. Without that IFF, we were open to attack from friendly fire. We were two to three hours from base and worried that our own anti-aircraft guns or fighter planes would simply finish us off when we returned."

As they made their way toward home and crossed the coast, the crew spotted two Spitfires in the sky above them.

"They circled and took a good look at us," Doc recounts. "We saw them turn and then come straight at us from behind. We were completely vulnerable and our adrenaline was really pumping. Like most RAF Spitfire pilots, these were superb fliers and they closed in on us quickly. They were almost on our tail before they cut back on their throttles.

"Then they just eased right in beside us, one on each wing, setting us up in a tight formation. I could see both pilots clearly through my cockpit windows. They gave us the thumbs-up signal, and I signalled back. What a colossal relief. As soon as we got over base, the Spitfires peeled off.

"I remember reading a quotation once. I forget who wrote it, but it was someone who knew about war. His statement was: 'There are no atheists in foxholes.' That certainly was the case for me. I was very grateful to see the landing strip at our base that day." (Second World War journalist Ernie Pyle first used the phrase in one of his dispatches before a sniper stopped short his courageous life near Okinawa in June 1945.)

The friendly thumbs-up from the Spitfire pilots was one of the most welcome sights Doc had ever seen; yet they weren't home free. Doc's damaged leg was still tied to the rudder, and the weather was extremely rough, producing a tough crosswind. Having outwitted the German, Doc was not about to succumb to Mother Nature. His will and skill pulled rank over the weather and the pain.

"By this time, my legs had essentially seized up, but I did manage to land the plane safely. They untied my leg from the left rudder pedal, carried me to the ambulance, and got me to an American field hospital." Although Doc received excellent care, he first went to the end of a waiting line that would have many modern patients complaining to the media.

"I remember lying there for three hours before they took me into the operating room, but that was all right. There were lots of soldiers back from the front with more serious injuries than I had. Will Fletcher was buried in a local military cemetery. McGlade and Thorpe attended the burial, along with other buddies from the squadron. Will was a good young Brit," Doc adds quietly. "He didn't deserve to go out so young."

Doc at first thought the attacking plane was a Junkers Ju 88 (hence his logbook entry), but McGlade and Thorpe later convinced him it was a Messerschmitt. The account of the firefight is spellbinding: Doc, hemorrhaging badly as his left foot remains firmly tied to the rudder, all the time swallowing considerable pain as he struggles to remain fully alert and fly home; the surviving crew achingly aware that if Doc blacks out, their lives are lost. And in back, the radio operator, Fletcher, tragically felled by a shell that had passed right between Doc and McGlade, missing Doc by a thread.

"The shot-up aircraft and the dead crewman that could just as easily have been Doc. The pandemonium. The courage. Amazing," Bercuson declares after Doc relates the story.

Even though he would recover fully, Doc's injuries were his one-way ticket back to Canada if he wanted to cash it in. He knew this at the time, but did not give the option any thought.

"I suppose I could have asked to be grounded," he reflects now. "The injury to my leg was quite serious because a bullet had clipped the tendons. It would have been easy to say I had a pinched nerve and the pain was unbearable. But I went there to do a job. The cause was well defined. The enemy was well known. It was a real challenge … and at that age, you never even considered that anything could happen to you. Awful things could be going all around, but you would just say, 'Well, that's not going to happen to me.'"

There was another consideration, too: the shame of being labelled a coward. "Your file could be marked 'LMF' — lacking moral fibre. If there was any suspicion that you were chickening out, you got that designation. It was a disgrace." Doc Seaman had no appetite for disgrace, and he certainly had given ample proof that he was not a coward.

After a month of recovery, most of it on crutches, Doc was released back to his unit on April 28, 1943 — his twenty-first birthday. He quickly returned to active duty, with a Canadian named Archie Henderson replacing Will Fletcher as one of the two WAGs.

When they started flying together again, the crew wondered whether they might receive some kind of recognition for the remarkable return from the U-boat raid. Others had been decorated for less. But this never happened. "There was a good chance it was just overlooked," Doc says. "We were a Canadian crew, and most of the commanders tended to look down on us a bit."

Doc got on well with almost everyone then, as he does today, but sometimes he feels a bit of resentment toward the RAF's casual sense of superiority. He remembers flying near the Atlas

Mountains with an RAF pilot, holder of the Distinguished Flying Cross, who almost got them killed because he was flying too low. "All of a sudden he realized, 'Golly, the tops of these mountains are 5,000 feet and we're flying at 3,000 feet.' On go the full throttles and he started to sweat and finally we got up to 5,500 feet or so and there was this big sigh of relief. But the guy was pretty shaken up. When we got to Tafaroui, he just about crash-landed." Doc laughs. "I could have done better myself."

But the commanders began to realize who was getting the job done, even if they weren't generous with medals. Doc and his crew, now ranked as senior in the squadron, began to pull the most difficult missions. "This was particularly true in bad weather, when navigation was of extreme importance," he says. "McGlade was an exceptional navigator. Using dead reckoning, and with the aid of radio or astral fixes at night, we consistently got back to base safely. This wasn't always the case with other crews. A number of them got lost and had to bail out, abandoning their aircraft."

The crew would eventually receive a citation from the Free French in North Africa, under the command of General Charles de Gaulle. On September 3, 1943, Doc and his crew were sent out to find two French fighter pilots who had been shot down in the Mediterranean. "By flying on the deck we found the two pilots in the seas, floating in their Mae Wests." Doc quickly alerted sea rescue, who picked up the men; one was already dead, but the other survived. Doc's flight log notes: "sighted dinghy, U-boat — no attack."

In North Africa, Doc and McGlade befriended another Canadian, Robert "Sam" Turner. "Sam was from Edmonton," says Doc. "He sometimes crewed up with us when Eddie Thorpe or Archie Henderson were sick."

For months to come there would be many adventures and near misses. Doc recalls one thunderstorm that was so severe "we were being thrown all over the sky. I was transfixed by the storm, with my head out of the cockpit, and began to lose control." Quickly his experience kicked in, and Doc turned his full attention back to controlling the aircraft. Was he remembering those stunning storms of his prairie youth where the scorn of the sky would set his adrenaline on high? Perhaps Doc recalls this episode so vividly (and with a touch of remembered fear) because he so rarely lost focus. Indeed, it's memories of the things Doc could not control that seem to trouble him most today — not the thought of being shot down or blown up, but the brushes with dying in a senseless accident.

"I remember one time — and it's stayed with me longer than anything — we took off in the middle of the night from our base in Tafaroui, and it was really rough," Doc says. "I told my radar operator to let me know as soon as we crossed the coast, because I wanted to get down out of the rough air. So we crossed the coastline all right, and I got down to about five hundred feet. Then I looked out the port window, and here's one of these huge uncharted rocks jumping out of the ocean. I had but seconds to react and get clear."

Bercuson, who was present for this conversation, commented, "Unadulterated luck. One degree one way and you're just a slash on the rock."

One of the most tension-filled sorties Doc ever flew came one night when the crew was sent out from Bone (now named Annaba), a base on the northeastern coast of Algeria, near Tunisia, for a reconnaissance flight over Italian waters. The Italian fleet had been bottled up by Allied aircraft, but new intelligence revealed they were planning an escape from Taranto, in southern Italy, to Marseilles, on the southern coast of France.

"The first two crews sent out from Squadron 500 were never heard from again — no distress signals, nothing. We were the next ones scheduled to fly," Doc says. They took off with a potent mixture of adrenaline and apprehension.

"Eddie 'Mast-High' Thorpe was especially edgy. Once we got there, we circled throughout the assigned area and patrolled for several hours. We were extremely vigilant and, as it turned out, fortunate, because we returned to base, incredibly, without incident." Amid the anxiety, they had managed to escape their mates' fatal misfortune.

More than forty-five years later, a vivid remembrance of the Italian mission came to Doc's mind. He was sitting in the office of his urology specialist in Calgary. "I'm sorry, I have some negative news," Dr. Edwards told him. "The tests confirm you've got prostate cancer." Doc turned his chair and looked straight into the doctor's eyes. "What is your prognosis?" he asked. "I would estimate you've got about eight years," Edwards gently replied.

"I just sat there for a few moments, weighing the gravity of his words," Doc recalls. "All kinds of memories flashed through my mind, but then I settled on that reconnaissance mission of the Italian fleet. We were just kids back then, being sent out with the prospect of only a few more hours to live. Now, here I was at sixty-nine, not only having survived but having lived a wonderful life. And I was still active. Somehow, eight more years didn't sound too bad to me."

As of 2008, the years had stretched to seventeen.

By September 1944, Doc had flown an astonishing total of eighty-two combat operations over eighteen months. Since training began in Canada, he had been flying steadily for almost three years. Nearly everyone in wartime gets a break long before racking up numbers like that. Someone in the command structure might finally have realized this, because on February 23, 1944, Doc and his crew were posted to a communications squadron for what he calls a "rest leave" — even though they remained on active duty, ferrying military materiel and high-ranking personnel around North Africa. The war was being won by then, and flying was more relaxed. At one point, they were slated to fly Winston Churchill, who was visiting the base in Italy. "That would have been quite an honour," says Doc. But the schedule changed and Churchill flew with another crew.

In early September, McGlade was sent to visit Canadian personnel officers at Allied Headquarters at Caserta, north of Naples. "When they learned we had been overseas for three years, and in the Mediterranean for almost two years, they decided we should have a rest leave," Doc says. On September 23, 1944, they caught a ride on a Dakota from Pomigliano to Florence, and then to Hendon, England. That flight would prove to be the final entry in Doc's military logbook.

In England, they were granted leave "and spent a few weeks at a nice home in the Lake District of Cumberland, organized as a rest home for air crews," says Doc. "We then received word that we were heading back to Canada for an extended leave." Doc sailed to New York on the liner *Aquitaine* — by amazing coincidence, the same vessel that had ferried his father, Byron, back from the First World War.

Remarkably, Doc and McGlade still didn't believe their war was over. They'd decided to ship out to the Pacific to fly Mosquito bombers against the Japanese. When McGlade made the request at RCAF headquarters in Ottawa, the response was a firm "No," probably delivered with the conviction that these men were both incredibly brave and very fortunate to be alive. Fliers with their records of service were not expected to go back on active duty, and few wanted to. They were told they could either stay in the air force as instructors or demobilize. Neither man was interested in being a trainer; indeed, Doc had already turned down an offer to be a flight instructor in Europe, even though accepting it would have removed him from combat.

Finally they decided to leave the military and participate in one of the best things to come out of Canada's war — the program to help thousands of veterans get a university education. As Bercuson says, this was crucial to the growth of an educated middle class that perpetuated itself through the original students' children and grandchildren, contributing mightily to Canada's prosperity.

At first, both McGlade and Doc thought they'd go to McGill University in Montreal, but Doc finally decided on the University of Saskatchewan in Saskatoon, where his parents had moved. Both his brothers were students there, and his sister, Dorothy, had graduated from the school. He was going back home, finished with the air force and mostly done with flying.

Doc flew very little in later life because he didn't have time to keep up his training. Typically, he decided that if he couldn't fly with dedication and high skill he wouldn't fly at all. "I knew an American fellow who had a drilling company; he crashed and was pretty badly injured. One of my friends was killed because he instructed the pilot — against his own best judgment — to let him fly. They crashed in a squall and killed themselves. You have to be doing it every day. I had a sense that I shouldn't. Later on, when our company had a plane, I would occasionally fly as the co-pilot, but I never flew as captain."

Doc's final act as a military man had nothing to do with flying, but would show his character as vividly as any of his wartime feats. Although he was entitled to a lifetime pension because of his war wounds, he turned it down.

"The medical officer in Regina said I deserved a pretty good pension, but I said no, I didn't want anything, I just wanted to make it on my own," Doc says. "He couldn't believe it. But it was the correct thing for me to do psychologically, because I did not want to take any handouts and feel as though I might be handicapped, and therefore dependent. I did not want to feel that the government or anyone owed me anything."

To Bercuson, who has studied the war records of hundreds of Canadian servicemen, Doc's military history is truly astonishing.

"People in Bomber Coastal Command had less chance of survival than infantrymen," Bercuson says. "One in six would die.

They spent a lot of time out of touch over water. The aircraft would fail and there would be no survivors. Also, after 1943, the Germans would arm their U-boats with all kinds of anti-aircraft guns. The policy had changed from diving to staying on the surface and fighting it out. It wasn't that difficult to hit a plane with a machine gun, especially if you were coming in low and slow.

"The odds of disaster went up with every sortie, because the aircraft technology wasn't comparable to today's. Lots could go wrong up there … when you look at Bomber Command and the numbers of crew that were lost in training accidents or because of mechanical failure, and compare them to the number lost on missions, it is a high percentage. The more you flew, the more the odds were stacked against you.

"Doc, in my view, should have received some recognition. To fly eighty-two missions in that war, with those planes, is absolutely unbelievable." A Distinguished Flying Cross would have been entirely in order, he says.

More than many other veterans, Doc was able to turn away from war to a healthy new life. Some veterans were horribly wounded or psychologically scarred — often both. Veterans had high rates of alcoholism and severe mental distress. Unable to shake the terrifying dreams of death and destruction, thousands were haunted to early graves.

Doc surely didn't come out unaffected, but somehow he had the ability to take the best lessons from the war and set the rest respectfully to one side. He never forgot his wartime friends or the lessons he learned from them. "I have many fond memories and everlasting respect for my comrades who were my crewmates and best friends on many hazardous missions," he says.

"All of us matured quickly even though we were fairly young. We took on difficult assignments. It was a great confidence booster to know that we competed favourably with our peers around the globe. That was where I learned to pick people out pretty quickly.

You could tell who the guys were who had the real stuff and who did not. You became harder to scare, too. I've always enjoyed risk in business. I still do. I love to drill wells, and not the easy ones. When you have risked your life, as opposed to risking dollars, risking dollars becomes a pretty easy choice."

And risk he certainly would.

PART TWO

~

Building a Global Empire

Chapter Three

The Water-Jack

How old would you be if you didn't know how old you are?"
— Satchel Paige

After tempting fate with a phenomenal eighty-two sorties, Daryl Seaman's war was finally over. "We had a job to do," he said, and now that was done. The Allies had defeated Hitler, thanks in considerable measure to kids from places like Rouleau, Saskatchewan, and those soldiers — young in age but veterans in courage — would return to create modern Canada.

"What they were doing was an extension of the national will, and that's very different than today," notes military historian Dr. David Bercuson, who worked on two hour-long films called *Coming Home* for the sixtieth anniversary of the war. "They had a sense of purpose, a sense of community. World War II had an amazing impact on this country. For the films, we talked with a lot of people, including artist Alex Colville [who chronicled the war on canvas], about that transition, the last months of the war and the first months of the peace, and what it meant for our country. There was almost boundless enthusiasm that people had at the end of the war."

In conversation with Doc, Bercuson described how the war experiences of people like him were the determining factor in building a future for themselves and their country. Doc replied, "We said that often. I was given the chance to do something, and so many others were not. I thought I must do something meaningful with my life."

The veterans would use the skills and good fortune that had allowed them to survive to transform Canada into an industrial power. In war, says Doc, "judgment of people is a big thing. You have to rely on your mates to perform whatever operation is assigned." The instinct to pick the right crew and to make that team work was key to survival in many aerial dances with death.

Bercuson points out that these skills, honed in war service, were remarkably well suited to business. "Problem solving, multi-tasking, and multi-roles" were vital, he says. So were calm nerves while taking huge risks, as well as the will to survive and fight again.

Branded by the horrors of war and relieved by its end, Doc now intended to make good his childhood pledge to those ravaged men who had ridden the rails across the country desperately looking for work. He also vowed to repay the debt to his fellow servicemen who didn't make it home.

For a veteran looking for opportunity and education, there was no better country than Canada to come home to. The federal government showed its gratitude by investing $1.5 billion over five years — a mammoth total in those days — in veteran benefits for post-war education, business start-up support, and land grants. Given the veterans' recent sacrifices, and their incredible storehouse of talent and experience, the federal spending was well targeted. "Six years after World War II ended, 52,000 applications had been approved under the Veterans Land Act; 80,000 veterans received vocational training; 54,000 attended university; and more than 7,000 received financial support to start up businesses under the Veterans Business and Professional Loans Act."[3]

Bercuson says, "How were people going to get a higher education in the 1940s? Canada's universities were small institutions at that time. Along comes the government and says they are going to create this opportunity, and the schools followed suit." They expanded to accommodate the flood of students, gradually evolving into our modern post-secondary system.

For every veteran who enrolled, the institutions picked up $150 from Ottawa. As long as they remained in school, veterans paid no tuition and collected a monthly stipend of $60 if single and $90 if married.

Canadian campuses quickly became crowded. The University of Saskatchewan, with 8,705 veterans enrolled, was no exception. To ease the burden, a former RCAF Service Flying Training Station on the outskirts of Saskatoon became No. 4 Campus.

Doc arrived in Saskatoon for Christmas leave in 1944, but because his military records remained in the Middle East, he wasn't demobilized until August 1945.

"I went to the Veterans Affairs office in Saskatoon. They told me I could go to McGill [with Tom McGlade] if I liked, but they were starting a Vets program at the University of Saskatchewan and there was a class opening in January. My parents were there and my brothers were in engineering at the university, so I stayed in Saskatoon. The government paid my tuition, and I received $60 dollars a month." That covered Doc's board, and with summer school he was able to complete his four-year engineering degree in three years.

Mechanical engineering seemed to be the logical choice for Doc. He'd had a lot of practical experience on construction crews, and his brothers, Don and B.J., were enrolled in the program. But this background and his natural aptitude didn't make his studies any easier.

"To get back to civilian life was an adjustment, particularly as I had graduated from high school before the war, when I was seventeen," Doc says. "Then I came back into a science degree, and suddenly had to remember all the forgotten formulas: trigonometry, geometry — it was a struggle. I worked hard at it."

University life at the time, heavily influenced by young men who'd survived hardship and danger many of their professors could scarcely imagine, was very different from today's campus scene. Former military mess halls housed crews of students eager to digest every morsel of knowledge the professors offered. It was a happy lifetime away from the mess halls of war, where each meal could be the last. "The service guys were deeply serious about their studies, and they really worked," says Doc.

In his spare time, Doc enjoyed a robust game of gin rummy. To this day, he's an avid player with the same zeal to win he has always shown in everything from academics to war to sports. He also began to earn extra money playing baseball, and at this point his teammates branded him with his indelible nickname after they spotted the satchel he used to carry his gear.

In 1945 and 1946, he played first base for Saskatoon's Army, Navy and Air Force Veteran's team. The players were hard to miss in their distinctive red uniforms, but it was their game that had opposing teams on the run. "It wasn't a classic baseball uniform, but the ANAF Vets sure were a good team," recalls Doc.

In fact, the Vets were good enough to win the North Saskatchewan senior baseball championship in 1945. Doc might not have been quite as fast on the base paths as he'd once been, but the war injury to his Achilles tendon didn't affect his hitting — Doc regularly led the Vets in both batting percentage and home runs.

Although they loved the game, baseball was money as well as sport for Doc and the team. A popular prairie Sports Day would feature a first prize of up to $2,000, a sizeable amount for the time. Second place carried $800 to $1,200. Even divided among twelve players, the amounts were substantial. "You could earn more money playing baseball than pounding nails," recalls Doc. "My summer construction job paid $1 per hour. In baseball, we were almost always in the money and we had some good paydays."

Baseball was the most popular summer sport on the prairies in those days. Almost every community had a team, and the calibre of play in the top tier was considered to be as good as Triple A baseball in the United States. North Battleford had a contingent of American servicemen who were still stationed in Canada, some of whom had played ball in college and professional leagues in the United States. And a few towns brought in African-American players from the Negro Baseball Leagues. Occasionally, teams of black players would travel north to Canada on barnstorming tours.

"The Kansas City Monarchs came up and played an exhibition game against our Vets team in Saskatoon in 1945," Doc recalls. One of the Monarch's top players that year was a second baseman named Jackie Robinson. "It's hard to imagine today," Doc says, "but it wasn't until 1947 that Jackie Robinson broke the colour barrier. Up until then, some of the best players in the world were banned from playing in the majors."

During the 1940s, the Monarchs also featured Leroy "Satchel" Paige. By combining enormous pitching talent with showmanship and storytelling, he had become a near mythical figure. Joe DiMaggio once called him "the best and fastest pitcher I've ever faced." Despite this, Paige didn't realize his dream of playing in the major leagues until 1948. As one of fifteen children born to a domestic worker in Alabama, Paige's age was surrounded by uncertainty, adding a further dimension to his mythology. New York Yankees' Manager Casey Stengel used to call him "Father Time," but Paige's plaque in the Baseball Hall of Fame indicates he was, in fact, born in the summer of 1906. In 1965, he made a brief promotional comeback to the majors. Defying the years lost to the colour barrier, at age fifty-nine Satchel Paige pitched three scoreless innings against the Boston Red Sox.

Other teams the Vets competed against featured National Hockey League players who were back in Saskatchewan for the summer.

"The little town of Delisle had a great team with five of the hometown Bentley brothers. Max and Doug Bentley played together with the Chicago Blackhawks on one of the most famous lines in hockey. They were both small in size but were terrific athletes," Doc recalls.

Terrific indeed. Raised in a farming family of thirteen kids, Max and Doug Bentley rose to stardom during the 1940s in Chicago. Max was traded to Toronto in 1947 and became an immediate fan favourite, helping the Maple Leafs win three Stanley Cups over the next four years. Both Max and Doug Bentley were inducted into the Hockey Hall of Fame and in 1998 were ranked by *The Hockey News* among the one hundred greatest hockey players of all time.

"I also remember Emile 'the Cat' Francis playing shortstop for Delisle," Doc says. Emile Francis started his NHL career as a goalie with Chicago before moving to the New York Rangers, first as a player and later as coach and general manager. Francis, an avid baseball player, was the first NHL goalie to use a trapper catching glove. During the 1945–46 season, he began experimenting with a first baseman's glove by adding a cuff to protect the rest of his hand and wrist. His innovation was the prototype of the present-day catching glove used by net-minders all over the world.

"Wild Bill Hunter was around in those days, too, and was always trying to organize games and big tournaments," Doc recounts. One summer before the war, Hunter had triumphantly organized a seventy-eight-game baseball tour of the Prairies for his school team: Père Athol Murray's famous Notre Dame Hounds. Wild Bill went on to bring professional hockey to Edmonton with the Edmonton Oilers, even forming a rival World Hockey Association for eight years when the National Hockey League wouldn't allow them in. By the time the NHL relented and admitted the Oilers, Wild Bill had sold the team.

Despite the extracurricular activity, Doc proudly graduated with his Bachelor of Engineering in the spring of 1948, following B.J. (1945) and Don (1947).

Armed with their engineering degrees, the Seaman brothers could have settled on safe career paths in the skill-hungry economies of Central Canada. All three worked stints in either Ontario or Quebec. In the end, though, they would risk every crumpled bit of cash they could scrape up to build a dynamic and independent Canadian resource company, Bow Valley Industries Ltd.

Bow Valley would become "the most actively traded stock on the American Stock Exchange for a number of years in the 1970s," remembers family friend Thomas McGlade Jr., an investment banker in Connecticut and the son of Doc's wartime navigator and close pal. "During the first oil embargo in '73, BVI [the company's stock symbol] was an incredibly hot stock with huge trading volumes." But there were many hurdles to jump before Doc and his brothers achieved that success.

B.J. was first off the blocks after earning his degree. He had been hired by Cam Sproule, the head geologist for Imperial Oil, to work with a subsidiary during the summers of 1943 and 1944, and full-time after graduation in 1945. Within a year, Imperial wanted B.J. in South America for seismic work, so he started south.

"I made it as far as Miami and got cold feet — or hot feet — and came home," laughs B.J. "I met a fellow who'd just come back from Magdalena, and he was all skin and bones. I figured I would be better off in Saskatchewan — at least there I would get enough to eat!"

Upon his return from Miami, B.J. worked for his father's small harvesting business and then spent a term instructing at the University of Saskatchewan, where he honed a natural gift for public speaking. Then he headed east for a year to British American's refinery at Clarkson, Ontario.

When Don Seaman graduated in 1947, he moved to Shawinigan, Quebec, and later Kingston, Ontario, to work for Canadian Industries Ltd. That summer, Doc trekked to Hamilton with the

Steel Company of Canada but turned down the firm's permanent offer after he graduated in 1948.

While the Seaman sons were looking east, a monumental event was occurring west of their home province. On February 13, 1947, Imperial Oil made a giant find near Leduc, Alberta. This groundbreaking oil discovery, after 133 dry holes had been drilled, showed the tenacity of the early oil players. Leduc No. 1 oil well was to put the province firmly on the world oil map.

At about this time, Doc was thinking he might buy some heavy equipment and get the family construction business going again. He went to the Legislative Building in Regina to see what kind of construction work would be available. Nothing seemed promising, so Doc and B.J., with their dad, Byron, hopped into the grey 1939 Buick and headed west, with the idea of checking out construction projects in northeastern British Columbia. But very quickly, Doc was gripped by the oil fever raging through Alberta.

"I had read about the Leduc discovery early in 1947, and it was something I was curious about," says Doc. "So I decided to go to Edmonton and take a look at what this exciting new stuff about the oil patch meant. We went north as far as Fort St. John, B.C., but I liked the atmosphere in Edmonton. It was buzzing, compared to Saskatoon, and there were lots of trucks going back and forth hauling equipment. It was something new and exciting, and I've always liked risk."

The Seamans quickly hauled themselves back to Saskatoon, where Doc and B.J. packed their bags and made the fastest turn-around they could manage back to the buzz of Edmonton.

The boys put their names into an employment office, and within a week Western Geophysical had hired Doc as a surveyor and B.J. as an instrument operator on the seismic crew. They spent a few months in Edmonton, but most of the first year they toiled in the town of Athabasca, one hundred miles to the north. It was to be a cruel winter.

"The temperature dropped to forty below zero and stayed there for days on end. The company we were contracted to, Standard Oil of Indiana [which later amalgamated into Amoco Corp.], ordered us to keep working, but it was tough to make much progress," says Doc. "Our trucks kept breaking down, and bulldozing trails through the frozen muskeg was really hard on equipment. The crew was mostly Americans from Texas and Oklahoma who had never experienced a cold winter. It was a nightmare for them. I didn't think we would be able to run a survey instrument in that kind of cold, but we managed by leaving the truck heater off so the temperature remained the same inside the cab as outside. I bought silk gloves to wear under my heavy mitts. I'd work with one mitt off, adjusting the survey instrument and making notes until my fingers got numb."

While Doc and B.J. were freezing in the Athabasca bush, their hearts were warmed by thoughts of their sweethearts still in Saskatoon, Lois DeLong and Evelyn Shirkey. On Labour Day 1948, the two Seamans took matters into their own hands.

"Lois and I went to university together. She was in what was then called Household Science. B.J. married Evelyn on Labour Day, and Lois and I got married a few days later. B.J. got two days more of a honeymoon than I did," laughs Doc.

Doc drove to Athabasca with the two brides in the front seat and B.J. squished between the gifts, packages, and suitcases in the back. When they returned a day late, the boss delivered his own wedding gift — he docked B.J. and Doc a day's pay.

Doc needed no further reminder that he should determine his own destiny, build his own business, and, finally, create the jobs he'd silently promised the Depression's rail riders. He would make his move, but not before gleaning every kernel of knowledge he could find on the job.

His crew routinely crossed the Athabasca River to their work site on the north side. On the ferry, Doc noticed a young man named George Bennett, who owned a shot hole rig being used nearby.

Compared to the Western Geophysical rig, Bennett's equipment seemed outdated, yet he was fully employed as a contractor. "On the several trips over the river, I asked him about his business, how he got started, how much money it cost, and how well he was doing," Doc says. "He was a very personable fellow. I got sort of the lowdown on what it would cost to enter the business."

Operators of shot hole rigs are crucial in the early stages of finding oil and gas. They drill shallow holes, drop in dynamite, detonate it, and then measure the seismic waves that reveal underground rock formations with potential to trap petroleum. Doc soon decided to plunge his Air Force savings into shot hole drilling, but he knew he'd also need both a loan and a partner.

A truck-mounted shot hole rig requires two men to operate: a driller, who is responsible for the operation and maintenance of the machinery, and a water-jack, whose primary job is to load the water truck and take it to the shot hole locations for use in drilling.

Doc found the first partner of his business career in Bill Warnke. "He had been born and raised in Alberta, the son of Russian parents who had come to the province at the turn of the century from Brazil," Peter Foster wrote in *From Rigs to Riches*.[4] "After war service, he had been working in a lumber camp when the Leduc boom hit."

Warnke got his start in the oil industry as a water-jack on a seismic crew and quickly moved up to become a driller. When Doc approached him about forming a business partnership, Warnke decided to put up every penny he had — $1,500 — for a 25 percent share. Doc took out a pencil and drew up the deal on a piece of paper. Armed with little more than a few stark facts but considerable faith in Doc, Warnke signed on.

"After all," Warnke told Foster, "what have I got to lose but $1,500?" — even though it was hardly an insignificant sum at the time.

Doc had saved a good portion of his military earnings from five years in the Air Force. "As an officer flying a plane over North

Africa, the pay was $125 a month. Because we were living in tents, we got another $25 hard-living pay, so I had $150 a month. We didn't have much opportunity to spend our earnings. We were also rationed one beer and an ounce of Scotch a day. That I didn't save," laughs Doc.

Between Doc's seed capital of $6,000 and Warnke's savings, they had a total of $7,500, half of what they needed.

"But the banks wouldn't loan us any money then," Doc remembers. He didn't let that slow him down. During spring break-up in 1949, Doc hitched a ride into Edmonton and met with a company called Seismic Service Supply, which represented the Mayhew line of equipment. They told him if he could make it down to Calgary, he could talk business terms with Percy Smith, who ran the company.

Through Smith, affectionately remembered as a "big old cowboy," Doc was able to find out all the relevant details, including how long it would take for them to manufacture a rig at their plant in Dallas, Texas. He chose the Mayhew line of equipment because of its modern features and also because Seismic Service Supply had a method of financing their rigs through a small Calgary insurance company, Tait, Lowes & Mirtle. Now Doc could finance his dream.

"I resigned from Western Geophysical, ordered the rig, flew the milk run to Dallas, and spent nearly a week waiting for the rig to be ready. I used to go over there every day and got to know the fellows putting the finishing touches on it."

He also got to know everything about the rig itself. When it was finally mounted on the back of the new three-ton truck, Doc keenly climbed into the driver's seat and started the long, slow haul back to Canada, occasionally tipping the speedometer at 60 miles an hour. It was mid-June 1949, and the sun burned hot in the Deep South. Doc drove all night and slept in the heat of the day.

"The thing I remember is that I didn't have much money for living expenses. The schools were out for the summer, so when I got tired each day I would watch for a schoolyard where I could park the rig. I bought an army canvas cot for a few dollars and put it underneath the rig and slept there. I had a blanket or something, and I slept in my clothes. It was summertime, and I didn't need to worry about getting cold. That worked out quite well. I didn't have to stay in a hotel. I could just wake up and start again."

The highway to home was humdrum until Doc got to Coutts, the Canada–United States border crossing. The very day that he arrived, July 4, the border was closed. It seems the Americans were celebrating a little holiday. "So I spent one long day there that I didn't have to. Making every minute count and then suddenly having to stop with Calgary so close, those twenty-four hours felt longer than all the days on the road."

When he finally arrived at Seismic Service Supply on 9th Avenue East, there wasn't even time for a celebratory drink. Doc was off to Malpass and Sons in the city to pick up the water truck — crucial to seismic shot drilling — that he had also purchased.

"Bill Warnke was the driller, and I drove the water truck — I was the water-jack," says Doc. "I also handled the dynamite."

Doc knew all about being a water-jack from his Western Geophysical days. He had become an expert at loading the seismic shot holes with a string of ten to fifteen pounds of dynamite and connecting the charge. "We got pretty handy using dynamite," he says. "And we took a few shortcuts."

Before Seaman and Warnke could strike out on their own, the partners needed contracts. At the beginning the promises appeared as erratically as tumbleweeds, and rolled away just as fast. Doc lived cheaply and kept plugging.

"I stayed at the YMCA on 9th Avenue and 1st Street," he says. "I allowed myself a dollar and a half a day for living expenses: a dollar for the Y and fifty cents for meals." Doc also leaned on brother B.J., who had remained with Western Geophysical, for a short loan.

When the first contract materialized, Doc was so delighted he still remembers the moment vividly. "I got an early education into how fast the oil industry worked. For more than two weeks, I'd spent a good part of each day canvassing all the companies and telling them where they could contact me. Then one Saturday morning, a manager with Canadian Exploration Company came up to me and said, 'Is that your rig over there?' I responded, 'Yes, it is.' He said, 'You want to go to work?' I said, 'I sure do. I'll be ready first thing Monday morning.' He said, 'The hell you will. If you want a job you're going right now. Get your butt up to Hughenden. It's on the Camrose line, south of Wainwright.'"

So Doc was off to Hughenden, and the start of a lifetime career in the rush of risk and the weight of responsibility. In August 1949, Seaman and Warnke Drilling Contractors Ltd. was officially born. By the end of the year, B.J. was on board, heading up a second rig thanks to cash from their dad, who believed in both his sons and the business opportunity.

"It was fundamentally a family unit that made it work," says Doc. "We used all our own resources to do what had to be done. That was the ethic of hard work and loyalty that we brought with us."

Brother Don, who was still working with Canadian Industries Ltd. in Shawinigan, Quebec, also decided to join the business. He married his beloved Eleanor Lee on November 4, 1950, in Regina. They had met in university, where Eleanor received her degree in household science, as had Doc's wife, Lois.

Like his brothers, Don spent time as a water-jack, learning the business along the way.

"Our uncle [who lived in the U.S.] put his $600 war certificate into the business as a loan so I could buy my share into the company," says Don. "I paid him back. My monthly salary was $300, and he used to get 25 percent of that. I remember how Doc didn't sleep much at night. He'd lay awake and come up with ideas, then B.J.

and I would carry them out. We were a pretty good team; there was always something for us to do."

Doc recalls the time vividly: "I would think of something during the night and could barely wait for daylight so I could get into work and try it out."

Doc's original partner, Bill Warnke, didn't share his vision for achieving their dreams, however. More averse to risk, he wanted to pay for the rigs as they went along and began to balk at the cost of growth. Debt worried him. "Bill Warnke was an excellent man," recalls Doc fondly, "but I wanted to move a little too fast, I guess. We kept buying rigs, and Bill said, 'You guys don't have enough money and you're taking more risks.' I didn't have any more money than Bill, but I was willing to risk what I had."

A split was inevitable but proved to be completely amicable. The Seamans bought out Warnke and changed the company's name to Seaman Engineering and Drilling Co., soon referred to as Sedco.

One of their earliest and best clients was Frontier Geophysical, founded by Ted Rosza, a pioneer in the post-war oil industry. Rosza had a degree in geology from Michigan and had worked extensively for Shell Oil Company managing seismic exploration. In 1950, one year after relocating to Calgary, he left Shell to start his own company.

"We worked for Frontier for many years," recalls Doc. "Then one day the public accountant we had retained came in to see me. He said he had been reviewing our books and couldn't find a contract to cover our work with Frontier. Well, that was because we didn't have one. Ted and I had simply reached a verbal understanding and proceeded to get on with the work. Since this arrangement had worked well, I didn't see the need for anything different, but the accountant was insistent. So I went over to see Ted and told him about our accountant's request. Ted was quite affronted. 'We've trusted one another for years, Doc,' he said. 'We've given each other our word. We don't need a contract.'"

Ted Rosza and Doc Seaman never did draw up a written agreement. They continued to do business with each other the way they always had. Both believed that an understanding between gentlemen was better than a legal contract.

"Ted was an exceptional person," Doc says. "He and his wife, Lola, were really generous with their time and money and were among the leading patrons of the performing arts in our community."

Doc already had plans to offer more services. "It wasn't long after forming Sedco that we decided to go into structure test drilling, which involved larger equipment," he says. "Instead of drilling shot holes, we drilled structure test holes as deep as two thousand feet. We supplied our own survey crew and logging truck and delivered a complete job. It was an integrated service, and we did a lot of work for Hudson's Bay Oil & Gas."

He was always a keen student of cutting-edge technology and kept abreast of fresh ideas in the seismic business. He was struck by the new science behind the Stettler oil field discovery, where the logs of shallow horizons indicated that reefs with oil- bearing potential existed below.

"The reefs are prominent structures, and the overlying formations drape over them. With our structure test rigs, we would drill small-diameter holes on a grid pattern to depths of around two thousand feet. By running electric logging tools, we determined the subsurface elevation of key formation markers in each hole. Using these data, we could then map out an approximate model of the reef located thousands of feet below the markers," says Doc. "What we were doing was kind of a 'poor-boy' 3D survey. All this has been superseded by today's incredible advances in seismic technology, but some good discoveries were made in those early years using structure test rigs."

Doc also spotted the opportunity to create a small seismic company that multi-tasked everything: shot holes, recording trucks, and interpreting crews. And so another brainchild, Seismotech, was born when the Seamans partnered with a former colleague, Mac Baker. Doc's concept of elite teams leading the company to self-sufficiency gained ground as he expanded and diversified services. He invested in Stan Rokosh's firm, Rokosh Engineering. With Ernie Rice, the brothers established Rice Machine Services, which serviced Sedco and other rigs. The company was becoming a hotbed of ideas, and Doc was always on the innovation trail to design and create an edge.

"Muskeg was a bearcat to work, particularly after spring breakup," notes Doc. "To get year-round work we co-operated with Bruce Nodwell on the notion of a machine that would move more easily over muskeg."

Nodwell, born on a Saskatchewan homestead east of Saskatoon, eventually went on to create his "tracked truck." Known as the Nodwell, the machine was able to conquer severe muskeg, nature's northern quagmire.

The passion for exploring was every oilman's dream, and for Doc, the lure was impossible to resist. He wanted to get the company into oil well drilling and would begin with Cardwell trailer rigs.

"They were more compact and portable than conventional drilling rigs, and you could move most of the rig with one truck," says Doc. "They rigged up much faster, and we could move quickly. Most of the times it took us seven or eight days to drill a well, and then we'd move on and drill another one."

The Seamans were working in the new oil fields of southeastern Saskatchewan, where they seemed to be adding a rig every year. They had geared up for an active drilling program in the Midale Field in 1956 but were hampered by one of the harshest winters on record.

"At times the snow on the side roads would pile as high as the telephone wires. It was difficult getting crews back and forth. There were times when the crew that went out at four in the afternoon would have to stay overnight and keep everything going until bulldozers could clear snow off the road and we could get another crew in. They would work sixteen-hour shifts until they could get relief. It was a tough winter."

Nothing seemed tougher, though, than getting cash to buy rigs. Everything Doc owned, earned, and mortgaged was tied up in the business. It still wasn't enough, and credit seemed impossible to secure. The eastern banks didn't believe the western oil and gas business was sustainable. But Doc's friend Tom McGlade, who had studied at McGill and then worked for Sun Life Insurance in Montreal, had joined a small underwriting firm on Wall Street called Shields and Co. His contacts in Toronto managed to secure Doc a hearing, but it was no use. The banks said he could have the money for a new rig if he could present a three-year drilling contract. But in the frantic day-to-day atmosphere of the oil and gas business, the only contracts available were hole-to-hole.

The bankers wouldn't budge; a rig in the hand was worth more than two in the bush, if it had a long-term contract.

"When I think back how great a risk it was, really," says Doc, shaking his head. "The banks weren't at all eager to lend money unless they had absolute, total, solid collateral. It was very difficult in the early 1950s. I had no luck at all with any of them in the venture capital business."

Defeat was not an option, and Doc refused to set out empty-handed. He pursued every hint of a willing merchant banker, until he finally came face-to-face with Bill Hulton. He recalls, "I ran into a British firm called Charterhouse Canada run by this British fellow. He rather liked our stories and had a good financial mind, so he invested some money."

Of course, like all venture capitalists, the principals of Charterhouse insisted on their price: in this case, 25 percent of Seaman Engineering and Drilling. Hulton and his aide, D'Alton "Sandy" Sinclair, also ended up on the board of directors. But Doc was pleased. "My philosophy is about taking entrepreneurial risks to produce something of value and to create jobs," he says. "I get a lot of satisfaction out of that working."

For Doc, it was time to take the next risk. And for Charterhouse, that meant moving into the public market, a watershed move that Doc was initially apprehensive to make. He preferred remaining private, where contracts were won by one's good name and hard work. "The Seamans made their reputations in exploration drilling through a number of innovations and through simply working harder, faster, and more cheaply than the opposition," wrote Foster. "They outbid other drilling companies first, by offering to take a piece of the exploration action in lieu of cash — always attractive to explorers hungry for funds — and second, by offering 'turnkey' contracts."[5]

The turnkey operation promised a fixed price for everything involved with drilling and casing a well. If they encountered problems with a well, the Seamans would be at risk. If they could drill more efficiently, they would retain a bigger profit. By giving incentives to their crews and through their own ingenuity, the brothers were able to prosper even when times were tight.

Turnkey contracts were attractive to a wide range of investors, too, and this allowed the Seamans to keep their crews together and gainfully working. They were rapidly adding rigs, but still didn't have enough.

Enter Hi-Tower Drilling, an active public company run by Hart McIvor and admired for its crews and equipment. Hi-Tower's origins could be traced back to a larger-than-life pioneer of the Canadian drilling business, Ralph Will. Armed with a degree in geology from the University of Oklahoma, Will worked for years on drilling rigs in the United States before moving to Canada in 1937 with the Anglo-Canadian Oil Company. When Anglo-Canadian decided to withdraw from Canada in 1945, Will bought their rigs. Two years later, his gamble paid off when Imperial struck oil at Leduc. By expanding his rig fleet through the boom years, Ralph Will made a fortune and went on to serve for two years under Federal Cabinet Minister C.D. Howe at a dollar a year. Later, he was appointed by Alberta Premier Ernest Manning as the first president of Alberta Gas Trunk Line, later known as Nova Corporation.

"In order to buy Hi-Tower," says Doc, "Bill Hulton organized what would today be called a reverse takeover. In effect, one company uses another company's money to purchase it." A reverse takeover involves a smaller business purchasing a larger one and is often the route that a small private company takes to go public. That's exactly what Sedco did with Hi-Tower.

Peter Foster described the 1959 deal in which Charterhouse and the Seamans bought 70 percent of Hi-Tower's shares for $1.2 million: "By the middle of 1960, [the Seamans] would be able to pay the money off when Hi-Tower bought out all the shares of Seaman Engineering and Drilling for $924,000 and 55,000 shares of Hi-Tower, worth $660,000. Although they were scrupulously careful to gain independent assessments of the value of their shares, and did not vote when the issue came before the Hi-Tower board, the Seamans had effectively used Hi-Tower's own money to pay for their acquisition of the company."[6]

The takeover was greeted with incredulity in the oil patch. Questions around town were not always politely packaged, but the message was: "What do those shot hole drillers know about the real drilling business?"

Undeterred, Doc became president of Hi-Tower, with B.J. and Don as vice-presidents. With their purchase, the Seamans picked up many of the best drilling people in the business. Joe Wark was appointed executive vice-president. Don Binney, who had worked for Ralph Will both before and after serving in the war, was named vice-president of drilling operations.

Initial misgivings among Hi-Tower employees about their new bosses soon dissipated as the brothers connected with them personally. Foster captures a sense of this in his account of a get-together with staff members and their wives at the Stampeder Hotel not long after the takeover: "Soon things really loosened up and some of the boys began to engage in some competitive events, such as 'squaw wrestling' — lying on their backs, linking legs, and trying to pull their opponents over. The big muscular guys from the rigs soon discovered that although the Seamans were far from bulky, they were wiry and strong — and they played to win. One of the Hi-Tower toolpushers would carry around his snuff tin between his knuckles and challenge anybody else to grasp it and take it away from him. Both Doc and Don did."[7]

Many of Hi-Tower's senior operations people stayed with the Seamans for the rest of their careers. Don Binney became a key figure in Bow Valley, earning a reputation as one of the most knowledgeable drilling experts in Canada. Later, Doc relied on him to oversee construction of the company's first offshore rig in Norway. When Binney left Bow Valley, it wasn't to join another firm but rather to make a career change. Following in the footsteps of one of his forefathers, the first Canadian Bishop of Nova Scotia, he joined the clergy of the Anglican Church. B.J. affectionately called him the "oil patch pastor," but Binney himself described his new role in more pedestrian terms. "When the guys I worked with turn feet up and there has to be a funeral," he told *Oilweek*'s Gordon Jaremko, "they call on me."

Little more than a year after buying Hi-Tower, Doc went on the acquisition trail again. He picked up six more rigs in two separate transactions.

Doc also pulled together a group of companies to form Western Rockbit, and then acquired the Canadian interests of Cardwell Manufacturing Company, an equipment supply house that sold the trailer-mounted rigs the Seamans had used in their earliest exploration drilling ventures. To run Cardwell, Doc hired Bob Phibbs, who had once captained the Canadian Olympic basketball team.

In 1962, Hi-Tower was officially renamed Bow Valley Industries to reflect the company's diversification and vision for the future. The Seamans kept the Hi-Tower tag for their deep drilling division. By 1964, the brothers were the second biggest drilling contractor in Canada.

Bow Valley's accountants carefully researched Canada's tax laws and concluded that companies involved in metal fabrication were allowed to offset their taxable income against drilling projects. "We had our own machine shop, Rice Machine Services, that made drilling tools, and we built a home heating furnace called Flame Master," Doc recalls. "We also bought Mainland Foundry & Engineering in Vancouver that created sophisticated machinery for the forest and mining industries. They all earned money, and that gave us a larger budget to drill more oil and gas wells. That in turn increased our drilling company income, allowing us to spend even more on drilling."

Other acquisitions included interests in a small northern airline run by Cam Sproule and a Calgary-based computer software company owned by Rod McDaniel. Before the 1960s ended, Doc added Bullock Helicopters and Connors Drilling, a diamond drilling company, to his portfolio.

When he went public through the Hi-Tower acquisition, Doc's focus on risk and growth was one the stock market amply supported. While he now appreciated its advantages, he fully understood that the power of rumour could sink a stock faster than drilling a dry hole.

"The essence of business is being able to measure risk and make it work," Doc told journalist Gordon Jaremko. "Your enthusiasm and willingness to take risks is tempered by the amount of money you have. You have to know you can stand the hit from a dry hole and continue to go. It stays the same no matter how big you become. You don't want to sabotage yourself."

The Seaman company had a number of successful wells in southeastern Saskatchewan, often surprising the big companies from which they took farm-ins: Imperial Oil, Regina-based Tidewater Oil, and Central Del Rio (the precursor to PanCanadian Petroleum and then EnCana). Doc remembers the kick from a high-risk discovery and the immediate urge to do it again.

"Spending $100,000 in those days was huge, and to bet that on a well was quite exciting," he says. "One in ten would be a reasonable percentage of success on a wildcat exploration well. So if you're able to beat those odds, then you've been lucky."

By doing the homework and placing every dime and scrap of effort he had into a well, Doc was clearly creating a lot of his own luck.

"To make the system work takes a lot of dedication and effort," he explains. "The mechanics of starting up and building a business are mostly the same in any industry, and so is the level of personal commitment. You really do not have any time off. There is a lot of sacrifice."

Despite his growing success, however, Doc also felt stymied by the system. As contract drillers, his company couldn't compete with customers like Imperial who got the choice exploration parcels in Crown land sales. Clearly, a separate exploration and production company was the way to break into the production sector of the industry.

He soon connected with Alcon Petroleums, initially conceived by another Canadian industry icon, Harley Hotchkiss, in co-operation with Harry Van Rensselaer, a Connecticut blue blood working on Wall Street. Alcon was named for the Alberta and Connecticut homes of its principals. "Doc was interested in expanding beyond drilling and getting into the oil and gas business," says Hotchkiss. "Harry was very much interested in the Canadian oil business. I was coming to the realization that maybe my future wasn't in going to Toronto and being a banker, because I was walking away from my geology training and experience here."

Like Doc, Hotchkiss would abandon corporate security for an entrepreneurial life of high risk but unlimited reward. "That was a really interesting and challenging part of my life because I left probably the most secure job in the world at the Bank of Commerce in Calgary, with trips to Dallas and Houston and membership in the Petroleum Club," says Hotchkiss. "Here I am with four kids and no money and trying to make a way. I often look back and wonder, was I crazy? How did I do that?"

Hotchkiss was no crazier than all the other oilmen gambling their livelihoods and even their lives. Then as now, rig work was as big a risk to personal health as investment in it was to the bank balance. But the land was buzzing with the optimism of a new industry — volatile and seductive all at once.

The Seamans invested their oil and gas properties, which gave them 75 percent of Alcon, while Hotchkiss, Van Rensselaer, and their American partners held the rest. "So we had some modest income," recalls Hotchkiss. "I became the president, but I also swept floors and went out and sat on the wells. I've always been a hard worker, but I worked as hard then as I ever have in my life."

Van Rensselaer's role was to convince his Wall Street colleagues and wealthy friends that the Canadian oil patch was a worthy venture. Americans investing in Canadian oil and gas wells could deduct the amount from their American income tax. Canadians couldn't, until the law was changed years later.

"Under Canadian tax law, profits from the drilling business could be spent in oil and gas properties, and those costs could be deducted against their drilling income, because that definition was broad enough to include drilling," explains Hotchkiss.

Alcon had three sources of funding: drilling revenues from Doc's rigs, the company's own oil and gas properties (which had come from Sedco), and the investments of people whom Van Rensselaer had contacted.

Alcon's growth was steady, and it eventually boasted a major discovery in a farm-out well at Crossfield. One of its early wells flowed at rates of nearly seven thousand barrels a day. Years later, when fully developed, the field eventually produced around one trillion cubic feet of natural gas.

"I had a wonderful relationship with Doc," says Hotchkiss. "Doc was the kind of guy that gave you all kinds of room to run. I ran. I put the plays together. I would often go to Doc to bounce things off him, but really, he let me make the decisions. That was one of Doc's great strengths. He knew when to leave you alone, but he was always there to help if you needed it."

In 1967, after eight years, Hotchkiss left Alcon and established Sabre Petroleums with a wealthy German investor, Baron Carlo von Maffei.

"The reason I left was that I had gotten a taste of independence with a small company close to the action," says Hotchkiss. "I realized that was what I liked to do, probably what I was best at doing. So I went to Doc and said, 'I'll stay with you as long as you want me and need me. But I really want to do it on my own.' He understood that, and I left on a very friendly basis. They bought me out."

Hotchkiss adds, "Doc and I have maintained our close friendship over the years and have worked together in a whole variety of ways." Indeed, the two, with B.J., would later bring a National Hockey League team, the Flames, to Calgary. They would also collaborate on a number of philanthropic ventures.

Another lifelong relationship developed out of the Alcon connection too. In its earliest years, Alcon shared a two-room office on Calgary's downtown 8th Street and also some drilling ventures with T. Boone Pickens, who went on to create Mesa Petroleum, BP Capital, and his own American business empire.

Like Doc, Harley Hotchkiss and Boone Pickens are still actively involved in multiple business interests. Each has his own separate corporate entities, but all three still enjoy teaming up to hunt pheasants and quail.

Once his flagship company was in place, Doc invited Harry Van Rensselaer to join Bow Valley's Board of Directors. Van Rensselaer worked furiously with his friends on Wall Street to raise funds for the company.

"He was a great guy," says Doc. "He was from an old established family in Greenwich, Connecticut. We called him Harry the Hawk. He was a market-oriented fellow, and he was always swooping around. Any time the market was bad, we had visions of Harry jumping out the window."

Van Rensselaer gave Doc an advantage in finding American capital, especially when Canadian banks weren't lending substantial funds. The Hawk's contacts, and Doc's dreams, would soon thrust Bow Valley into the tumultuous waters of the international energy giants.

Chapter Four

The Huntsman

"We rarely find anyone who can say he has lived a happy life, and who, content with his life, can retire from the world like a satisfied guest."
— Horace

Relationships, often carved in war or on the rigs, became the bedrock for Doc Seaman's business success. Doc's word was his bond, and a handshake sealed a deal.

"We used to do contracts verbally, just two people," recalls Doc. "All our seismic work with Ted Rosza at Frontier Geophysical was done without a written contract." Rosza was a self-starter like Doc who believed in honour, respect, and sharing success with his community.

"It was the same way with Ernie Latham at Murphy Oil," says Doc. "We went for years by handshake. If we had any differences we would sit down and work it out."

It wasn't that way with the banks, which simply did not believe in the oil patch as a source of future growth and profit. Even into the 1960s, Central Canada's banking establishment eschewed western achievers like Seaman in favour of the mainstream industries clustered around Bay Street. That's why, to Doc and others in the oil business, friendship and loyalty were so important.

"It really exemplifies the importance of relationships and those that are long-term," says Harley Hotchkiss. "Harry Van Rensselaer was absolutely instrumental in Bow Valley's financing when it needed to raise a bunch of money later on. That kind of went back to those early days. It is interesting to see all that fit together."

Going from a small private enterprise to a substantial public company listed on senior stock exchanges ultimately helped give Doc and Bow Valley the access to elusive capital.

"But our relationship with Harry Van Rensselaer was crucial in that respect, because it was very difficult for small Canadian independents to access money for whatever reason," recalls Doc. "We certainly tried."

Even with Bow Valley on the market charts, Doc felt constrained because they were primarily drillers and not explorers. Alcon Petroleums had given Doc the taste for discovery. Now he wanted the chance to bid on and explore choice acreage. Doc was chewing at the bit. But he could neither explore nor bid outright for promising land parcels, because Bow Valley Resource Services (BVRS) drilled wells for the exploration companies. Hence Bow Valley Industries would be considered direct competition if it wanted choice parcels for exploration. BVRS was a revenue generator, and Doc didn't want to jeopardize that.

"There wasn't an opportunity to get prime acreage," recalls Doc. "We were drilling contractors here and pretty much forbidden to go to Crown sales. If we'd been able to bid and if there had been a discovery by another company, we wouldn't have been able to get any drilling contracts. That's because we'd be pretty much competing with our principals at the same Crown sales."

Besides the unavailability of land, there was another problem for smaller prospective explorers. The majors acquired acreage in large blocks and were allowed to simply sit on it. Alberta Tory Premier Peter Lougheed, who swept to power in 1971, succeeding the long-serving Social Credit government, changed the law and encouraged homegrown companies to compete. Lougheed's government decreed that the large leases had to be either drilled or surrendered.

"The land was mostly held in big licences and required only a minimum amount of work to hold massive acreage," recalls Doc. "They could do a little seismic or drill one well and hold it for a ten-year period. So Peter Lougheed devised a plan where they either had to do a certain amount of work or put the land back into circulation. That allowed some of the smaller companies a chance to get going."

By this time Doc was certainly going — and going strong — with his company listed on the stock exchanges in Canada and the United States. Bow Valley had expanded into diverse but related businesses.

"We were a bit of a conglomerate," Doc says. "We had the drilling rigs and a fair amount of oil and gas production."

But capital was still elusive. "The biggest challenge was always money," he explains. "It was difficult to get money. You had to travel either to New York or Toronto or Montreal. My buddy Tom McGlade was able to sell to his Wall Street partners that we were worth taking a bet on. So they took the lead in underwriting. Greenshields, a Montreal-based firm, joined them for a small piece of it. It was our first successful public financing."

Tom McGlade Jr. reinforces this. "It's remarkable that two guys would come face to face in an airplane hangar in England, crew up, and end up with incredibly successful lives," he says. "They rose together to amazing statures in business and elsewhere. What an extraordinary set of coincidences. They were step for step with each other; as my dad's career took off, so did Doc's."

The war that had transformed their youth now inspired their careers.

"All the way back to the very beginning, Doc was taking responsibility and leading, and he just continued to scale that up with the business," says McGlade Jr. "He's a natural-born leader. The BVI values and behaviour — everything came down from Doc. His leadership was mind-boggling. It was always very impressive to me to see that in person. He took so much satisfaction from creating jobs for people and running an organization with integrity."

That was the very reason Doc was able to attract inspired characters like hockey great Bill Hay, who served Bow Valley in a number of executive roles.

"Doc is refreshingly unpretentious. He has an even-handed manner, and he relates to rig workers, cowboys, and prime ministers in the same unaffected way," Hays says. "After my wife, Nancy, met Doc, B.J., and Don, she said, 'Bill, it will be very difficult to find a better group to work with.' I agreed. We liked the job, we liked the people. We liked their simplicity, we liked their competitive drive. They didn't act like all-stars. There were no personal trophies around the office. They didn't aspire to material things, and they didn't drive big cars. They weren't flashy. They were friendly and had a lot of fun, but they worked hard. Boy, they worked hard. It was the work that they loved to do. You don't meet very many men like that, and that's one of the big reasons I stayed with Bow Valley."

And yet, with choice western Canadian acreage securely fastened to a few multinational oil companies, Doc was stymied as an explorer and frustrated by the deals the majors offered along the way.

"We continued to follow the same form — try to get farm-outs from major oil companies," notes Doc. "It became increasingly difficult as land blocks were in larger holdings. You had to take more risks to get something that made sense."

As he told veteran journalist Gordon Jaremko, "We were stuck looking for that little edge of the geological reservoirs and hoping we could make something out of it. This scavenging was a pretty darn risky business for the rewards we could get."

For Bow Valley to grow, it also needed to go global. Doc started looking east, far beyond the Canadian borders, to a place he had once known only from the air — the United Kingdom's North Sea.

"I had a chance to go over to the North Sea," continues Doc. "A fellow by the name of Angus Mackenzie had a company called Syracuse. Angus had applied for some licences offshore both in the Norwegian and the British sectors of the North Sea."

Mackenzie was another of the great oilmen who refused to follow convention. He partnered with Calgary lawyer Jim Palmer, and the two went off to London to take on the majors at the black gold rush that was heating up in the North Sea.

"To bid in company with the Seven Sisters, the corporate rulers of the world oil, was an act of almost unparalleled bravado," wrote Peter Foster. "To some, in particular the big oil companies themselves, it appeared at best as an act of irresponsibility; at worst something close to downright fraud. At the operating meetings, the buttoned-down executives from Gulf or Chevron would look down their noses at Mackenzie and Palmer as if to ask: 'Who are these guys?'"[8]

"These guys" would soon be joined by another of their kind — Doc Seaman. They would carry their Canadian entrepreneurial spirit into uncharted global hunting grounds, reconciling the risk with the power of innovation.

As Mackenzie and Palmer acquired acreage further east, in Abu Dhabi and Indonesia, Doc decided to buy something even more formidable — Syracuse itself. The company had everything: solid assets and solid exploration management in the form of Dick Harris and Fred Wellhauser.

"Harry Van Rensselaer was instrumental in helping us get together with Angus Mackenzie," says Doc. "It was actually a merger. In the end, we bought them out for stock."

Naturally, the details were more complex. To get to the actual merger on April 30, 1971, serious discussions had begun six months earlier.

"Angus Mackenzie and Jim Palmer are longtime friends of mine," Doc notes. The respect is mutual. "Employees at Bow Valley loved Doc," says Palmer. "They would have done anything for him. That impressed me. It didn't matter what they were being paid. Whatever Doc said, people accepted. He listened carefully to everyone on the board, but Doc made the final decision, always in a nice way."

Syracuse had licences in the Norwegian and British sectors of the North Sea. It was a hunting ground that appealed to Doc, and in June 1970, he travelled to London with Bobby Brown Jr., who created Home Oil. A fabulously successful company, Home Oil had discovered the massive Swan Hills field in northeastern Alberta.

"My friend Maury Paulson was head of production for Home, and I told him about our interest in the North Sea. I had a chance to talk with Bobby Brown about it too, and he got quite excited to have a look. We went over to London together and took rooms at Inn on the Park [now the Four Seasons]. You know, I don't think it would be out of place to say that Brown was flashy and flamboyant — he took the whole top floor of the hotel," laughs Doc. "I got myself a small single room."

The objective was to obtain licences, and bravado was the order of the day, especially for the small companies. But the British government recognized the value of risk takers in their frontier waters.

"They allowed smaller operators to have licences there," recalls Doc. "They realized that in most cases, we were more anxious to drill. The majors tended to sit on acreage for a period of time, whereas the smaller independent companies created a lot more activity."

Brown knew many of the big players in the North Sea and subsequently joined a different consortium of explorers. However, Doc and Brown did unite with two Norwegian companies to construct the Odin Drill, a massive semi-submersible rig under Bow Valley's management.

"After we'd all done our geological and seismic work we had the opportunity to submit proposals on any number of blocks, ranking them in our order of preference," recalls Doc. "Bow Valley was awarded the block we had listed as our third choice. Home Oil's group won the rights to the block that seemed to be everyone's top pick, and they had the first slot on the drilling rig. They drilled a dry hole. The group awarded the second block also drilled a duster. We were next up."

The Bow Valley consortium's block lay about 150 miles off the east coast of Scotland under 350 feet of water. With two dry holes on choice blocks, everyone was apprehensive, but there was no retreat. Bow Valley, as rig manager, positioned the Odin Drill and spudded the well on September 19, 1974. The fury of the North Sea took its toll on the drilling schedule and on the partnership's bottom line. Plagued by some of the worst weather in the North Sea and by difficult downhole conditions, that single well took almost eight months to drill and test. It ended up costing a staggering US$16 million, making it one of the most expensive wells in the world up to that time. To darken the drilling days, initial indications were not encouraging. Based on a lack of oil shows in the drill cuttings, Bow Valley's operating partner, Pan Ocean Oil (later taken over by Marathon Oil U.K.), telexed the group that the well appeared to be dry.

Pan Ocean's initial assessment was wrong. Electric logs indicated five hundred feet of potentially oil-bearing sandstone. On test, the well flowed an astounding 22,000 barrels a day. Doc's Bow Valley drillers had bagged an elephant. The five Brae Fields would eventually boast nearly 800 million barrels of oil reserves and 2.5 trillion cubic feet of natural gas.

In the end, Doc's decision to explore in the North Sea would elevate Bow Valley to international status as a hunter of no small consequence. Pan Ocean held the majority position, while Bow Valley took an initial stake of 35 percent. This dropped to 28 percent after Britain's National Coal Board exercised its option to buy into Brae. A smaller interest was owned by Sunningdale Oil, controlled by Angus Mackenzie and Jim Palmer. Merchant banker

Hambros would put its stake "into the flotation of Bill Siebens's British company, Siebens Oil and Gas U.K."[9]

"Participating in that first Brae well was the most important decision in our company's history," explains Doc. "Because of the turbulent weather, that first well cost Bow Valley essentially all of the its cash flow for 1975. But the reward sure proved to be worth the risk."

At first, this huge financial risk depleted the company's coffers, as the tempestuous North Sea controlled the drilling agenda. "It took us quite a long time to drill that first well," recalls Doc. "We went way over budget because floating rigs weren't as stable as they are today. There happened to be a lot of storms in the North Sea that winter, and we were hit fairly often with fifty-foot waves. We'd get all rigged up for a drill stem test, and as luck would have it the weather would thump us again. Then we'd have to rig down all the testing tools and wait for the storm to blow over. That happened several times until finally we could successfully test the well — and what a find! We had a thirteen-hundred-foot oil column there, whereas five feet is often considered a good pay section here. Our Swiss geologist, Fred Wellhauser, would come up every morning and say, 'We're still in the goodies.' That's what Fred called the pay section. When the boys laid out a printed copy of the electric log, the pay section ran the full length of our boardroom table."

Once the exhilaration of the discovery died down, the cold reality of needing to raise enormous sums of capital set in. Two more successful wells were drilled. Facing an aggressive drilling program to delineate the field and then massive development costs, Bow Valley desperately needed money.

"We travelled around the world to find a partner," adds Doc. When asked if he considered walking away from his Brae discovery, Doc replies, "Oh no, I don't think so. No, I'm pretty risk-oriented. We were bleeding a bit, but I knew we had a valuable asset to work with." Doc's tenacity paid off, and by May 1976, he found a partner who was willing to meet his terms.

Bow Valley assigned half of its 28-percent interest in three blocks to Ashland Oil. In return, Ashland agreed to pay approximately $15 million to cover past costs and provide a loan for Bow Valley's entire share of development costs. The loan was non-recourse — in other words, Bow Valley's repayment obligations were confined to Brae production revenues. Further, the deal was structured so that Ashland would receive a maximum of 70 percent of Bow Valley's share of net revenues, thereby giving Bow Valley an income stream long before its loans were repaid.

As events played out, Doc's agreement with Ashland proved to be a brilliant move. Peter Foster later called it "the sweetest farm-out deal" in Bow Valley's history."[10]

After the first three wells, Brae had been touted as one of the North Sea's biggest finds. Shockingly, the next well was dry. And the next. Instead of being a single long structure, as initially thought, Brae proved to be a complex of five separate fields. Fortunately, Bow Valley didn't have to have to provide any more up-front money.

At 13,000 feet, the reservoir in the discovery well at Brae was one of the deepest in the North Sea, and the oil and gas were trapped under high pressure and temperature. This added to the cost and lead times required to construct the offshore platform and processing facilities.

"It was a big undertaking, to obtain all the government approvals and then complete the construction and installation," Doc says. "From the time of the initial discovery, it took us another nine years until we got it into production in 1983."

The ongoing development costs must have seemed as insurmountable as drilling that first Brae well in near-hurricane winds. With its huge capital costs, frontier exploration and production is a ride that even many thrill-seekers spurn. No wonder. By 1984, Bow Valley's 14 percent share of project costs would be a staggering

US$1.4 billion. Three years later, Doc would declare Brae to be "Bow Valley's greatest asset."

Eventually, after all the difficulties, the huge blast of petroleum from the Brae Field brought fortune to Bow Valley. The perseverance of a small upstart company from Canada discovered and put into production an enormous field that had eluded the majors.

The Ashland farm-out later produced another sweetner for Bow Valley too. Kaiser Resources bought Ashland and then sold the Brae stake to British Columbia Resources Investment Corporation and Louisiana Land & Exploration (LL&E). In December 1985, these two companies negotiated an end to their financing support for Bow Valley's future Brae development costs. "Their $450 million loans to Bow Valley were largely forgiven," states a Bow Valley Industries Brae Field profile. "The Company recorded a $360 million gain on the transaction."

To extricate LL&E from its future commitments, CEO Leighton Steward flew to Calgary. "I remember LL&E arriving at our offices with an army of lawyers and accountants," says Doc. "When they filed into our conference room, it seemed like they'd never stop coming. I took Leighton Steward aside. 'Leighton, we'll never get a deal done with this many people,' I told him. 'How about if you pick one of your guys and I pick one of mine and the four of us just sit down and work this out?' Fortunately, he agreed. I chose Charlie Fischer, who was in charge of our corporate planning at the time and now is CEO over at Nexen. Steward picked one of his staff and asked the others to go back to the hotel. We drafted up an agreement, and the LL&E team flew back home that same day."

Doc's North Sea venture didn't start with the astonishing Brae discovery. In December 1972, Bow Valley and its partners had found the Heimdal field around 100 miles off the Norwegian coast, under 375 feet of seawater. It initially promised 1.7 trillion cubic feet of natural gas and 49 million barrels of gas condensate. But by the time the thrill died down, so had the size of the find. With additional drilling, the reserves diminished while capital costs escalated. Political decisions made in Norway and elsewhere in Europe concerning natural gas marketing created lengthy delays. The Heimdal project eventually came on stream in mid-1986. "It's interesting that both the Brae and Heimdal fields are still in production," notes Doc.

Frontier euphoria was also gripping Canadian explorers, and the Arctic Islands charged onto the petroleum scene like a bull elk. Doc wasn't as enamoured as the others because drilling and exploration conditions were tough and getting the oil to market would be tricky. But it did offer Bow Valley opportunities for its drilling company and a chance to be part of a pure exploration play of over 50 million acres.

In 1969, Doc convinced the Bow Valley board to take a 2.26 per-cent piece of Cam Sproule's Panarctic Oils consortium, in which the federal government also had a stake. Later that year, Bow Valley could boast two rigs working within the cruel climatic confines of Melville Island: its subsidiary, Hi-Tower Drilling, and its joint venture partner, Commonwealth Petroleum Services (a subsidiary of United Westburne Industries), led by John Scrymgeour. While Panarctic's exploration indicated 17 trillion cubic feet of gas and 500 million barrels of oil in their acreage alone, getting the com-modities to production and then to market is still proving illusory forty years later.

By 1975, Doc had decided to sell the Panarctic stake to the Quebec government's Société Québécoise d'Initiatives Pétrolières (SOQUIP). The Panarctic partners were fine with the sale, but the federal government balked. The deal with SOQUIP stalled, likely because Ottawa didn't want rising separatists in Quebec taking control of the asset.

"The deal was dead," said Doc. "I resigned from their board. Panarctic was acting more like a civil service department than a frontier exploration company."

The Mackenzie Delta offered a more compelling story, so in 1968, Doc took a timely farm-in with Bill McGregor's Numac Oil & Gas, which held 320,000 acres in the vast delta region leading to the Beaufort Sea. Harry Van Rensselaer, always concerned about raising Bow Valley's profile on Wall Street, supported the Numac deal, partly because American investors loved the call of the wild north. Just a month later, Prudhoe Bay was discovered, and stock analysts quickly sharpened their pencils and Bow Valley's share price. Three years later, discoveries close to Bow Valley's acreage consistently bumped up their stock.

By 1973, the majors were brazenly courting Doc for a frontier farm-out: they wanted Bow Valley's Delta acreage. Doc chose to deal with Sun Oil. The farm-out was a tour de force for Bow Valley.

"Sun Oil paid $3.5 million for our seismic and technical data, plus $1 million annually for eight years," recalls Doc. "We were released from all financial obligations, but we kept a 27.5 percent stake."

One reason frontiers like Canada's north and Europe's North Sea were attractive hunting grounds was pure geopolitics. This was the era when the Organization of Petroleum Exporting Countries (OPEC) threatened to hold the Western world hostage to rising oil prices. By the beginning of January 1974, OPEC pumped its price from $3 to $11.65 a barrel.

Canada was locked in its own energy wars as Alberta Tory Premier Peter Lougheed clashed swords in the 1970s with federal Liberal Prime Minister Pierre Trudeau. Lougheed wanted the same deal for energy that central Canadian mining companies enjoyed: world prices. Trudeau responded with a made-in-Canada price for domestic consumption and the OPEC price for U.S. export. To further fuel the political fire with Lougheed and Alberta, Trudeau added an extortionate export levy that taxed the difference between the two prices.

Meanwhile, Lougheed raised royalties — ultimately three times — and Trudeau responded in typical fashion. He declared the royalties not deductible for companies filing corporate taxes. Producers decided to deploy their capital elsewhere and fled to fairer regimes. The stock market for Canadian producers followed suit, and Bow Valley saw its share price plummet. It didn't help that they had huge financial obligations in the North Sea.

In the midst of the energy wars between Lougheed and Trudeau, Harry the Hawk decided to take flight. Van Rensselaer, the trusted money man, grew weary of the political fights and endless airplane flights. He sold his Bow Valley stock. The old money followed, and Doc had to move quickly to avoid a calamity.

"We were vulnerable for a takeover, as our stock had taken quite a hit. We had strong assets, like Brae in the North Sea, but their value wasn't reflected in the share price," recalls Doc.

Bow Valley needed some new friends fast. It found them in Charles Bronfman and his family, who were familiar with the North Sea through their holding company CEMP, headed by Leo Kolber. Doc knew about CEMP's stake in Pan Ocean Oil and contacted Kolber. When Marathon Oil U.K. bought Pan Ocean, the Bronfmans decided to stay in the North Sea and invested in Bow Valley.

While the focus had been on oil, the forgotten fuel — natural gas — was about to come into its own. Natural gas was clean burning and transportable to the east through the TransCanada Pipeline and to the west via the Westcoast Transmission line. In addition, feeder lines had been constructed to the important American markets, whose access finally made the readily available commodity profitable for western Canadian producers.

"In fact, between 1970 and 1977, when the domestic consumer price for gas increased more than two-and-one-half times, the price to the producer, before royalties and taxes, increased by a factor closer to ten!" wrote Foster. "Export prices increased even more sharply, as did export demand."[11]

Meanwhile, Doc continued his global quest. In Indonesia, Bow Valley joined its operating partner, Asamera, to make a significant discovery in the Corridor block of southeast Sumatra. But first there were other adventures. In Abu Dhabi, they had an interest in an offshore concession through the Syracuse acquisition — Angus Mackenzie had earlier struck up a friendship with the ruling sheik and presented him with a white falcon as a sign of good faith. Bow Valley went on to partner with the American company Amerada Hess and found the Arzanah oil field. In Vietnam, they found plenty of intrigue but no oil, as wells in the South China Sea proved dry.

Doc's point man in Southeast Asia was Lloyd Flood, whose contacts ran the gamut from Viet Cong to CIA. Flood's love of the Far East echoes in the colourful stories of his exploits. He understood the languages and cultures and knew how to sidestep danger.

During the spring of 1975, Bow Valley had an offshore concession and was getting ready to move its drill ship in. In April, the North Vietnamese won the war against the Americans, and the intrepid Flood flew out of Vientiane, Laos, on a dilapidated Russian-built turbo-prop.

"We made it to Hanoi," recalls Flood. "As I headed off the airplane down those long step walkways, there were all these guys standing in a row, with red-starred Mao caps and creamy yellow uniforms holding AK-47 rifles. I said, 'Flood, you fool, you're forty-eight years old. What are you doing here?' I couldn't get a taxi, but a Polish newsman took pity on me and offered to drive me in. Once we left the airport, the road was filled with a familiar chaos: buses honking at cart drivers and cyclists; dogs and chickens running amok; and people everywhere. I said to myself, 'Relax, you're back in Asia.'"

Flood started working for Doc in the winter of 1969–70 and was on the ground with Bow Valley's biggest success story in the Far East — the Corridor block in Indonesia. The block had been spurned by many, but in 1980 Bow Valley took a 40 percent piece of Calgary-based Asamera's Corridor acreage. Initially, the $17 million spent on drilling and exploration looked like wasted money.

"We were right down to the nubs, and this is where Seaman is incredible," recalls Flood. "It was ten at night, so the same time in the morning in Calgary. Doc was on the phone with Bill Tye, and Bill, being a good CFO, went through the list of work and its results. We got to the end of the story. Doc said, 'Well, what do you think about that, Lloyd?' I said, 'I think Bill's summary is fine; but he just didn't put any value on the land. We still own 40 percent of 3 million acres.' 'What's land going for?' Doc asked. 'Fifty dollars an acre,' I told him.

"After a short pause, Doc said, 'We still have some value there. We'll go on for a while.' In early summer of '82, I came to Calgary to face the music over the budgets. I get a phone call at 4:00 a.m. Buddy De Luna, our exploration manager, says, 'Do you want the good news or bad news?' I said, 'Well, we've got enough bad news, give me the good news.' He said, 'The well is flowing nearly 1,400 barrels a day on a drill stem test.' I said, 'I don't want to know any more' and hung up.

"Doc left a lot of things to the guys he put in charge. But he always had his finger on what the heck was going on. He knew about those things that could seriously affect the business. His foresight and gambling instinct led to a lot of success in South Sumatra. The reality is that Doc realized we hadn't quite finished there and we had a few more prospects to drill."

The multi-million-dollar bet paid off. Further wells cemented Asamera and Bow Valley's success. "We made some big discoveries," says Doc. "More than 80 million barrels of oil and condensate were found. We discovered a lot of natural gas too, but there was no market for it in those days. Indonesia was a good experience for Bow Valley."

And the major finds in the Corridor block were certainly good for Indonesia. Initially there was no viable market for natural gas, but Doc's gamble became a huge asset for the state oil company, Pertamina, and another Canadian company, Talisman

Energy. Talisman bought Bow Valley's assets in 1994 from controlling shareholder British Gas and continues to enjoy the fruit of Doc's Indonesian investment. Gas reserves greater than seven trillion cubic feet in South Sumatra are now connected by long pipelines to buyers as far away as Singapore.

Although Bow Valley's biggest international successes eventually came from the North Sea and Indonesia, Doc was always on the lookout for opportunities to expand south across the Canadian border. He was comfortable doing business in the United States, and Bow Valley dabbled in exploration activity in the oil states of Louisiana, Oklahoma, and Texas. In 1977, Harry Van Rensselaer's groundwork on Wall Street resulted in exposure to a potential American acquisition.

The prey was Flying Diamond, whose assets ranged from drilling equipment, petroleum, and coal to ranching and property management. "It was a conglomerate of a whole bunch of things," recalls Doc. "They held coal mines in Kentucky. There was an oil and gas operation in Virginia and an oil field in Utah."

Gulf & Western Industries owned 39.6 percent of the Denver-based company, but were eager to sell for $40 per share in cash, or cash plus stock. Doc was determined to buy — at Bow Valley's price of $30 per share in cash. It would take tenacity, teamwork, and a certain element of tranquility to wrestle control of Flying Diamond from G&W's founder, Charles Bluhdorn, and his deputy, Martin Davis. (When Davis succeeded Bluhdorn at G&W, he built a Hollywood powerhouse, renaming it Paramount Communications.)

"Davis told *Fortune* in 1984 that he was 'thrilled' to have made the magazine's annual list of toughest bosses. *Fortune* quoted a business associate saying, 'He exceeds all of the qualifications for the category of s.o.b.'"[12]

Doc was no stranger to hearing tough talk and was unmoved by Bluhdorn's bullying tactics. "He was blustery," recalls Doc. "He'd suddenly phone and say, 'I'm pretty busy right now. What about the $40?' And I'd say, 'We're still thinking $30.' And he'd slam down the phone. Ten minutes later, he'd call again and begin, 'I'm pretty busy. There are a bunch of cameramen here wanting pictures. What about the $40?' And I'd repeat our offer, and he'd yell so I would have to hold the phone away from my ear, and then he'd hang up."

Doc called Dick Harris, Bow Valley's president, and asked him to go through his numbers once more to confirm that $30 was a fair price, given Flying Diamond's varied assets. His response reinforced Doc's resolve. The phone rang one final time.

"When after some minutes of ranting and raving, it became clear that Doc wasn't going to budge, Bluhdorn said: 'All right, you can have our stake for $30 a share. You're the toughest goddamn Canadian I've ever dealt with,'" Peter Foster recorded.[13]

The fight for Flying Diamond became legendary, and Tom McGlade Jr. remembers Doc standing up to the intimidating Bluhdorn. Both had built their companies with their own sweat and cash, putting everything on the line to grow. Even though they shared the role of risk taker, the similarity ended there.

"Doc is quiet and reserved," notes McGlade Jr. "He's clear-eyed and displays a beautiful instinctive understanding. He has the ability to make impeccable decisions all the time. Doc almost has a military mind, like that of Dwight Eisenhower or Colin Powell. You see the discipline of his military training where those leadership qualities became part of his character."

Flying Diamond held a few surprises for Doc, including a real estate division and several hundred thousand acres of ranchland. There were also eight thousand sheep. "If they'd been cattle, I would have been inclined to keep them," quips Doc. He sold the ranches and sheep, but kept land adjacent to the towns for future housing development. Bow Valley developed the Utah oil field, but focused more closely on the 8,000-acre coal concern in the Appalachian region of Kentucky.

"Our coal division manager, Clyde Goins, was quite a character who in earlier years had acquired a reputation for facing down militant union leaders. Clyde always kept a pistol nearby, either in his pocket or in the trunk of his car," recalls Doc. "We developed the coal mines from about 2,000 tons a day to around 4,000 tons. We had contracts with Florida Power and a number of other utilities that were generating power on the East Coast of the U.S."

Bow Valley's coal mining venture was such a success that Governor John Y. Brown Jr. gave Doc a virtual key to Kentucky. The plaque from the "Commonwealth of Kentucky" awarded "Honorable D.K. Seaman" the "commission of Kentucky Colonel on 14 July, 1982." Brown signed the tribute, which states: "I hereby confer this honor with all the rights, privileges and responsibilities thereunto appertaining."

Coal wasn't the only mineral making the boardroom hot at Bow Valley. Uranium was suddenly glowing in their suite of assets. Bill McGregor from Numac had shown Doc a prospective uranium deal that intrigued him at Midwest Lake, 640 kilometres northeast of Saskatoon, Saskatchewan. Imperial Oil was the operator, and Bow Valley was offered 20 per cent.

"We made a large uranium discovery in 1978," says Doc. "There were 36 million pounds of recoverable uranium oxide. Imperial was negotiating a contract at $50 per pound. They were close to closing when the price collapsed."

The Three Mile Island nuclear disaster struck on March 28, 1979. All the while, strategic arms limitation talks were occurring, with SALT II signed on June 18, 1979. Eventually, the resulting treaties freed uranium from the hell of nuclear arms to the heat of nuclear power plants. In the short term, the price of uranium plummeted to $10 per pound, and Imperial's contract talks collapsed with the market. Bow Valley was forced to sell its stake.

"Oh, I would have liked to keep it since we made the discovery. We sure should have," chuckles Doc. "But we were hard pressed to keep all the other things going, and uranium wasn't our main interest. It later became a big asset for Cameco in Saskatchewan." In 1999, Cameco sold its remaining stake in Midwest Lake to the French company Cogema, now named AREVA. Neighbouring mines in northern Saskatchewan are the largest source of uranium production in the world today.

Bow Valley had become a thriving global venture, because its leader wasn't afraid to take the trail less trodden.

By 1980, the energy industry was thriving in Canada. So were Alberta coffers, with royalties boosting the Heritage Trust Fund, a savings account established by Premier Peter Lougheed to ensure a future for the province when renewable resources ran dry. Prime Minister Pierre Trudeau's government had just returned to power. Now Trudeau and his ministers were looking at the province with money on their minds. They soon bludgeoned the energy business and Alberta with the most punitive tax system ever to hit an industry or a province. The National Energy Program (NEP) would ultimately pull $100 billion (in 2005 dollars) in revenue from Alberta and drive energy investment dollars out of the country. It was a power grab of astounding proportions. Trudeau's trusted advisor Marc Lalonde was the energy minister responsible for putting the NEP in place. As if to add insult to serious injury, parts of the plan were conceived during a federal cabinet retreat in Lake Louise.

"You had the NEP and then came low oil prices," notes Gerry Maier, who became chief executive of Bow Valley in 1982. "The whole industry went into dormancy." When the NEP was announced, Maier, then chairman of Hudson's Bay Oil & Gas, flew to Ottawa with Dick Haskayne, then its president.

"Their arrogance and lack of knowledge of the industry was astonishing," adds Maier, referring to both the politicians and the federal bureaucrats. "Our company was run by Canadians. The majority of our shares were held by Canadians. Our largest single shareholder was Hudson's Bay Company — you can't get much more Canadian than that. Yet, as part of his feeble justification for the NEP, Marc Lalonde represented incorrectly that a South African company, Hudson Bay Mining and Smelting, was our major shareholder."

Maier notes, "There were two solitudes: Ottawa and the West. Trudeau's Liberals were clearly bent on stripping money out of the western provinces to make political gains in Central Canada. It was hard not to be angry, but you realize you're powerless to do anything in the short term."

Doc shared this feeling of helplessness. He saw the NEP as an economic disaster for the oil industry and for Canada, but it was now the law of the land. He knew he needed to work within this new reality and try to salvage a future for his company.

The Trudeau government was placing huge emphasis on exploring Canada's frontier areas. Doc and his colleagues had overcome the most demanding conditions in the raging North Sea. The Brae discoveries, while expensive both to drill and to bring on-stream, offered the Seamans and their colleagues an extraordinary advantage. They had their own offshore drilling rigs. What better tools to tackle the untamed ocean off the east coast of Newfoundland?

"While the feds were primarily after the major oil companies, their new programs also hit the Canadian independents hard," Doc recalls. "One of their goals was to increase the Canadian content of the oil and gas business, but this was ill-conceived, ineffective, and ultimately very costly for Canadian taxpayers."

To achieve its grand objectives, the government introduced Petroleum Incentive Payments. These PIP grants were aimed at Canadian companies and were paid for out of the revenues they extracted from the industry. In order to qualify for PIP grants, a company had to have 75 percent Canadian voting control.

Many Canadian-born and bred energy companies, including Bow Valley, didn't qualify. Doc had no choice but to sell certain assets to adjust Bow Valley's ownership structure. The stress was palpable in the Bow Valley executive suite as the company, flirting with collapse, finally bumped over the crucial Canadian ownership marker and qualified for the PIPs.

In 1979, before the introduction of the NEP, Chevron had discovered the Hibernia field about 320 kilometres northeast of St. John's, Newfoundland, after taking a farm-out from Mobil. With his revised shareholding, Doc was determined to venture off Canada's eastern seaboard, where PIPs could be used to uncover the kind of fields the North Sea had yielded.

"Since we were in the North Sea and had our own offshore drilling rigs, I had the idea this was something we could tackle," says Doc. "I went to Bob Blair and talked to him about the possibility of using PIP grants to explore for oil fields beyond Hibernia. Bob was chairman of Nova, which had taken over Husky Oil. We already were partners with Nova in Western Star Trucks, a company we had bought to custom-build heavy diesel trucks, and now we were discussing a fifty-fifty joint venture to explore for oil and gas off the East Coast with Husky as operator."

Doc explained that the PIP grants paid for 80 percent of the cost of drilling an exploratory well. Blair, a staunch Canadian, was excited about the hunt in a new Canadian frontier, and the two agreed. They also decided to add a third semi-submersible rig. The government pushed to have it built in Canada rather than in Norway where the Seamans had previously worked with experienced rig constructors. Despite his nagging doubts, Doc agreed to build the Bow Drill 3 rig in Canada, mostly in Saint John, New Brunswick, at the shipyards owned by the Irving brothers.

"The government encouraged us to build in Canada, at considerably more cost to us, and promised preferential acreage to anyone who did that. We even built one of our supply boats in

Vancouver because of their promises. We kept our word. They didn't keep theirs," recalls Doc, still shaking his head at the betrayal.

"I remember one occasion when Jean Chrétien was in Calgary for a conference," Doc continues. "He was minister of energy at the time, and we had met with him several times before on account of our East Coast commitments."

"'Mr. Minister, we need a short meeting with you,' I said. 'Ten minutes should be enough. Can we sit down with you while you're here? I could drive you to the airport and we could talk in the car if that would work for you.' But no, he wouldn't meet with us here. He didn't have time. He gave us an appointment in St. John's, and we had to fly all the way to Newfoundland to have a ten-minute meeting.

"The way our own federal government dealt with us during the 1980s was worse than anything we ever encountered with a foreign government anywhere else in the world. The fact that it turned out well for us was a bit of serendipity, I guess."

The choice acreage the ministers and bureaucrats had promised Bow Valley and Husky for their pricey made-in-Canada Bow Drill 3 did not materialize. Essentially, Bow Valley and its principals were double-crossed by a company of the Crown. Petro-Canada, founded by an act of Parliament as a Crown corporation in 1975, was suddenly awarded what were considered to be the best prospects. Canadian companies founded through sweat and sacrifice were left to pick through the leftovers.

"We had to do what I would call a fairly difficult deal with Mobil Oil," says Doc. "Before we signed the deal, we set up a meeting with Energy Minister Chrétien. I recall that Dale Beischel, who headed up our exploration, and Bill Clark, who was in charge of our land department, were with me. Bob Pogontcheff accompanied us to represent Husky. I asked Minister Chrétien if they would assure us of the PIP grants. And I still remember Chrétien saying, 'the PIPs will be there.'"

But Doc's interests were side-swiped again after the Liberal government, under the new leader, John Turner, lost the 1984 federal election. The voters swept Conservative Prime Minister Brian Mulroney to power. As the Tories had promised to do, they began to dismantle the NEP — including the PIP grants.

"Well, that left us with continued obligations to the drilling company and commitments to Mobil Oil," says Doc. "Again we found it extremely difficult. We really had to gut up to continue that program and live up to our commitments. However, the East Coast was a good hunting field, and our Bow Drill semi-submersible drilling rigs sure did their work. On the fourth well, we discovered White Rose."

Doc and Blair's team had found another elephant. Husky and Bow Valley were the first independent Canadian companies to make a discovery in the Grand Banks. White Rose, located 350 kilometres east of St. John's, has an estimated 440 million barrels of crude reserves and 2.7 trillion cubic feet of natural gas. A year later, in 1985, the team discovered North Ben Nevis.

Today, White Rose is primarily in the hands of Husky Energy, which is controlled by Chinese billionaire Li Ka-shing. Husky operates White Rose with Petro-Canada as partner and produced its first oil from the floating platform in late 2005. Production is expected to peak at 140,000 barrels per day.

The Ben Nevis discovery will be developed in conjunction with the Hebron field; construction is scheduled to begin in 2010. With reserves estimated to be in excess of 700 million barrels, the combined Hebron-Ben Nevis project will be even larger than White Rose. ExxonMobil, Chevron and Petro-Canada are the major interest holders.

Cancelling the PIP program midstream was a huge blow to companies that had committed large sums of capital to Canada's oil and gas frontier. Bow Valley was especially hard hit, as it now had three large floating rigs and a fleet of supply boats at risk. Doc saw this clearly as a breach of the deal the government had made with him.

"We wanted them to extend the commitment that the previous government made," says Doc. "I met with Pat Carney, the new energy minister, and explained that we took on this big obligation off the East Coast as a result of a commitment from the government. It was the government that had made a deal with us, not the political party in power. They made a partial concession and allowed us to drill one more well under the PIP program. The wells were costing $300,000 a day."

The 1980s were brutal for domestic drilling companies, especially the smaller ones. Trudeau's initial attempt to develop and control the Canadian energy industry created havoc. Drillers were hard hit when producers bolted south to a warmer reception. Doc was especially concerned for the small family rig companies and formed a working group to deal with some of the bedlam.

"He worked with other drillers and particularly with the banks to seek solutions to the economic chaos being created for rig operators," remembers Bill Tye, who became Bow Valley's CFO in 1980 and seven years later was appointed president and COO.

The aftermath of the hated NEP was western Canadian mistrust, fewer Canadian independents, and much doubt in the minds of all producers. Alberta Premier Lougheed worked furiously to bolster the industry that the federal Liberals seemed so intent on tearing apart.

"We knew that we needed to come up with incentive programs that would offset the negative impact of the National Energy Program and encourage companies to explore," says Lougheed. "The Alberta government couldn't conceivably come up with a plan without consulting the industry as to what would work. It was important to have advice from people who knew the industry and to have an incentive plan that people with calibre, understanding, and awareness, like Doc Seaman, believed would work. And it did."

The government had off-the-record meetings with Doc, J.R. "Bud" McCaig, Jim Gray, and other industry leaders. There was no publicity or media. The goal was to stimulate the energy industry that the NEP had effectively stifled. Lougheed called Doc's advice "invaluable" because he knew the business intimately and understood precisely how incentives would generate activity.

As many businesses floundered, Bow Valley's global operations helped keep it afloat. "Fortunately, we had the international revenues," says Doc. "By this time, Brae was producing, and we had an ongoing program there. Because of our diversification into the North Sea and Indonesia, plus the sale of our assets in the U.S., we were able to survive all this. It wasn't easy."

Doc believes that governments must provide a fair landscape for business. Before governments decide to make any material changes to fiscal terms, there should be in-depth discussions with the industry involved so they know what the effects will be. Investing in multi-million-dollar projects is risky enough without the rules changing midway.

"It's important for government leaders and senior civil servants to recognize the contribution that entrepreneurs make to an economy," Doc says. "Alberta has in many ways provided a model environment where people can succeed through hard work, ingenuity, and risk taking. I hope this continues. Prudent business people will not put large sums of money at risk if governments take away the upside potential."

Early in 1981, Dick Harris resigned his position as president and COO. A year later, Dome Petroleum purchased Hudson's Bay Oil & Gas, and its CEO, Gerry Maier, moved over to Bow Valley while Doc stepped back to the position of chairman.

"Doc is very adventuresome, willing to take great risks and gambles," says Maier. "Bow Valley Industries' prior decisions with BVRS had some huge financial risks with the investment in offshore drilling rigs. When I learned what their exposure was on the Canadian

East Coast, I was really concerned. They were relying a hell of a lot on the producing company using super depletion allowances — PIPs — from the federal government to do the East Coast work. And based on my dealings with the Trudeau government, I felt Bow Valley was depending too heavily on promises that were liable to be broken."

Many felt, like Maier, that the PIPs were essentially designed for the likes of "Smilin' Jack" Gallagher, who built Dome Petroleum, and "Wild Bill" Hopper, who headed the Crown corporation Petro-Canada. The two Liberals lobbied for their own special brand of Canadian energy companies. They were awarded huge acreage advantages that eluded long-time Canadian oilmen.

Maier respected Doc's leadership style: hands-off in terms of running the daily operation, but hands-on in broad strategy. "I feel an unwritten kinship with Doc," says Maier. "In some ways we're very much alike. We're quick decision makers for better or worse."

Nexen's president and CEO, Charlie Fischer, had worked at Hudson's Bay Oil & Gas and joined Bow Valley in 1982. He appreciated Doc's instinct for any changes in the energy environment.

"Doc has an uncanny sense of timing," says Fischer. "We evaluated many potential deals, and when Doc believed we were working on the right one strategically, he'd find a way to get it done. In his quiet way, Doc works through complicated issues to define good solutions, which he then leaves for others to execute. He can do more on one piece of paper than anyone I've seen. His goal is always to work out a deal that provides reasonable returns for all parties."

When Fischer came to Bow Valley, he was a bit startled at its uniqueness. Unlike most large public companies, Bow Valley began as a service company and kept its roots even as it grew to have twenty-three affiliates involved in other businesses, including mining, manufacturing, and real estate.

"You just wouldn't do that today. The diversity would be too distracting," notes Fischer. "When they invested in environmental issues, they were ahead of their time, particularly in regards to dealing with wastes. Doc invested in technologies and new businesses he believed would be important as the world evolved. Today you have a very structured market pushing companies towards becoming pure plays. When you look at shareholders today, they're more engaged in interacting with management than they were then, and they prefer to build their own portfolios rather than rely on others to do it for them."

From an initial investment of $7,500, Bow Valley had grown dramatically through drilling, exploration, and acquisitions to achieve an asset value of $2 billion — and this in spite of high interest rates and low oil prices. Times were increasingly frustrating for energy companies as interest rates soared to 20 percent in 1980 and the price of oil collapsed in 1986. That July, oil dipped to below US$9 on the British Brent crude oil benchmark. By then, the full effect of the 1980 National Energy Program had put Canadian companies on the brink of collapse. Some were ruined. While Bow Valley had escaped that fate, it was forced to scale back its programs dramatically.

Bow Valley also had some sizeable debt due to its North Sea commitment. Doc decided to sell the American divisions, including the Kentucky coal mines, at a sizeable profit. It still wasn't enough.

"I was able to do some convertible preferred shares at a really drastic discount price as far as I was concerned, but we needed the money," recalls Doc. "They were converted into Bow Valley stock at a very low price. I hated to do it, but it was a necessity."

Bill Tye seized the challenge and dedicated himself to finding a financial balance by considerably downsizing the operations. "It was the only time I had to — was actually forced to — let some people go," says Doc, who looks crushed as he tells the story, even from a distance of many years. "It was a difficult time. I was always one for creating jobs, not letting people go."

Bow Valley restructured its company, management, and debt. "We needed to decouple Bow Valley Resource Services, which was 80 percent owned by Bow Valley Industries," recalls Tye. "We got BVI away from the service group, and our debt-to-equity ratio was much better."

Bow Valley Industries now owned only 40 percent of BVRS and was legally separate from it. The symbolic move away from its roots put Bow Valley Industries into a much better position to attract a strong stakeholder. This was becoming necessary, since the Bronfmans had decided it was time to move on.

"The turning point was CEMP wanting out. The Bronfmans had been the largest holders other than the Seaman family," says Charlie Fischer. "They had been in the sector for a long time and their intention to leave got the ball rolling, and that led to British Gas coming in."

At one point, the Reichmann family considered buying a stake. "They looked at us a couple of times," says Doc. "I remember Paul Reichmann coming to Calgary to have lunch with me and talk about Bow Valley. It was the week of the Calgary Stampede, and I had on my boots and Western hat. When I went to pick Paul up at the hotel, I said, 'How about wearing a cowboy hat for the Stampede?' Paul pointed to his skullcap. 'I've already got my cowboy hat on,' he responded, chuckling. I always enjoyed Paul's sense of humour."

While the Reichmanns passed on Bow Valley, Doc did find his investors. In 1986, TransCanada PipeLines called Gerry Maier with an offer he couldn't refuse, and Doc was pulled back into Bow Valley as CEO. The oil industry was reeling in the aftermath of the NEP, and oil prices had collapsed. In the midst of the turmoil, Doc took a suitor — British Gas.

Reuters published the details on August 6, 1987: "British Gas said Monday that it would acquire 29 million newly created Bow Valley shares for $575 million to increase its stake in the company to 33.3 percent, from 5 percent. Mr. Seaman said Bow Valley would use part of the new money to develop its 14 percent interest in the Brae oil and gas field in the North Sea. It has just spent about $350 million for its share of developing the North Brae Field, scheduled to start oil production next summer."

British Gas hoped to increase its stake to 51 percent at a price of $24 a share. There was a roadblock, however, in the form of Investment Canada, which needed to examine and approve any foreign deal above 33.3 percent.

"British Gas wanted absolute control, and that's where they had a lot of difficulty with the Canadian government," notes Doc. "They thought our government was being too onerous with them."

The deal was eventually done through a combination of common stock and convertible preferred shares that positioned British Gas at 51 percent. But no one was positioned for the Black Monday stock market crash. On October 19, 1987, the Dow Jones lost $500 billion, a drop of 22.6 percent. A month later, British Gas backed out.

On November 20, 1987, Reuters reported that the company had "called off its bid of $940 million, for a controlling interest in Bow Valley Industries. But British Gas said it would try to modify its offer to satisfy shareholders and the Canadian Government."

This was a harsh blow. Not only was Bow Valley a sitting duck for any predator, but, more crucially, British Gas was walking away from an agreement.

"A deal is a deal," Doc always said. In this case, a deal was in grave danger of being broken. Doc booked a flight to London and landed on the doorstep of British Gas. "They placed me in a waiting room and left me there cooling my heels for a good half hour," Doc recalls with a wry smile. "Then they ushered me into their boardroom. I took a chair on one side of this huge mahogany board table. On its centre sat a massive Canadian Inuit soapstone sculpture. Their chairman, Sir Denis Rooke, entered with half a dozen of his senior executives. He placed himself directly opposite me but right behind the sculpture. It was kind of comical. Every time Sir Denis spoke, he had to crane his neck so he could see me past the soapstone."

Everyone in the room knew there was only one item on the agenda: was British Gas going to proceed with the deal or not? Sir Denis Rooke was an imposing figure with a crusty manner. London reporters called him the "lion of British Gas" after his battles with the Thatcher government over the threatened breakup of "his" gas company during privatization. He was the defender of British Gas, and his remarks to open the meeting were polite but resolute. One of his senior staffers laid out the British Gas perspective on how the situation had unfolded and why they weren't buying. Then it was Doc's turn.

"Their facts weren't in dispute," Doc recounts, "so I got right to the point. I told them how I'd been in the Royal Air Force as a pilot during the dark days of the war. From those battles, I knew that the Brits were men of principle and integrity. Now we had done a deal. We all knew that stock markets went up and down. But I firmly believed they had agreed to do a deal with us, and I expected them to honour their word."

Sir Denis abruptly recessed the meeting. Before leaving London, Doc had his deal back in place. "As a result of that meeting, they honoured the deal," says Doc. "And that deal is now a matter of record. If it wasn't the largest single financing of that era in Canada, it was close to it. They put $1.2 billion into Bow Valley Industries. That was a huge amount for the times."

Doc chuckles at the notion that certain underwriting firms thought Bow Valley couldn't handle that much cash. He quickly proved otherwise.

"We bought the Hatton field in southwestern Saskatchewan and paid around $140 million. We started to develop it and ended up with about 25 million cubic feet of natural gas a day. Then gas prices collapsed, and we had to quit developing it for a while."

Doc retired as chairman of Bow Valley in May 1992. Just two years later, British Gas retired its interest in Canada. On May 18, 1994, the *Wall Street Journal* announced that Talisman Energy was purchasing Bow Valley for C$1.82 billion: "Bow Valley ... was quickly identified as a prime target, and with a willing seller in the form of 53 percent owner British Gas PLC, a deal was soon struck." The purchase made Talisman the third largest gas producer in Canada, but more importantly it gave the company substantial properties in the British North Sea and Indonesia.

Talisman would take Doc's discoveries and become one of the most important Canadian producers of the day. But it didn't keep all of Bow Valley's plays; the Hatton field in Saskatchewan was ultimately acquired by Apache Energy. "Apache says it's the best field in their system and producing 100 million cubic feet a day," says Doc. "It's shallow gas and has a long reserve life."

Doc may have left Bow Valley, but the company has never really left him. When British Gas sold its stake to Talisman, Doc retained the right to the Bow Valley name. In 1996, Bow Valley veterans Ken Stiles, Jim Cummings, Walter DeBoni, Bob Welty, Lloyd Flood, Rod Blair, and Les Beddoes joined Doc, B.J., and Don in creating the junior company Bow Valley Energy Ltd. Two other founders, Jack Peltier and Tim Swinton, had done business with Doc and his associates in other ventures. A feature article in the *Calgary Sun* announced on July 24: "Like the phoenix, Bow Valley Energy is rising from the ashes."

Today, the new Bow Valley's mandate is to become an "international, intermediate-sized exploration and production company." Doc's love of adventure and the hunt for the big prize have not diminished over the years. The company's focus is currently on the British and Norwegian sectors of the North Sea and Alaska's North Slope. Doc sits as chairman, with Gerry Maier and Jack Peltier as members of the board and Rob Moffat as CEO.

"Bow Valley Industries was a good head start in a historic company and in building a Canadian energy industry," says B.J. Seaman.

"We came out of a small town now called *Corner Gas* and yet we've been to every continent except Antarctica."

Brother Don Seaman is quick to agree. "Doc was quite an innovator," he says. "We had health insurance and stock options for employees. We looked at environmental impact and capturing wastes. We did sulfur recoveries. We had a stack monitor on sour gas plants that gave the operators an idea of how to control their emissions. We had five-year plans where we would double business in five years. This all began in the mid-1950s. Doc was ahead of his time."

Doc's career as the creator of a large-scale industrial enterprise was mostly over. Now he was developing an even more exciting business interest as a venture capitalist involved in dozens of smaller companies. In this role, he would be a mentor to oil and gas entrepreneurs of the twenty-first century.

CHAPTER FIVE

The Mentor

*"THE MEASURE OF OUR LIVES COMES FROM THE INTEGRITY OF OUR
SPIRITUAL JOURNEY, AND THE DIFFERENCE WE MADE IN THE
LIVES OF THE PEOPLE WE MET ALONG THE WAY."*
— EUGENE STICKLAND

Doc's moral compass points to job creation, and he can't sit still when offered a fine prospect or an intriguing idea. "I keep turning down things, and then something comes along and I have a hard time saying no," he says. Doc embodies ability, agility, and old-fashioned nerve. Risk taking, luck, and smarts have added intangible dimensions to his business wisdom. Trust and respect generated the success. Lifelong loyalty was the reward.

"If you could create jobs with your own capital and new ideas and innovations, then you had a responsibility to do that," Doc notes. "And so I guess I've done that in good measure, although I suppose it's for others to judge." His modesty will always underrate his accomplishments, but there are many business innovators for whom Doc is a model or mentor.

"Doc is a deep thinker who takes the larger perspective," says Calgary Flames co-owner N. Murray Edwards, president and owner of Edco Financial Holdings.

Edwards first set eyes on Doc at the University of Saskatchewan when Doc was receiving an honorary Doctor of Laws degree in

1982. Edwards was earning something of his own, a Bachelor of Commerce with Great Distinction. Doc chuckles as he recalls their later meeting in Calgary and Edwards' comment: "You and I graduated the same year." That graduation ceremony in 1982 had a deep impact.

"Here I saw this iconic guy — the founder of Bow Valley and a Calgary Flames owner. I was very excited and got to meet him at the awards lunch, and Doc left a lasting impression," says Edwards. "So when I was invited in 1994 to be a Flames owner, it was a real honour. Doc is very much an entrepreneur in the Western sense, with that pioneer spirit. He built the company from scratch when deals were done on a handshake and the back of a napkin. It was a different time and a difficult one, and Doc was able to do really well through business acumen and his engineering background and his personality. He's a charming individual."

Edwards agrees that Doc represents the generation that built modern Canada, but he also believes that Doc's philosophy is crucial for modern times. "The underlying value is hard work, entrepreneurial sprit, and being true to your word. Those things are still important. They are the hallmarks of Calgary and Alberta business, with today's added wrinkle of a lot more paper," he says.

Indeed. Today there's a plethora of paper for everything. The heart of the deal — a handshake — has been replaced by the heft of the deal — a pile of words on a vast mountain of paper.

"The Code of the West was the handshake, and it's not like that in the oil patch anymore," says Doc. "Ethical standards may be the same, but the contracts are much more formal. In the past, everyone knew one another and it was easier to get things done, even with government."

In Doc's early days, the principals sat down and worked things out. Today's demands for paper verification mean that work has broadened and intensified. Certainly there were areas where lax laws allowed the crafty and corrupt to create dishonest

Parents

Byron and Letha Mae Seaman ~ Wedding ~ January 1920

Byron

Hudson's Bay Cup Winners ~ 1938

Byron Seaman, Alex Sharp, A.W. Johnson, and W.A. Cochran

Siblings

Don, B.J., Doc, and Dorothy ~ At home in Rouleau

Dorothy, B.J., Don, and Doc ~ Letha Mae's 100th birthday ~ 1999

Top Gun

Doc with silk stocking scarf ~ RAF base in England 1942

Doc in Lockheed Hudson ~ RAF base in North Africa 1943

Bomber Crew

Eddie Thorpe, Doc, Tom McGlade, and Archie Henderson

Robert "Sam" Turner, Doc, and Tom McGlade ~ Tent camp in Algeria

Edinburgh Castle

October 1942
While stationed in England

Return visit 1991

Inspiration

Copy of pocket-sized card carried by Doc throughout the War

"I SAW THE MORNING BREAK"

The following poem by the late Sir Owen Seaman, which formed the close of the first speech made by the late Marquess of Lothian after taking up duties as Ambassador in Washington, was sung at the Memorial Service to Lord Lothian at Westminster Abbey. It was set to music by Dr. Ernest Bullock.

You that have faith to look with fearless eyes
    Beyond the tragedy of a world at strife,
And trust that out of night and death shall rise
    The dawn of ampler life ;

Rejoice, whatever anguish rend your heart,
    That God has given you, for a priceless dower,
To live in these great times and have your part
    In Freedom's crowning hour ;

That you may tell your sons who see the light
    High in the heaven, their heritage to take :
"I saw the powers of darkness put to flight !
    I saw the morning break ! "

Printed by the Canadian Y.M.C.A.

England.   *January, 1942.*

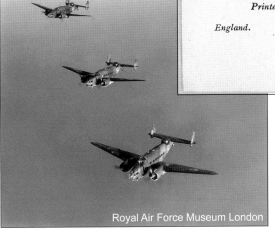

Royal Air Force Museum London

Lockheed Hudsons in flight ~ WWII

Baseball

Army, Navy, and Air Force Vets ~ Saskatoon 1945

Negro Leagues Baseball Museum

Doc

Satchel Paige and
Jackie Robinson
Kansas City Monarchs
1945

Family

Diane, Ken, Bob, and Gary

Lois, Evelyn, and Eleanor ~ Watching "the brothers" playing hockey

Bow Valley Brass

Doc, Don, and B.J. ~ Rouleau

B.J., Doc, and Don ~ Calgary 1985

Rig Crews

Southern Saskatchewan ~ 1960s

South Sumatra ~ 1980s

Northern Alberta ~ 2007
Rig Manager Len Nanaquawetung (centre) with Lakota crew

Operations

South Brae jacket under tow from shipyard in Scotland

Doc with
Rev. Don Binney
(former vice-president
of Bow Valley's
drilling operations)

Frontier Drilling

Arctic Islands

Offshore North Sumatra ~ Well Test

Bow Drill 3 ~ Saint John, New Brunswick Shipyard

North Sea Production

South Brae Production Platform ~ North Sea

Western Lakota

Lifetime Achievement Award
Elson McDougald
Chief Eddie Makokis and Chief Victor Buffalo

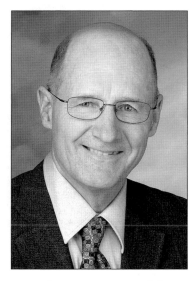

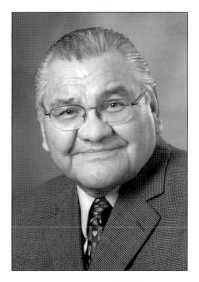

Elson McDougald

Victor Buffalo

The Next Generation

Diane ~ University of British Columbia Graduation 1970

Gary, Ken, and Bob ~ July 2008

deals. But now the U.S. Securities and Exchange Commission, responding to white-collar crime, has tied the regulatory process so tightly that companies can spend more time creating paper than wealth. Businesses listed on the Toronto Stock Exchange must also comply with SEC regulations. But many believe the regulators have gone overboard.

"Before we sold the original Bow Valley, our year-end board book would be no more than a half-inch thick," recalls Doc. "Now, I can show you our book and it's four inches. Instead of a meeting taking an hour for business, we're dealing mainly with words and making sure that everybody has complied with absolutely everything. It takes at least a day, or more." That's one reason companies like to remain private, simply because of all the paperwork. "It's so much easier to get things done," adds Doc, "and that's like the old days."

On the scientific side, though, the improvements are huge and beneficial in the petroleum business. Massive strides in science and technology create greater efficiency in getting the resource out of the ground. Along with this comes improved environmental awareness.

"We had mud pits in the old days, and all the refuse was put in them," recalls Doc. "I try to be a good steward of the environment, and the oil industry has improved its tactics."

As his brother Don noted, Doc didn't wait to follow the industry; he led with environmental initiatives before others began doing so just because regulation demanded such action. The brothers are ardent investors in CCR Technologies, a high-tech chemical purification company.

"We had a research division in Bow Valley that did a lot of sulfur recoveries, and that was an early stage of environmental technology," says Doc. "And CCR has gone beyond that quite a bit to reclaiming of glycols that are used in the gas production process. We do a lot of work for refineries, cleaning up their systems. Instead of dumping the waste somewhere, we reclaim it to 99 percent purity."

Elson McDougald is involved in CCR Technologies as well as a number of other companies in which the Seamans have invested. To McDougald, they personify "patient money," a trait that has passed on to entrepreneurial successors like Murray Edwards.

"The Seamans invested in all of the companies I'm involved in and were very patient," says McDougald. "I am really pleased to see that it has paid off for them as well as it has. Doc's been fantastic to work with. He has such an amazing insight into people and opportunities." McDougald is currently working on Decision Dynamics Technology, a business operations and management software company, as well as CCR Technologies. But the business that makes his heart beat with pride is Western Lakota Energy Services, which merged with Savanna Energy Services in 2006. Western Lakota was recognized as the leading energy company in promoting partnerships and training with First Nations and Métis communities.

"What distinguishes Lakota are the relationships," Savanna CEO Ken Mullen told the *Daily Oil Bulletin*. With the merger, Savanna adopted Western Lakota's First Nations' training and hiring program and is using it throughout their company while fostering future programs and ties. Michael Tims, chairman of investment banker Peters & Co., points out that Doc encouraged aboriginal training and hiring years before others in the oil patch promoted the partnerships.

"Having aboriginals in your workforce lessens the tensions," explains Doc. "They absolutely should be part of the scene when you're doing work on their land. Otherwise there can be problems. This has been one of the most gratifying experiences in my life, and the partnerships continue through our merger with Savanna. It's a great story."

Aboriginal hiring and training should have been an obvious choice for any company working in the energy industry. The people know their land, it's their home, and they intend to remain. Yet for too many years, aboriginals were ignored and discriminated against in their own place. McDougald saw an opportunity to right a wrong and, in the process, develop a successful company. Understanding diversity and building relationships were the keys. Then came the training and hiring.

"I love it when someone says you can't do that," notes McDougald. "The more they say that, the more I want to do it. With Doc behind you, the comfort of someone believing in what you're doing is so great."

Doc and McDougald had initially started Tetonka Drilling, which merged into other drilling and well servicing ventures. Within three years, they were part of drilling giant Nabors Industries.

"Not long after that, we started Western Lakota, and the idea was to be in partnership with First Nations," says Doc. "In most cases, they would buy 50 percent of the rigs because they were given grants by the federal government. We also organized a drilling and training program. That's worked extremely well. We started out with the Dene Tha', a large nation in northwest Alberta, northeast B.C., and the southeast end of the Northwest Territories. Then we partnered with the Samson Cree Nation."

With Doc's backing, McDougald mined his experience, skill, and passion to enhance Lakota's position and make the company unique. There was an industry shortage of drilling rigs, and EnCana contracted Lakota to supply three rigs over four years. As he travelled with some of EnCana's senior explorationists and landmen, McDougald listened to their plans for exploring on First Nations lands. Then, as he visited with different First Nations throughout northern B.C. and Alberta, McDougald learned about their dreams, their hopes, and their hurdles. He considered also what role the federal and provincial governments could play.

"I tried to design a win-win for all parties — with lessons from Doc where we want to do balanced deals that are good for those involved, including our shareholders," says McDougald. "We had five parties to please, and we had to find a fine line where everybody was a winner."

For the aboriginal communities, McDougald and Western Lakota focused on establishing long-term relationships. He wanted the community members to see a partnership that produced equity and/or cash flow as well as crucial employment. For the oil and gas companies, McDougald needed to cement his aboriginal relationships in order to present a solid performing rig.

"We were told by some of our early customers that we met and exceeded their expectations by twenty-plus percent," says McDougald. "Not only did we improve aboriginal relationships, we were turning the whole venture into a cost benefit. These aboriginal partnership rigs were, in fact, saving the energy companies money. For the communities, they were achieving long-term sustainable business and they were getting employment."

With the provincial government, Western Lakota established a training program for aboriginals. The company built a rig simulator to one-fifth scale with all the functions of a drilling rig floor. They mounted it on a tractor-trailer and took it to the reserves. Candidates were carefully selected, and everyone talked about expectations.

"That is what most of the industry is missing — what should you expect when you arrive on the job and what does the company expect of you?" says McDougald. "You bridge the gap because they grew up in a different culture. That's week one of the course. The following week is hands-on tool training — going over and over again how to work the tongs, how to work the slips, how to set up the pre-fabs, put them up, and tear them down."

The students conclude their basic training with certificates in first aid and hydrogen sulfide safety systems. The aboriginal graduates earn a Western Lakota diploma and are ready for the real rigs. The entire curriculum is designed in-house and endorsed by the Alberta government. Much of the program's success is due to the trainers, who themselves are First Nations people.

Western Lakota's training manager, Shauna Simpson, from the Bigstone Cree First Nation, worked with lead instructor Marci Potskin, of the Sawridge First Nation. The rig instructor is long-time driller Len Nanaquawetung, a Saulteau from eastern Saskatchewan. "Len had worked his way up through the ranks of the drilling business and became a rig manager, which is the highest field classification. He went out to the reserves, got recruits, and guided them through training," explains Doc.

"Doc has attended as many of our ceremonial signings as he could," notes McDougald. "Doc fits in everywhere you take him — to the rig floor, to the shops, to the boardrooms — wherever he goes he fits in so well. He is just part of the group."

Chief Eddy Makokis of the Saddle Lake First Nation agrees that Doc is "someone you can talk with." With his vast global experience, Doc respects cultural differences and encourages understanding whether it's across the ocean or over the mountains. From the Dene Tha' First Nation to the Métis Nation to the Saddle Lake First Nation, Western Lakota has forged partnerships of mutual respect and understanding.

"We are partners with at least thirty-two First Nations, and we took Doc's approach of having all the information right on the table," says McDougald. "We visit our partners every quarter and we table a report on financial results, marketing, safety, and employment — the whole works. We talk about any issues and concerns they might have. At our quarterly meetings, I have presented to 125 people in a school gymnasium. It doesn't matter. Bring them all if you want. We'll go through all the facts and lay it on the table — it's an open book. I think that has been a large part of our success — an open, honest flow of information and communication at all times, anytime."

McDougald's team also visits high schools on the reserves. They make a presentation but tell the students to finish school first and then consider the rigs as a career. The Western Lakota course has become so successful that the company is able to provide the names of graduates to competitors.

"We've had over 150 recruits, and we're booked to do about 100 more," notes McDougald. "We've reached 90 percent course completion and 82 percent job retention. It has been so rewarding to see this develop. Now we are getting calls from all across Canada — from Ontario, Quebec, and the Maritimes. We really can't keep up."

McDougald also championed aboriginal promotions within Western Lakota where two rigs are completely staffed by aboriginal workers, from rig hands to managers.

"They're really coming up through the company," adds McDougald. "They are earning their positions. That's the way we set it up. You've got to perform. There are no easy jobs, no corner office just because you're a partner. You earn your stripes. I tell them at the graduation ceremonies that I was just a kid off the farm in Saskatchewan. I didn't know a thing about the oil patch when I started on the rigs. I'm no different from them, and I did fairly well. There's no reason they can't do the same thing."

McDougald started on the drilling rigs in 1963; he came to Alberta in 1964 and worked for John Scrymgeour's Westburne International Industries. He met Doc in the late 1960s and started working with him in 1984.

"I travelled around and became partners with Doc," recalls McDougald. "When I meet people in Boston, New York, Philadelphia, Los Angeles and say I'm from Calgary, they usually mention Doc's name fairly quickly. Doc Seaman and Jim Gray seem to be the most famous people in our industry in Calgary. I've never come across anybody who had a bad word to say about Doc. He's a tough, honest businessman who does the best thing for his company. He doesn't give anything away but is very sincere and straightforward."

After decades in the oil patch, McDougald was convinced that ownership and employment were keys to northern development.

He talked to Doc, and both were keen on Lakota's program for aboriginal engagement.

"Doc has been very supportive," says McDougald. "When we started the aboriginal concept back in 2001, it was a brand new idea: going full-tilt at this partnership-training relationship. The competitors were against it, and the investors were very, very skeptical. They wouldn't touch the stock for two years. It was a penny stock, and it stayed that way. Doc Seaman and J.R. "Bud" McCaig backed me up throughout. Doc listened carefully and analyzed what I was trying to do and gave me the go-ahead to pursue the idea and see what we could achieve. I never could have got it off the ground without the support of those particular board members, including Doc's brother Don Seaman." It took two years for everyone to buy into the plan. Doc never wavered, and Western Lakota's First Nations partnerships took off. Doc and McDougald are delighted, as the brokerage community is finally showing its support and competitors are trying to copy Lakota's success.

"The big investors in Boston, New York, Philadelphia, wherever, I find that so many of them can spend a half hour on the figures, and they will sit and talk for as much time as you've got on the social aspects of what we are accomplishing," says McDougald. "So many times I have been asked, 'Can you bring your model in some fashion here and apply it in various parts of the United States?'

Chief Victor Buffalo of the Samson Cree Nation, who was on the Western Lakota board of directors, sits on Savanna's board. McDougald calls Chief Buffalo's participation "outstanding." For his part, Chief Buffalo notes in the Samson Community Connection for September 2007 that "his board experience with Savanna and other companies differs greatly from his time spent on Nation committees." Bridging that gap through partnering, understanding, and learning was an early goal of McDougald and Doc.

Western Lakota was recognized nationally for its innovations and its inclusiveness by Jim Prentice, Minister of Indian Affairs and

Northern Development, at an Ottawa conference on November 21, 2006. "In the oil and gas industry, First Nations are working in partnership with giants like Syncrude and EnCana," stated Prentice. "They are engaged in managerial and technical capacities, in joint ventures that provide vital services to the industry, and as investors. In Alberta, for example, ten of Western Lakota's rigs are owned in fifty-fifty partnerships with First Nations communities. And the Samson Cree Nation has partnered with a wholly owned subsidiary of Western Lakota Energy Services to operate five coil tubing service units. We are seeing more and more First Nations acting on their potential to generate wealth and opportunity for their community members and for Canada as a whole."

Doc says, "I've really enjoyed seeing our partnerships with the First Nations come to fruition. We've been able to have a positive impact in over twenty bands. Anywhere I've been in the world, I've found people who want a chance to improve their own conditions. I've always felt that developing a business venture where everyone has some ownership makes a lot more sense than pouring billions of dollars every year into social handout programs."

Doc's insight and McDougald's passion inspired one company to look beyond the ordinary. Understanding the commonalities of human nature in the face of cultural differences was crucial. The support of First Nations leaders encouraged Western Lakota to persevere and ultimately succeed.

"Doc has a mindset to help aboriginal people get into the industry and move up within it," says Bill Tye, who worked so closely with Doc during the Bow Valley days. "He's a pioneer in oil and gas."

Tye admired Doc's no-nonsense leadership style: encouraging discussion, grasping the essentials and potential, acquiring all the facts, and getting on with the job. He believes in brevity and simplicity. While Doc is very private, he's also a facilitator. Tye recalls that if something came off the rails, Doc, ever the engineer, looked for the problem and resolved it.

"Doc is a charismatic person who inspired colleagues with tempered enthusiasm and positive thinking," notes Tye. "He's very well disciplined and, in his quiet manner, almost self-effacing. Yet he got the desired results. When meeting people, Doc makes good eye contact, offers a firm handshake, and makes others feel at ease. There's no superficial aura."

Doc's door was always open, and he was determined to have the best vice-presidents so he could delegate tasks. "That's why I hire good people," he used to tell his executive assistant, Jean Brown. Doc was the CEO, but he gave his VPs a wide range.

"Doc has influenced many people," says Nexen CEO Charlie Fischer, a former Bow Valley vice-president. Fischer is one of many who have benefited from Doc's wisdom as he delves through issues and confronts challenges. Doc has supported both entrepreneurs with innovative ideas and chief executives with massive companies to run.

"Doc took the time to help me," Fischer adds. "He is truly a venture capitalist. If he sees people who have a good plan and they're the right kind of person to do it, he's going to bet on them. I think to a whole bunch of us, Doc's a mentor."

Bob Hindson was also a vice-president at Bow Valley Industries, in charge of the mining operations until he moved on. After an exciting stint as vice-president of Aber Resources when they discovered Diavik in the Northwest Territories, one of the world's richest diamond mines, Hindson founded Far West Mining in 1995.

"I wasn't interested in being a holding company," he says. "I wanted to do active exploration, so I purchased from Bow Valley Industries some Saskatchewan exploration properties in uranium and base metals, like lead, zinc, and silver."

Doc had already sold Bow Valley, but was told about the mining assets. He contacted Hindson and said, "I hear you purchased the Saskatchewan properties. I want in." Hindson agreed, and Doc asked him what he'd paid for the properties. "I didn't pay a lot, but for me it was a fair amount," Hindson told him.

"Doc said, 'I'll pay you half,'" Hindson recalls. "He wrote me a cheque for half. I said yes. I didn't bargain. Then the next day, Doc called and said, 'That was too easy a deal. I'll pay you what you paid. I'm sending another cheque.'" Hindson had taken the initial risk, and Doc was essentially showing his faith in him by paying full price for a half share.

This amazing story speaks to the loyalty Doc has nurtured throughout his storied career. Hindson already knew of Doc's fairness and support and his love for exploration.

"If you're in exploration, you need to be enthusiastic and eternally optimistic," says Hindson. "He's the consummate businessman, and he's fun to be with. Yet if things don't work out, Doc's the guy who says, 'Well, we'll just move on'. He's totally supportive, but he doesn't like surprises. He'll say he wants to know what's going on, good or bad. In that way, he's very hands-on."

Hindson appreciates Doc's modesty, noting that he has never heard him speak in terms of "I" or "me."

"Doc's track record is fantastic," adds Hindson. "His name is magic. A year ago, I went on a marketing show-and-tell to Toronto, London, and New York. I met people I'd never heard of before, but they knew about Doc."

Doc enjoys the hunt and has the energy of a twenty-year-old, which, for Hindson, is contagious. When they were travelling to the Northwest Territories, Doc mentioned to the bush pilot that he had flown bombers in the Second World War. The pilot handed Doc the controls, and the former warrior flew the whole way from Edmonton.

Hindson explains his unique relationship with Doc. "I'm always trying to please him. It's like my own dad. I'm always trying to meet his expectations, ever since I first worked for him in 1981. I think what we share is an enthusiasm for life, for sports, for business, for the excitement of finding things. We have the potential to make a major discovery. That doesn't happen to everyone. I've worked for a lot of people, but there's no one like Doc," he says. "You meet businessmen who aren't concerned about the personal lives of others. All they care about is making money. That's not Doc."

With his long track record, Doc continues to impress and inspire a variety of people with whom he has worked over his career.

Michael Tims first met Doc at Bow Valley Industries and recalls the strength of his handshake. "I'll never forget that," says Tims. "He's very much that type of person where the handshake is the deal. I always thought of Doc as larger than life."

Doc is the quintessential wildcatter, having led the hunt off the shores of Canada, the United Kingdom, and Norway. Even more than the risk taker in Doc, Tims respects his fairness. "Though he's a very good businessman, Doc is cognizant of the other person's side of the deal," he says. "He's trying to do transactions where everybody comes out ahead, achieving what they want, and not just to his own advantage. Doc also takes terrific interest in supporting other businesses and in moving them along. He gets great delight in fostering businesses with other people, backing those in whom he has confidence and being a mentor and partner in that."

Before Doc backed Robert Moffat as CEO at Bow Valley Energy, he had encouraged him in a junior company called Courage Energy. Similarly, Doc had supported first Mike Columbus and then Dave Johnson as CEO of Encal Energy. In 2001, Encal was bought by power generator giant Calpine, four years before it filed for bankruptcy protection.

Encal was the first energy company Doc started after Bow Valley Industries, and he grew it the old-fashioned way — by the drill bit — to 50,000 barrels of oil equivalent a day. The company had two other major investors, the Ontario Teachers

Pension Fund and the Green family, who owned Luscar Coal. They wanted out.

"So we put it up for sale to the company called Calpine," Doc says. "Encal was a very successful company. I wish to hell we had kept it." He laughs. "Calpine got caught in the aftermath of September 11, 2001, and then they were affected only two months later by the Enron deal. They all got tarred by the same brush. So, all the work we did at Encal … oh boy."

Doc was recuperating from an operation and was lying on his couch at home when he saw the tragedy of September 11 unfold on TV. As a man who had fought for peace, he recoiled at the horror, and he knew the panic that would ensue. But the uncertainty in the stock market was nothing compared to the global fear the terrorists had created.

"Doc absolutely amazes me at his insight into world situations," says Elson McDougald. "At the time of the second Gulf war with Iraq, Doc said, 'They're making a mistake.' I didn't grasp it that well at the time. He was right on. He knew exactly what was going to happen."

Rod Blair, who managed Bow Valley's offshore exploration ventures in Indonesia and spent much of his career living and working overseas, agrees. Born into an Alberta ranching family (and not related to the Blairs of Husky and Nova), he was attracted initially by Doc's global perspective. "When I joined Bow Valley in 1984," he notes, "it was one of only a handful of Canadian companies that had any success internationally. Doc isn't daunted by complexity. He has an unusual ability to think in both analytical and abstract terms."

Author and journalist Frank Dabbs has known the key players in the Canadian oil patch. "For me, a few men stand out because of their decisions and strategies," says Dabbs. "They know how to pick people and put the right people around the drilling rig floor and the table. That speaks to a particular business skill and sets them apart. We produced a lot of smart oil people in Western Canada, but only a handful of geniuses. Part of Bow Valley's insight and what made them a different and distinctive company was reflective of Doc having his own particular vision of possibilities and going out of the country."

Very early in the game, Doc got the idea that there were places to be besides Canada. Bow Valley was an independent Canadian company and, in the world scheme, very small. "But it behaved with the financial and corporate acumen of a large multinational," says Dabbs. "On the one hand, it was patient and disciplined, but on the other, it took intuitive bold strokes. The way Doc and his brothers have conducted their business affairs and lives, there are no loose ends. Doc is elegantly perfectionist in the way he's done business."

Veteran drilling contractor Tony Vanden Brink supports this. "The Seaman brothers have a long history of success in building companies," Vanden Brink notes. "It started with their drilling roots and getting into oil and gas in Western Canada. Then they went to the North Sea and discovered the Brae Field, and later were involved in large discoveries in Indonesia, as well as in northern Canada and off the East Coast. They were in the frontiers. And they helped a lot of people get started in the oil business, including me."

Jean Brown is only the second executive assistant in Doc's entire business career. His first was Betty Fisher, who had been Hi-Tower founder Ralph Will's secretary and who continued to travel from Okotoks to Calgary until she retired.

Brown's learning curve was sharp since she had no experience in the oil and gas business. Coming from the legal community, Brown was an oil patch rookie and knew nothing about the business or the stock market. Doc sat on a number of company boards. One morning, Brown directed him to a board meeting while she set off on some business errands.

"When I returned, I saw Doc sitting in our boardroom by himself. He said the meeting was cancelled. I hadn't called to confirm. Doc wasn't angry, although I felt terrible. He said that was all right. To learn under him was great. He was a good teacher. I kept calling him 'Mr. Seaman' and he looked at me and said, 'It's just Doc.' Mr. Seaman isn't him at all."

In March 2007, Jean celebrated twenty-five years as Doc's assistant. She remembered her first Stampede when she needed to secure a number of dinner seats for Bow Valley guests. It was the usual party-hearty downtown atmosphere, and Brown left the office at 10:00 a.m. and wasn't back with the reservations until 4:00 p.m. Yet Doc didn't mind.

"Doc's not just an employer, I care about him," Brown says. "His is a purposeful life. It's something he instills in others. He's very open, but he's also a very private man. Doc doesn't like his name out there, attached to buildings and things. The only one I know that has his name on it is a well drilled in Zambia, and they're calling it Doc's Well."

Humility is a family tradition for brothers B.J. and Don as well. Any programs or places named "Seaman," such as the ball stadium for the Okotoks Dawgs, which Don enthusiastically supports, or the Seaman Family MR Research Centre at the University of Calgary, have been named in honour of their parents.

Jean Brown notes that Doc "is always there for his people. During the 1980s downturn in the oil patch, Doc had to let some people go. You saw the sadness on his face every day. He wouldn't eat." For a man whose purpose in life is to create jobs, this was a dreadful juncture.

"Doc always takes the time with others," Brown says. "He mentors quietly. When he's here, every day I learn something. He's very stimulating. He says, 'I need you here when I'm here and I also need you here when I'm not here.' Then we both laugh."

Don Thurston, the president of Selkirk Portfolio Management, was hired by Doc as a Bow Valley vice-president. "Doc sets the direction and expects everyone to get the job done. That's how he leads. As a Second World War pilot in bomber command, he never wavered. One of the reasons Doc survived on his bombing missions was that he always made sure he was first guy in. The last guy in seldom made it because the enemy knew where you were," he says.

Thurston admires Doc for not becoming so obsessed with work that he forgot his friends. There could be turmoil, but then Doc and his pals would disappear and go hunting for the weekend.

"He set an example for the rest of us," adds Thurston. "Organize yourself so you're occupied in different things. That perspective gave him the chance to do ranching, oil, hockey, always with a strong community focus."

Thurston met Doc fifty years ago and says he's still the same guy he was then. Doc's friends run the gamut from colleagues to cowboys to politicians to rig hands.

"Wealth, fame, and fortune have not changed him," says Thurston. "That is major. I don't know anyone quite like him. He inspires people to do things, and you don't always know why you did it. Doc wanted a deal that was good for everybody. I remember the time I was with him in Vancouver where we were buying a small company. The price came up, and Doc mentioned a number. We had a chat with the fellow and went away. The man thought we were still in a negotiating situation. I thought the fellow was going to fall off his chair. The deal was done and it was fair for all. It was a good lesson in business for me."

Thurston also recalled Doc's close relationship with the Reverend Donald Binney as a man he could lean on, likely because they shared similar values. Binney rose from rig hand to senior vice-president and director of Bow Valley Industries. He left the oil patch to become an Anglican minister, and his reputation grew before his untimely passing.

"He just practices the oil field culture," wrote Gordon Jaremko in *Oilweek*. "Be there when needed. Be competent. Rather than preach, Binney serves a brotherhood. In the oil and gas community, Binney said, 'You bond together as a family to get it done.'"

That was certainly the culture of the Seaman brothers, who loved to compete at cards and sports but who connected around the company and the community. Thurston remembers the work Doc did for the vitally important Macdonald Commission from 1982 to 1985.

"It was very hard work," he says. "It wasn't Doc's natural environment. There was lots of committee work, lots of chatter, and lots of politics. He did it because he thought it was the right thing to do."

The Macdonald Commission ultimately helped form the foundation for Canada's free trade agreement with the United States. Doc's role during the endless cross-country deliberations proved far more crucial than he or any of the others might have thought.

The Royal Commission on the Economic Union and Development Prospects for Canada was headed by Donald Macdonald, the former Liberal finance minister. Prime Minister Trudeau appointed the commission to examine better trade relations with the United States. But in 1984, the Liberal government under the new leader, John Turner, was defeated by the Conservatives, led by Brian Mulroney, who had been an active critic of free trade. The Macdonald report, ready for its final printing, seemed to be rolling instead towards the dustbin. Prime Minister Mulroney eventually had a change of heart, and from the ashes of the commission rose free trade and NAFTA.

"The Report is chiefly remembered for its recommendation of Canada–U.S. free trade," states a C.D. Howe Institute communiqué from September 14, 2005. "It also called for sweeping changes in Canada's economic, social and constitutional make-up, social-program reforms, and strengthened federal-provincial relations. While a free trade agreement was concluded by 1988, other recommendations were implemented partially or not at all. The lessons from that experience, and the impact of new ideas and evidence since 1985, provide some insights about how Canadians might think about their current economic, social and political challenges."

Doc had thought he was stepping back from business and devoting his time to ranching. The rigours of the range beckoned, and Doc had serious plans for the OH Ranch. When he was asked to sit on the Macdonald Commission, he didn't imagine it would take three years of arduous meetings and debate. After all, it was during Macdonald's tenure as Liberal energy minister that Petro-Canada was born, that bane of Canadian independent producers.

"We were within a few months of writing the final report," recalls Doc. "Lo and behold, Brian Mulroney won the election. There was a fair amount of discussion, because this was a Liberal report and the Conservatives weren't going to finish it off and print it. We'd done a lot of work on free trade. That's one place where I did feel I could add some weight to the argument when they were talking about cancelling the program and not finishing the report."

In 1984, Michael Wilson became finance minister in the Mulroney government. Doc had met Wilson when he worked with Dominion Securities and Doc was raising money for Bow Valley.

"I was in Ottawa for Macdonald Commission meetings," Doc recalls. "I phoned Mike up and said, 'Can I come over and just have lunch with you?' He agreed, and when we sat down, I said to him, 'We've done a lot of work on this commission and spent three years and a fair amount of government money, but there's one thing in there you should really look hard at and that's free trade. Free trade with the United States makes so much sense.' And anyway he listened to me. Whether it had any impact, I don't know. But they did finish the report, and the Mulroney government was instrumental in putting free trade in place."

Former Premier Peter Lougheed remembers the dynamics behind the Canada–United States Free Trade Agreement. A report put together by the C.D. Howe Institute and its president, Wendy Dobson, described how it should be done. Then the Macdonald Commission had its recommendations.

"The Alberta government led the way with regard to constitutional amendments at the Regina conference in 1985," notes Lougheed. "We were moving toward the Free Trade Agreement, and that is what the report was about with the advantages for Canada."

Lougheed recalls Doc as a key part of the Macdonald Commission, and one who played a prominent role in the free trade consideration.

"My guess is that there were major dissenters and Doc played an important role in turning it around," says Lougheed. "Donald Macdonald was our nemesis with regard to energy when he was the minister, because he was part of many of these negotiations that were difficult for us. Then out comes the Commission in favour of the FTA. We were surprised and quite happy about it when we were facing Mulroney, who had initially been opposed to the FTA. To his lasting credit, Mulroney completely turned around on it."

Free trade's time had come. There was the intellectual drive of the Dobson/Howe study, the authority of the Macdonald Commission, and the Premier of Alberta taking the lead. Within the Commission debates, Doc Seaman quietly but firmly encouraged free trade.

In 2006, Michael Wilson was appointed Ambassador to the United States by Prime Minister Stephen Harper. From Washington, he recounted earlier visits with Doc.

"Doc was very helpful to me when I became the Conservative energy critic. This was right after the NEP came out," says Wilson. "One of the things I did at that time was to reach out to leaders in the oil and gas business. Doc was one of those. He was helpful in giving me perspective on the industry and some of the technical aspects. I had known Doc through my involvement in the securities business in the past. It was helpful to talk with someone who was a leader in that business."

The Ambassador recalls meeting Doc a few years later and discussing free trade in his capacity as finance minister. "We talked about a range of issues," he recalls. "The Macdonald report and its position on free trade was significant, and Doc's views on that were pretty strongly held. They had an impact on me."

Ambassador Wilson clearly remembers the free trade discussions within the Conservative government. The so-called Shamrock Summit was launched on March 17, 1985, in Quebec City, where Prime Minister Brian Mulroney serenaded President Ronald Reagan and the American delegation with "When Irish Eyes are Smiling."

"Doc's views, because of his role on the Macdonald Commission, were quite important to us because they had obviously studied it very hard before they made the recommendations in that report," adds Wilson.

The Reverend Don MacMahon, a long-time friend of Doc's, was a padre in the navy during the Second World War and has served as the armed forces chaplain in Calgary. He remembers all the work Doc put into the Macdonald Commission and the eventual reward of free trade. "Doc's counsel has been sought by all kinds of people," says MacMahon. "He has that inner instinct and insight. If he'd entered politics, I believe public life would have been enriched by the presence of a leader with such energy and vision."

Yet Doc's first love was always business. One of Alberta's greatest politicians, Peter Lougheed, says, "Creating jobs. That was in his heart. That was the essence of Doc." Soon he would turn his heart to other dreams he shared with Lougheed: bringing world-class hockey to Calgary and building an arena that would host the Olympic Winter Games.

PART THREE

~

The Purpose-filled Life

CHAPTER SIX

The Motivator

From the time Doc Seaman was a youngster, any ice that shimmered in a beam of light has beckoned the prairie kid to grab a stick and lace up the skates. Now that kid is in his mid-eighties and still eager to play. As the moon fights for attention with the four hundred fibre optic lights showcasing the Calgary Olympic Plaza, the former hockey player steps onto the ice.

As he glides around the storied rink, his quick dodge away from an errant skater recalls swift moves from another era. He had visions of becoming a professional hockey player after Père Athol Murray's persistent coaching and mentoring. The Second World War punctured those images for Doc, and for a generation of prairie dreamers.

When he returned from the war, he earned a degree in engineering, created a global energy company, and contributed to society. He took little time to think about beliefs beyond respect, responsibility, integrity, discipline, and hard work.

As for formal spirituality, he says, "I haven't been as disciplined about that as I have with other areas of my life. I don't know —

I think it's something you have to consciously work at. I haven't completely come to grips with my own mortality, I guess. I think you have to deal with that at some point in your life, and I'm going to, sometime soon. Not long ago, someone asked me about mortality. I hadn't even thought about it and I was over eighty." In war, the young pilot refused to consider any alternative to survival in the air. "You had to have the attitude that you were going to be a survivor. If you didn't, you wouldn't have made it, because there certainly was a lot of stress. You pushed yourself to handle it. You had to handle it."

Those wartime traits never left Doc, and only recently has he started to contemplate mortality and its alter ego, spirituality.

"My mother recently passed away at 107, and I just lost my sister too," he says wistfully. "I've had the misfortune to lose the two women that were always in my life. Sometimes I have doubts over the big questions in life. That's where spirituality comes in, and I will take the time to try and reflect on that over the next few years."

But there is a kind of informal spirituality in his many physical pursuits, from horseback riding at the ranch to skating or walking long distances on downtown Calgary paths alongside the Bow River, near his home.

"I remember something Albert Einstein said: 'My sense of God is my sense of wonder about the universe,'" he says.

He knows the tranquility, the deep sense of connection, that settles over the soul. Doc's main expression of spirituality, perhaps, is the instinctive honour and fairness he brings to his dealings with other people.

Doc gazes through the window of his twenty-third-floor boardroom and momentarily fixes on the mountains. To Doc, the peaks represent strength and perpetuity. Far removed from the entrepreneur's creed of wealth creation, they beg the immortal question: What do we leave behind?

"You leave behind your family," Doc says quietly, "And hope you've done a good job of being a parent and guardian and that they have successful lives. You try to do your best at that. By and large I've been pretty fortunate with my family. I think you also want to feel that you've been of good service not only to your community but your country. You want to believe that you've been a stalwart citizen and made a contribution to society in whatever you're good at and whatever level you're at. You want to have a comfort and well-being about what you've achieved or accomplished."

Don MacMahon's admiration for Doc goes beyond his community achievements. As an ordained United Church minister for fifty-five years, MacMahon has seen it all, from his Second World War service in the Navy to his parish duties from Nova Scotia to Alberta.

"I never had any use for the pious sanctimonious Joes," he says. "If ever there was a person who lived his basic faith, it is Doc Seaman. It's the kind I totally admire. It's his deep sense of humanity and humility. As far as Doc's concerned, he's just trying to turn back to the community and help others with what came to him. He never seeks credit for things. There are so many who give to get recognition. For Doc, it just comes natural to do good things."

As Doc sees life, you go on and achieve as best you can until one day you simply can't any longer. His motivation, both spiritual and practical, is the duty to contribute, and his enthusiasm encourages others to do the same.

"I've had prostate cancer for seventeen years now. My illness is an overriding thing, but I feel well and I'm active. It's something that hangs over your head. I'm going to continue to do as much as I can, based on my code of ethics and philosophy of things I can do for society," he says. "I always try to be a good person within our community and our country and hope to continue to do things that are beneficial to society as a whole. I want always to be of service."

Being of service means keeping the brain as active as the body. Reading, learning, and listening keep his antennae attune to new ideas. When Doc reflects on the ambitions that motivate him, there's one that stands apart from the rest.

"When I got started in the drilling business, I found out I could create jobs, which is what I always wanted to do," he says. "I ventured into a number of things because I realized how important creating new jobs really is. Generally it is small businesses that create new jobs. So many larger companies — although not all of them — grow by acquisition or mergers. They shed jobs rather than create new ones."

As he generated jobs and slowly built Bow Valley Industries, Doc attracted people who would become part of his life forever. One of those was Harley Hotchkiss, Doc's fellow philanthropist, Calgary Flames co-owner, business partner, and sports buddy. They've known each other for more than fifty years and trust each other implicitly.

"Doc Seaman has been one of my closest friends," says Hotchkiss. "I know where he's coming from. I know what a great brain he's got up there. And I know how he does business. If Doc called me up now and said, 'Hotch, I've got this deal and I'm going to take a piece of it and I think you should,' I'd say, 'Fine. And I'll find out about it later.' That sounds silly, but I would do it. There aren't many people I'd do that with, but Doc would be one, and one of the very few.

"To me, integrity is important in your life and in your business dealings. Integrity is one of the distinguishing things about Doc Seaman. You can count on Doc. If he tells you it is going to be a certain way, it will be that way. If it ever should happen that he can't do something he said he'd do, he'd call you up and come and see you and tell you why, and when he will be able to do it.

"I've been blessed a number of ways: One is a strong family with my wife, Becky, and our children. The other is with strong friendships, and Doc Seaman is a leading example of that. When I think of the things in my life that are really meaningful, that is right up there at the top."

Doc treasures his relationships with family and old friends and always has time to chat or play cards with the gang. He hasn't changed, say his friends. Yet the world has changed dramatically since Doc began his two-man drilling company, Seaman & Warnke, in 1949. Always fascinated by technological change in his own field, Doc embarked on an educational quest to stay receptive to innovation.

"Continue to learn," he says. "Read, understand the past, but also keep your mind alert to shifts that are occurring so rapidly now. My mother lived in parts of three centuries. She certainly had to adapt, big time. Think of the changes she saw — radio, TV, computers, the Internet, household appliances. Imagine the leap from a soap board to an electronic washer-dryer. I used to help my mother gather up the bed sheets from the clothesline outside and bring them in frozen. I remember that well.

"There are new gadgets every day. You need a cellphone and then a BlackBerry. There's continual turnover of new technology that people feel they need to have. Sometimes this creates real advantages. For instance, yesterday was a really busy day. I was talking to a CEO, who was skiing in the mountains. We had to do a deal and were able to get it done by long distance. Communications have been so enhanced, you can be in touch with everybody all the time.

"If people don't manage this wisely, though, I think they can become inundated with too much unnecessary information. I notice that some people's lives take on a frenetic quality. My feeling is that busyness doesn't always translate into productivity."

Work and other activities have consumed time so completely that holidays can foster guilt rather than relaxation. Doc learned the cure even as he masterminded deals, created companies, extinguished corporate fires, and discovered oil and gas reservoirs that thrive today.

"Doc never wavers, but he also doesn't become obsessed," says Don Thurston, who worked with Doc at Bow Valley. Years ago, the Seamans bought an old house and moved it down the highway to a popular hunting area near Brooks, Alberta. Every fall, Doc, B.J., Harley Hotchkiss, and a whole crew of friends go pheasant hunting.

"We'd load up on Friday afternoon with steaks and some beer and go down to Brooks, where we'd cook the steaks, drink the beer, and play poker," says Hotchkiss. "We'd get up early Saturday morning, hunt pheasants, and then come back on Sunday. We did that many, many times."

Friends, family, and community are the bedrock of Doc's being. Growing up in the Depression and dust bowl of 1930s' Saskatchewan meant hard work and neighbourly reliance. Everyone pitched in to help one another. There was no distinction between town and farm folks. "I saw the dust bowl as a youngster, and our family lived through it," recalls Doc. "It was a hard time."

As the harsh realities of deprivation and world war subsided, prosperity pulled its wagon over the horizon. The comforts were compelling, but as society rode the wave of bigger and better, the kinship of community got lost in the swell.

Starting a business is certainly easier today than when Doc began. The oil industry is a proven entity, and raising funds isn't as daunting or discouraging as it was in 1950. The market has changed dramatically, as has the availability of capital.

"If you have a good business plan and can demonstrate ability, money is available," notes Doc. "I had to risk my life savings and mortgage the family home just to have a chance to do something. It's hard to compare. Those were the days when a cup of coffee was a nickel."

Today, there's no such thing as a nickel cup of anything. A tall (which is really a small) cup of Starbucks coffee will cost you $1.65.

There are all kinds of instant and frozen foods that are supposed to ease responsibilities at home. Like nearly everyone else, Doc often succumbs to the lure of convenience.

"I'm not saying it's the best, but there are a lot of pre-cooked meals you can buy at the supermarket, and I 'bach' quite a bit," adds Doc. "In my mother's time, she'd finish breakfast and then have to think about getting a hot lunch for us coming home from school. And on it went."

Finding a balance between family and work is as challenging as it's always been.

"There is a big demand on home life for all executives, because you do have to be away a lot," says Doc. "We got involved in the North Sea and other jurisdictions around the world. I can remember a few times when you thought you were going to be home that evening and instead you were on a plane to London. There are demands on home life, big time."

Doc's daughter, Diane Lefroy, remembers a typical family where her mother stayed home while her dad went out, "working, working, working. I thought what a treat it was for us to go to dad's office on weekends."

The kids loved heading to their dad's building with the welding shop next door. They'd romp around the rooms, explore between the machines, and watch the sparks sizzle from the welding rods. It was all very exciting, and no one paid much attention to kids running rampant on the shop floors. Those were different times, but the children soon learned to get out of the way of scalding metal and scolding tongues.

In Doc's day, the daily responsibility of child rearing fell on the wife, but children were expected to grow up much faster. Doc recalls sending his boys out to the drilling rigs after high school.

"You had to be able to keep your end up or you wouldn't be there," he says. "It was a good lesson in what makes the world go around. It doesn't have to be drilling rigs. In the summertime, at the ranch near Millarville, I gave the kids ten cents for every post they put in to build fences. They had to earn it, and if they put in one hundred posts a day, I gave them ten dollars."

Diane recalls vividly the values her father instilled, and work was at the top of her list. "It is certainly something that shaped everything that was expected of us," she says. "We were encouraged even as children to work hard. If you don't value hard work, you're in trouble in a family like mine. We always had jobs to do. Every Saturday morning I had a huge basket of ironing to press. I had to iron my brothers' stuff and my dad's shirts."

The Seaman family motto could have been "Work hard, play hard." All the kids were active in sports, including basketball, volleyball, baseball, and track.

"Everybody just did it," says Diane. "We lived right across from the school. Dad got us kids on the ice and he'd take us flying around. My brothers played hockey, and I took figure skating. In the summer, we caddied a lot for my dad, and my brothers became pretty good golfers. I never got into golf, but I learned how to caddy."

Diane loved the summers when they'd head out to Millarville for a two-month stretch.

"My dad still has a garden. When we were young, he'd say, 'Make sure you get the peas and beans picked before I get home.' We spent summers at the ranch. What a fabulous opportunity to have that. Again, Dad would drive off to Calgary to work and we'd be given jobs: watering the trees; painting endless miles of fences. It sticks in your consciousness. Now I don't have a garden and I really miss it. It's a way to get rid of stress."

Like any kids, Diane and her brothers, Bob, Kenny, and Gary, would have preferred to loaf and play on those long summer days. But they did their work first and then headed out for fun.

"We had time to do our own thing," adds Diane. "I learned to love solitude and be out in nature by myself. My brothers spent a lot of time together fishing, swimming, riding horses. It was a fabulous opportunity, and today it sounds rather idyllic."

Bob Seaman remembers waiting for his dad to return from work, driving from Calgary to the ranch in Millarville. "That was a challenge in the 1960s, since the road was all gravel. When he got here, we'd go out and shag golf balls. He did all the sports things fathers like to do with their sons. He would always say, 'Winning isn't everything. As long as you've done your best at what you do, then you should be happy whether you win, lose or draw. So always do your best, no matter what you do.'

"He has allowed me to do what I wanted as long as I did my job, and I've been able to branch out and do all kinds of other things. A common complaint of sons who have had successful fathers is that they are never around. That was true at times, depending on the era, but I certainly remember a lot of good things I learned from him and from him being around.

"We faced our own challenges growing up because of our successful father. I'd always say, 'I'm not trying to measure up. I'm just trying to be my own person and do what I've been trained to do and do it well.' Egos were never really a part of our family."

Bob remembers all the time he spent with his grandparents listening to the harsh realities of their younger lives. It made them tougher and often less able to express their feelings for loved ones.

"In hindsight, I realized my father wasn't as emotional as some of the people who hadn't had those experiences," says Bob. "He would say that he never really heard his mother say she loved him, but he knew she did. I'm not sure I ever heard my dad tell me that, yet he expressed it in many ways."

This was the generation that Tom Brokaw called "the Greatest Generation." In his brilliant book, Brokaw described how they sacrificed as they went to war and won the freedom the next generation too easily took for granted. They were a generation that loved deeply and gave generously, but as individuals, they often kept their emotions embedded within.

"My mother was the maternal glue who kept the emotional side more active than he did. Doc was busy, and he had had life experiences that had hardened him," says Bob sympathetically. "While I'm probably a little more like my dad than my mother, I picked up a lot of good things from my mother."

The Seaman children were well aware of being but a generation away from the Depression. It coloured their parents' view of the world: they knew what it was like to do without.

"To be afraid that there wouldn't be enough work and money to live is difficult to appreciate," says Diane. "You had to live by your wits and use everything you had. We grew up after the war where everything was pretty easy and good. We didn't have to think about not having and doing without."

Bob Seaman also believes it's hard to fully appreciate what his parents and grandparents lived through.

"I don't know how you could go through what they did: the Dirty Thirties, having very little, facing a war at eighteen and nineteen years old, and seeing your friends killed in front of you. No wonder things in Dad's life seemed a lot less difficult than the war experience. Who knows if I could ever think in the same vein of volunteering to go fight a war? I have no idea if I could face that kind of a challenge.

"The things that came out of his life experiences that he's taught us, the one word that would describe it is 'discipline.' Discipline is such an important thing in life. That's where I've learned more than anything. The discipline that you have is a core value. He harped on that a lot," says Bob. Then he grins and adds, "Doc says you don't know anything until you're fifty, so you better keep your eyes open. Dad has softened as he has gotten older, and he's become more of a family type of guy."

But Doc is also as determined as ever to share his deep conviction that to stop work is to finish a life prematurely. "Never quit," he tells his kids.

Doc's children quickly learned that an idle life is a life without purpose. They were encouraged never to cruise through life but to take account of their world and make it better. Theirs was an ethic of excellence in persistence. "Don't sit back and say, 'That's done and I can stop now,' even if all the evidence is to the contrary," says Diane.

She learned the value of education and remembers visiting her grandmother, who would tell stories about Doc in school. Then she'd retrieve his report cards for the grandkids to see: "She saved all the report cards and would get them out. We'd see all the good marks and were expected to match up. They were held up as an example."

Diane always had a passion for reading and studying. It was something that came naturally to her, and she carried it to graduate school, earning a Master's Degree. Her first job was as a French teacher and she enjoyed going back to school.

Another value that was instilled early on was community and giving back. Doc and his wife, Lois, didn't talk about it to the kids — they simply led by example.

"I don't know if it was something we were even conscious of," Diane says. "When things are done a certain way, you just assume that's the way everybody is. My mother always was working in charitable and community organizations. For example, at Halloween, we'd go out with pillowcases and fill them up with candy. Mother made us give half to the children's hospital. She said, 'There are other people less fortunate and you have to share with them.'

"We were always conscious that dad grew up in a less fortunate financial situation than we did. Sometimes, we thought we should be given more things because our friends had them. But we didn't just get what we wanted. Today, I have a hard time enjoying having more than other people. It's part of my consciousness. When you're fortunate to have, you need to remember that."

Doc also didn't talk about the war to his kids. Like many who had faced the brutality of battle and survived, he didn't want his children to know the horrors he had seen.

"He's always kind of shied away from that," says Diane. "I remember the photo of my dad in his uniform that was sitting out in my parents' bedroom. He must have been nineteen or twenty. For a young girl, he was like a god to me in a way. As the only daughter, he was up there on a pedestal. You think about your father being a hero. I remember stories about him getting shot. It's really hard for us to imagine that, and for him at that age, they were all so young."

One summer, Diane was given the job of organizing all of Doc's war photos. She asked him about the people in the pictures, and then he would talk about his best friend, Tom McGlade Sr., whose son eventually became like one of the family.

"I was sort of Tom McGlade Jr.'s mentor," says Doc. "He kind of drifted around like a lot of young people today, and I put him on the rigs just as I had with my boys. He went to the Arctic. Tom tells me that was one of the best experiences he's had. Tom has become a very successful partner in a securities firm and has done really well."

Tom and his dad often visited Doc and the family in the late 1960s, when the McGlades were living in Connecticut. "My dad and Doc sometimes talked about positive things they remembered from the war years," McGlade Jr. says. "While they were training with the RAF in England, they spent their days off in museums, movies, galleries, and the occasional pub. They shared a love of history and culture, and soaked up as much atmosphere as war-torn England could offer."

In 1972, the old friends decided to recreate their wartime romps in England and Scotland. They visited the places near their former bases before finishing up with golf at two historic courses.

"We travelled to London first and spent some time there going to the war museums, especially the RAF Museum west of

London," Doc recounts. "Then we travelled to Scotland because McGlade liked to golf and so did I. We played St. Andrews and Gleneagles. Afterwards, we went to a pub with a few Scottish friends, and they all said, 'You Canadians don't know anything about playing darts.'"

Doc recalls that during the war, there were plenty of darts in the mess hall, and the two Canadians had become pretty proficient. "So those particular Scots we were playing against sure got a surprise," laughs Doc. "We beat them at darts."

The Scots were not about to be bettered by the two Canadians. They challenged Doc and McGlade to a game of golf at Gleneagles the next day. The lead changed hands several times, but by the time they reached the final hole, the score was tied.

"My friend Tom, because of his handicap, had an extra stroke, the only one with a stroke on the eighteenth hole. And he parred it, putting us one under. So we beat the Scots again."

The jubilation of the win took the war buddies from the course to the hotel, where they celebrated into the night. Early the next day, Doc checked out and left for London. He never saw his best friend again. McGlade moved on to the grand old Turnberry golf resort. He played a round on the links course, enjoyed his evening, and went to bed.

"The next morning, my father didn't come down from his room," says McGlade Jr. "Dad died on that golf trip in Scotland. He had severe angina and couldn't walk down the street without chest pains. He talked about going in for a transplant but never did. Dad took massive amounts of nitroglycerin to expand his arteries."

Tom McGlade Sr. had died in his sleep of a heart attack. Doc was travelling, and the news took two days to reach him. He was stunned and rushed to be with family at the funeral in Smiths Falls, Ontario. "My father never lost his Canadian spirit and values," notes McGlade Jr.

He believes that Doc felt some responsibility for his father's death. "Dad was also a smoker. Doc never smoked. He always told my dad that smoking is silly and it's a waste of energy. He's had the health and clarity of mind that come with not smoking."

Why wouldn't Doc smoke? He lived in an era where it seemed that everyone smoked. The perils of lung cancer weren't yet known to be caused by tobacco. The great stars of the day smoked their way through their careers; cigarettes were the main prop for every film from the 1930s to 1960s. Smoking was as natural as dining and drinking. Only when Humphrey Bogart began dying of cancer did the *Zeitgeist* start to shift.

"In Rouleau, I had a friend whose dad owned a grocery store, and they had everything there," says Doc. "So he went into the store and got a plug of chewing tobacco. We all thought we were big guys — I guess I was about ten years old — and we all had a fat chaw. Half an hour later, I turned green and was as sick as I could be. I don't think I ever touched tobacco after that. I maybe shared a cigar or two when I was in the air force."

McGlade was only fifty when he died in 1972. In his short life, he became hugely successful as an investment banker and was key to Doc's business financings in the United States. Each motivated the other, and McGlade was instrumental in Bow Valley Industries going public on the American Stock Exchange.

Doc was devastated by the death of his best friend, but a year later an even greater blow left Doc numb with grief. His wife, Lois, "the emotional glue of the family," suddenly passed away.

Lawyer Patricia Leeson was a university student working for Bow Valley executive and financier Harry Van Rensselaer.

"Mr. Van Rensselaer was such a cheerful man but came in one July morning deeply subdued. He said, 'It is a very sad day. Mrs. Seaman has died.' There was a deep pall over the office."

Doc was in despair. For the most part, he kept his deepest thoughts to himself, but he wrote a long letter to his friend Reverend MacMahon.

A year later, Tom McGlade Jr. spent his first full summer with Doc at the ranch. The Seaman kids had grown and left home. Diane was living in Vancouver but was able to visit occasionally. Bob had just married Shannon and was running the cattle operation at the ranch. Ken dropped by when he wasn't busy, while Gary was away working.

"I'm sure my mother was in touch with Doc," says McGlade. "Lois had died the previous year. Doc was still in mourning and in a very private place."

There was little social life at the ranch that summer. Like the Seaman boys, McGlade Jr. found himself painting fences. When Doc came home, they'd make dinner, then Doc would drink a Scotch and Tom would have a soda.

"Often we'd play tennis at nine at night on the court Doc built for the kids," says McGlade Jr. "We spent a lot of time together. That summer was very interesting; I was only fourteen, but I was his companion. I think I was a comfort to him after his loss. He loved my dad, and we got along great. We had so much fun that after that summer, we were best friends and have been friends ever since."

McGlade also became close to Doc's children.

"Tom adopted our family," says Diane affectionately. The fondness is mutual, as McGlade is also a great friend of Bob's, jokes with good-natured Kenny and his wife, Roberta, and praises Gary and his wife, Val. Her father, Jim Palmer, is another Calgary mentor to a generation of high-powered lawyers, not to mention Liberals.

Doc heads a large extended family. He's proud of his daughter, his boys, and their partners, and he adores his grandchildren and great-grandchild, Isiah.

Gary and Val have two children, Oliver and Jarrod. Kenny and Roberta — known as Bobby — have one daughter, Jessica, and three sons, Kenneth, Cory, and Jeffrey. It is Jeff who made Kenny and Bobby grandparents and Doc a great-granddad to Isiah.

Doc encouraged his children's independence, and all have forged their own distinct paths. He is supportive of his grandchildren's directions and tries to keep connected to a brand new generation of Seamans.

But one is missing, and a vast sorrow stretches across the Seaman family, starting with Scott Seaman's mother, Shannon, father, Bob, sister, Kelly, and granddad, Doc.

Scott Seaman was exceptionally bright, outgoing, and funny. He excelled in sports, was a fine speaker, understood what giving back was truly about, and also loved a little prank or two.

Scott had finished Grade 12 at Strathcona-Tweedsmuir School in Okotoks and was entering university. He suddenly took ill with what everyone believed was the flu. In fact, it was a rogue virus that ravaged the lining of his heart and took Scott on March 25, 1997. The tragedy tore at his family.

As he had done when Lois died, Doc turned to Don MacMahon and expressed his feelings in a letter. "I just was there with him," says MacMahon.

Over a decade later, the sorrow is still fresh for the family. Jack Hay was Scott's teacher and mentor at Strathcona-Tweedsmuir School, and his poignant words at Scott's memorial revealed an exceptional student on the cusp of success: "Scott Seaman was my kind of guy ... He was, from the beginning, more than just a presence in my class. Over the next three years I came to appreciate and enjoy his quick wit and wonderful sense of humour.

"In class one day I made a statement that said, 'Among other reasons, it is important that Quebec stay in Confederation because a large majority of Alberta's beef exports go to this province.' The next day, Scott arrived in class with something that looked suspiciously like a research article in his hand. He said to me, 'Sir, did you say that a majority of Alberta's beef goes to Quebec?' I replied, 'Yes, I said that.' Then he showed me the article from the Alberta Cattle

Commission that said considerably less than a majority of our beef actually does go to Quebec.

"Later in the week, I made another statement that I thought was factual, and then I quickly added, 'Seaman will probably show up tomorrow with another article that will contradict what I have just said.' Scott never hesitated. He replied, 'No, I won't, sir. I think it's important that you have some time to build your confidence back up.'

"Students spend one afternoon a week for half of the school year doing community service work … Scott was assigned to the Cross Cultural Day Care Centre … Scott was in his glory. He had a captive audience every Friday afternoon … In the evaluation notes given to me when the term ended, the director of the centre said, 'Scott made an outstanding contribution to our program. His good nature and his love of fun brightened the lives of our children.'"

The school newsletter said, "Scott Seaman brightened the lives of many of us at Strathcona-Tweedsmuir School. The teachers and students who knew him loved him for his wonderful ability to make us feel good. We will miss him terribly."

Life's fragility has never been a mystery to Doc, but the impact shatters even the most stoic. Doc learned early to value every starlit sky whether seen from the Caterpillar tractor he drove as a fourteen-year-old boy, the Hudson bomber he piloted as a twenty-year-old airman, or the river path he walks as an eighty-six-year-old entrepreneur. What can't be measured in material gain is all there is to cherish. For Doc, wealth is assessed by strength of family and friends. Life is gauged not by how much you own but by the people with whom you've grown. Depth of character is never calculated in cold hard cash.

Family feuds over money and power are foreign to the Seamans. Doc's brothers, Don and B.J., are among his closest friends, and they continue to trade stories and share confidences just as they have all their lives.

"Blood is thicker than water, and the brothers coalesce beautifully," says Don Thurston. "They're very, very competitive and, along with their dad, were superb curlers. Each brother plays to win." Then Thurston starts to laugh. "You should see Doc and B.J. at gin rummy. Does B.J. ever win? Not according to Doc." Of course, B.J. begs to differ.

When the three brothers are together, as they often are, since they occupy the same suite of offices, they still act like they're off to the rink in Rouleau, full of fun and mischievousness. Doc's personal staff members have become loyal friends and part of the gang.

"Doc says and believes this: 'I'm where I am today because I had a good work ethic, came to Alberta at the right time, and met some like-minded people,'" notes Jean Brown, his assistant for more than twenty-five years. Doc's only other executive assistant, Betty Fisher, remained with him for thirty-five years. She never married, and they stayed in touch until she passed away.

"Doc always includes his old-time buddies in everything," continues Brown. "They're very important to him. Personal wealth was never a factor with Doc and never will be.… Doc helps others get things done too. Once he wanted a lawsuit settled — something he wasn't involved in but knew the parties — before it went to court. He simply called the people. Doc just jumps in to help."

Over the many years of working closely with Doc, Brown has seen him angry only once.

"There's a kindness and gentleness to Doc, and he never says anything to hurt people's feelings. He's always a gentleman," she notes. But one day Doc returned from a meeting clearly annoyed: "He picked up the phone, and I heard him tell this person that he should never, ever have spoken to him in that manner. A little while later, this man hurries to our building, rushes past me, bursts into Doc's office, and apologizes."

Doc attributes much of his vigour to his lifestyle. His tastes are spartan and his pleasures simple: a hearty soup that he's created from a brisket or ham bone plus broccoli, celery, and noodles ("but if I have time and ingredients I do cook good meals"); an appetizer of tomato sauce and crackers ("I've read that it's beneficial for prostate cancer"); a short glass of Scotch in the evening ("one but never more than two"); the daily papers, as well as the *Economist* or *Time* magazine and perhaps a weighty tome on one of his heroes, such as Winston Churchill; the Calgary Flames home games; hockey on TV; six hours of sleep; a breakfast shake ("with fruits, half a tumbler of wheat germ, two types of ground flaxseeds, oat bran, and two powders of fruits and vegetables plus a protein booster, all blended with some orange juice, vanilla yogurt, and soy milk"); plus a daily snack of unsalted almonds or dark chocolate ("they're both good for you").

Doc's heroes are those who refuse to waver against colossal odds. A photograph of Winston Churchill, by the great Canadian portraitist Yousuf Karsh, hangs in Doc's office. Karsh took the famous portrait of a scowling Churchill in 1941, just after he addressed the House of Commons in Ottawa at the height of the Second World War. Churchill, not wanting his picture taken, lit up his cigar. Undaunted, Karsh removed the glowing cigar from the glaring Churchill, muttered, "Forgive me, sir," and got his photograph.

"I greatly admired Winston Churchill, and we all listened to his speeches," says Doc. "I subsequently read a lot of his books. To think how one man could inspire a nation and the world to go against the German forces that had already occupied France, Poland, and had enticed Italy to be behind them as well. At times, it looked hopeless. How he was able to rally the British people during the Battle of Britain. Their lives were unspeakably tough: there wasn't enough food for everybody, and everything was rationed. Yet they remained in their homes in London and the other cities that were bombing targets. It was amazing how he was able to keep their spirits up. By circumstance, Churchill arrived at our Allied airfields in Italy when I was there. While it was just a short visit, I'll never forget it."

Doc also came to admire Dwight Eisenhower, but not simply for his role in the Second World War and later as the American president.

"General Eisenhower said that he would be happy and feel good about his life if he left one piece of ground, one piece of land better than he found it," says Doc. Eisenhower was talking about the small ranch he had retired to near Gettysburg. "That one simple thing after all he had done in his life as commander-in-chief of the armies in Europe and then president of the U.S."

Canadian leaders whom Doc admires start with Peter Lougheed. The former Alberta premier laid the political and economic foundation for Alberta's strength in twenty-first-century Canada. It was Lougheed who famously said there are doers and critics, and Albertans are doers.

"A trademark of Seaman is that he makes things happen," says journalist Gordon Jaremko. "Doc's not interested in becoming personally famous. His is a generation that was not about the money but about creating community and a society where people could have work."

People felt that it was almost a fundamental right as well as a responsibility to make a living. Doc would consider himself one of the more successful examples only because he had made a living by creating jobs and allowing others the same opportunity to work.

"A guy down the road who works for wages is no less of a person because he works for wages," adds Jaremko. "That's very different from the next generation. As long as you worked and were honest in what you did; that was a legacy of the 1930s." In today's greedier world, people who follow that ethic are often considered fools.

Doc's generation lived through the market crash; consequent-ly, they weren't as fearful of government taking some responsibility for the welfare of its citizens. This was the generation that founded medicare and social assistance. They weren't ready to vilify governments that offered hope and incentives to new industries. They opened up frontiers and literally paved the road to modern Canada. This was a more public-spirited generation, and Doc's goal of creating jobs meshed with it perfectly. It was a generation proud to share; the worst sin was to portray them as victims. They were victors over a Depression sandwiched between two world wars. They knew what it was to need and to give, and knew what a person gained from both. They also knew the crucial role of the entrepreneur in taking risks to build a better Canada.

As Père Athol Murray told his Notre Dame College Hounds: "Adversity, gang — that's what gives you strength — adversity."[14]

CHAPTER SEVEN

The Trailblazer

"Retire to What?"
— George Burns

On the eastern slopes of the Kananaskis, the panorama encourages the imagination to fly. The sky sends its silken gaze over the mountain fortress, and the land basks in its eternal radiance. On the serene southeastern edge of this landscape sits the OH Ranch, a historic cattle spread where Doc Seaman rides the range through some of the most magnificent scenery on the planet.

To the BlackBerry-toting visitor, the land soothes away the stress and hearkens to an earlier time of horses, buggies, and dirt trails.

"I found that if I was feeling worn out and having too much going on, my best therapy was to get on my horse," says Doc, who has had only two favourite steeds over the last forty years.

"The first one was Smoke. He'd been a bit of a renegade in a way." Doc chuckles, recalling this kindred spirit. "Before I rode him, one of the cowboys said he'd better try him first. When he got on, Smoke bucked all over the pasture. Being a good rider, he stayed on. It was my turn next, and I thought there might be some more fireworks. We looked one another over intently, and then I climbed on. Smoke craned his neck to take another good look at me. He seemed to wonder: What should I do with this guy? Then he turned to face the trail and we just went on our way."

For twenty-five years, Smoke and Doc went on their way. Smoke didn't buck with Doc in the saddle that first day or any day afterward. They seemed to have an instant bond of trust and respect, two qualities that characterize Doc's relationships with a vast array of four-legged and two-legged critters that have crossed his path.

Smoke was a horse like no other. Doc laughs as he recalls the close relationship that every horse lover comes to treasure if they're lucky enough to find the right animal.

"Smoke would come to me any time I called him. Even if he was out in a pasture with other horses and I whistled to him, he would come running right up to me," says Doc. "I could saddle him up anywhere and away we'd go. After a few hours, I'd find a little space with a clump of willows and the sun shining, drop the reins, hop off, lie down, and have a snooze. Smoke would stand there looking down, watching and waiting for me to wake up. I never had to tie him up."

That's unusual, even for those whose bond with their horse it's almost sacred. On the ranch, cowboys normally run the horses into a corral and pick out their own to ride, throw a halter on, and then saddle up.

"That's true for Remington, the horse I have now," says Doc. "He's a particularly hard horse to catch, but after you have a halter on him he's very quiet, and much like Smoke. I think we have the same relationship of trust. Once he's saddled up, he's gentle as can be." Still, Doc knows that Smoke was the horse of a lifetime and there will never be another like him.

Today, as often as he can on weekends, Doc takes a light lunch and rides the open range with Remington, reaching the extraordinary Highwood Pass.

"I can't remember getting on a horse and riding with a group or by myself where I didn't come back feeling quite refreshed with a sense of well-being," Doc says. "It's good therapy. Always has been. I'm a cowboy addict in a way. While I'm not really a cowboy, I like the cowboy way of life."

Doc could have made this his life's work. But he had an even more powerful calling than a life on the range: creating jobs, a goal he has pursued throughout his long career as an oilman.

When he sold Bow Valley Industries, Doc briefly envisaged a genteel retirement as a rancher. With his critical role on the Macdonald Commission from 1982 to 1985, life after Bow Valley still would have been very full indeed. But despite the pull of the ranch, Doc soon decided that he could never really retire. He loved business and philanthropy and the goal of contributing even more to the Canada he loved.

Doc was fortunate to have a budding cattleman at his own dinner table: his son Bob, who gradually rode into a major role in running the ranch. It was a logical move with Bob's formal education in agriculture, his practical education handling cattle, and his ongoing interest in studying and applying cattle genetics.

Doc's brief brush with retirement made him ponder the powerful Canadian view of leaving work as a blessed entry point to a golden life of leisure. He soon decided that for many the reality of retirement is depressing and even destructive. He was worried about his old friends from the boom-and-bust days, the Calgary Ratpack, some of whom were retiring about the same time. They had all been vigorous CEOs and senior executives who'd had a profound impact on Canada's burgeoning oil business.

"Some of the fellows were forced to retire at sixty-five, and I noticed that a few who had been vital in business went downhill so fast. It was hard. Perhaps it was a loss of self-worth. It happens to too many, where they seem to get depressed and just don't know how to get out of it. It's very sad," Doc says.

He decided he would not let an arbitrary age limit his curiosity and risk taking. He cautioned his friends to rebuff the lure of a golden age of rest and relaxation. It's all a chimera, he felt, like the lure of fool's gold.

At about this time, a close brush with tragedy put Doc in the same room with a like-minded man to question the deeper issues of life and mortality. Doc already knew Dr. Bill Cochrane, one of Canada's most honoured physicians and a former president of the University of Calgary. Doc's youngest son, Gary, and Cochrane's second son, Paul, grew up together and were school chums. As they drove home from skiing in the B.C. interior, their Jeep skidded over black ice on an infamous stretch of the Trans-Canada highway and flipped over.

"Bill Cochrane called me sometime around midnight," Doc recalls. "By this time, they had gotten Gary and Paul to the Foothills Hospital in Calgary. Bill said, 'I'll see you there at five in the morning.' I rushed to the hospital, but Bill wasn't in the lobby. I saw a nurse and said, 'Where's my son Gary?' I went straight up to his room. Bill was a bit agitated when he arrived because he had wanted to prepare me a little before. Gary had a severe brain injury and was in a coma."

Paul Cochrane was also in the hospital with cuts and a mild concussion, but he was not severely injured, so the physician was able to focus his complete attention on Gary and Doc. They shared many long vigils in the hospital, waiting to learn of Gary's fate, desperate for news of any sort of progress.

"I found a father who was deeply concerned about his son," says Cochrane. "He was able to control his emotions well and was very cool, in a sense, but also sensitive to his son's injuries. He didn't have the outward fear that some people show, but you could feel his anxiety."

Doc had learned to suppress fear in wartime, but this was different. His stomach churned with a feeling of helplessness. He dreaded the doctor walking through the door and wanted just one thing: his son, safe and well and home.

A parent's worst nightmare was staring Doc in the face, and the hours turned into a psychological no man's land of worrying and waiting.

Mercifully, Gary came out of his coma and started to recover. As their fears subsided, Doc and Cochrane turned to more general conversations about health, life, and then retirement. From Doc's practical experience and Cochrane's medical studies, the two suddenly found themselves saying the same thing: Never retire.

"I said to Doc, 'Why would you want to step aside or retire if you're still healthy, physically active, and intellectually strong?'" Cochrane notes. "Why would you even want to think about that? You've got your wisdom and experience with all that you've done, as well as the mistakes that we all make that can strengthen us."

Cochrane cites copious medical literature showing that physical exercise and mental stimulation, along with a healthy diet, adds years to life. But participation in work or community (or both) is also crucial.

That's fortunate indeed, because many studies show that baby boomers are balking at traditional retirement. BMO Capital Markets Chief Economist Sherry Cooper says that baby boomers' energy and creativity "will redefine retirement." They will likely work beyond age sixty-five, and their work will reflect their healthier lives. "We can actually regenerate rather than degenerate," she says in her book, *The New Retirement: How It Will Change Our Future.* "Labour shortages and rising healthful life expectancy will encourage boomers to work longer, helping to meet the financial demands of this 'sandwich generation.'"

Cooper's work underscores research that BMO unveiled in November 2006, which revealed that boomers recoil at a fixed retirement age. Those who don't intend to stop working after reaching age sixty-five total nearly 75 percent. In Ontario, the number of retirement-averse boomers jumps to 91 percent if they face the prospect of running out of retirement funds.

A report by Sue McPherson, published by the C.D. Howe Institute in 2005, focused on aging, identity, and work. She argues that because people live longer, the idea of mandatory retirement needs to be re-examined. "Work is not just a means of making life more financially secure, but is a way of spending time that can be meaningful, or a way to gain benefits that accrue from having a recognized status in society that contributes to the individual's personal and social identity. Work is a major component of identity."

In 2005, when he was seventy-five, writer William Safire retired from his *New York Times* column not because he felt he was too old but because he knew it was time for him to do something else. Safire moved into a new career as chairman of the Dana Foundation. "Nobel laureate James Watson, who started a revolution in science as co-discoverer of the structure of DNA, put it to me straight a couple of years ago: 'Never retire. Your brain needs exercise or it will atrophy,'" Safire wrote on January 24, 2005. "Never retire, but plan to change your career to keep your synapses snapping — and you can see the path I'm now taking."

Examining the effects of retirement on mental and physical health may well make any prospective retiree reconsider. Researchers Dhaval Dave, Inas Rashad, and Jasmina Spasojevic found "that complete retirement leads to a 23–29 percent increase in difficulties associated with mobility and daily activities, an eight percent increase in illness conditions, and an 11 percent decline in mental health."[15]

Creative, healthy work stimulates mental, physical, and social engagement. At the simplest level, it's good for your health. As the NBER paper points out: "Retiring at a later age may lessen or postpone poor health outcomes for older adults, raise well-being, and reduce the utilization of health care services, particularly acute care."

The call to avoid retirement does not imply that a person should continue with an unspeakable job. Finding the right career and the proper work is essential. If one career brings unhappiness, illness, and stress, then clearly it's time to cross over to a job and life that stimulate rather than terrify.

The media now regularly reports on workers beyond the age of sixty-five who are fulfilled and intend to keep working. Tool making entrepreneur Peter Hedgewick retired at age seventy-two and promptly acquired and then sold another company. At ninety-two, he works five days a week — even longer if the muse strikes as he's designing highway reflectors. "You have to wait for ideas to come, you know," he says. "They can come anywhere."[16]

Waiting for the muse is the life of musicians, but they do know how to chase it. American jazz great Louis Armstrong said, "Musicians don't retire; they stop when there's no more music in them." Canadian composer John Beckwith isn't likely to stop any time soon. At his eightieth birthday in March 2007, Beckwith was busy composing music for the rare ninety-six-tone microtonal piano. "It just seemed natural to me," he told *Globe and Mail* music critic Robert Everett-Green. "There were unexplored musical aspects of living in Canada, so why not explore them or try to find them?"

When Leonard Waverman was appointed dean of the Haskayne School of Business at the University of Calgary at age sixty-five, a few were surprised. The *Globe and Mail*'s Gordon Pitts gave the skeptics a voice with when he said, "But at sixty-five, you are a bit long in the tooth." Waverman quickly scored a bull's-eye: "The new business dean at Georgetown University is sixty-seven. If you look around, you see a variety of deans. Some have long track records with the wisdom from doing a number of things — and a lot of them are young. So there are two different models. There is no reason that we people with a little grey hair and who still have boundless energy can't continue to do these things for years and years. That's the way society is going."

Merchant banker Hans Vontobel, the patriarch behind the Swiss-based Vontobel Group, established the Creative Age Foundation in 1990 to encourage innovation and creativity in those over age sixty-five. As a thriving man who's past ninety, Vontobel urges society to discard its stereotypes about age and embrace the vitality and complexity that seniors bring.

"A new phase of life starts when someone retires. This opens up many opportunities," says Dr. Vontobel whom Doc knows through business ventures. Vontobel, whose philanthropy is global, believes "it is important to comprehend that giving creates more happiness than accumulation. Money generates a feeling of security; happiness has to be secured in other ways." (Quotes conveyed through Thomas Amgwerd e-mail, June 27, 2008)

In many cultures, the aged are revered and their counsel is sought. They are accorded high status for overcoming challenges, sharing their experiences, and bringing a wealth of knowledge. Canada's First Nations in particular have never abandoned the wisdom and spirituality of their elders, who occupy a crucial role in all decision making.

Bioethicist Margaret Somerville of McGill University in Montreal urges all of society to see the value and wisdom age brings. "When, as a society, we saw elders as fonts of wisdom, the paths of elderly people went somewhere," Somerville said during a University of Calgary lecture in October 2006. "That somewhere was a contribution to both the present and the future — it was a legacy. Old people were valued, respected, helped others, and could experience hope to the end of their lives."

Somerville urges society to go beyond the search for physical longevity through scientific advances to also explore the widespread emotional, psychological, spiritual, and intuitive human possibilities. In particular, she points to the teachings of nature.

"We now know that animals — and in all likelihood, humans — have genes that must be activated (imprinted) during a critical period when they are young, failing which the genes shut down permanently," she argues. "Might we also have genes that cannot be activated before a certain relatively advanced age, genes that allow us to experience realities that result in wisdom?"

Somerville also wonders if the normal loss of memory associated with aging is adaptive for society, so that seniors see the collective picture, while youths see and respond to the individual matters within it. She cites neurological research that reveals age distinctions in specific mental acuity. Younger people performed better on tests that involved exact precision whereas older ones scored higher on those that required a comprehensive understanding.

"Perhaps," she surmises, "this might be a manifestation of a group survival mechanism, one that allows a society to have a range of skills at its disposal, especially for input into critical decision making."

Former South African president Nelson Mandela brought that insight into a global perspective as he invited other Nobel laureates and world leaders to Johannesburg to foster peace and justice. Taking a cue from the elders' role in traditional African cultures, Mandela established The Elders on July 19, 2007, just a year before his 90th birthday. With British entrepreneur Richard Branson as facilitator, The Elders include Elie Wiesel, Archbishop Desmond Tutu, and former U.S. President Jimmy Carter.

"Together we will work to support courage where there is fear, foster agreement where there is conflict, and inspire hope where there is despair," Mandela said, and then looked at The Elders beside him. "They don't have careers to build, elections to win, and constituencies to please … I wish them well and hope that they succeed in bringing light to some of the darkness that affects our world."[17]

An Inuit elder, Enoki Kunuk, brought light and more to his community and to Nunavut — he brought his life. The eighty-one-year-old hunter left Igloolik alone and headed north to hunt caribou. The week-long trip turned into a twenty-eight-day quest for survival when his snowmobile and sled slid through the slush of spring thaw. But a lifetime of experience had taught Kunuk to be well prepared with clothing, shelter, ammunition, and food. While he didn't bring a communication device, he was equipped with an elder's essentials: wisdom and common sense. He was found four weeks later in excellent health. "He went by the shore and figured sooner or later people going fishing would have to run into him," his son, award-winning filmmaker Zacharias Kunuk told reporters.[18] This calm common sense, born of decades of experience, kept a man of eighty-one alive and well in the frigid wilds that would have killed most youngsters.

When Buster Martin retired at ninety-seven, he quickly decided to return to work. Boredom was not his style. Pimlico Plumbers of London, England, was delighted to take him back; and the company prides itself on the calibre of its employees and their work. Three years later, at one hundred, Martin was still going strong. Managing director Charlie Mullins favours hiring "Bronze Age" plumbers, those who are over sixty-five. "I always prefer to hire older and more experienced people for this company, because they bring a level of ability and a commitment to their work that you don't find elsewhere," Mullins told reporter Doug Saunders. "What I want are the people who have the longest experience and the most maturity."[19] In Buster Martin, he found his ideal employee.

Working beyond sixty-five does far more than improve the worker's bottom line. It encourages social and intellectual stimulation and is a sure cure for boredom.

"You've got to stay active physically and mentally," says Doc Seaman. Current studies in health and wellness certainly support Doc. Boredom is a ticking time bomb that can explode into physical and mental failure.

Dr. Leonie Bloomfield is a researcher with the Australian government. Her pioneering study into why men die earlier than women resulted in a startling conclusion: boredom kills. "Killing Time — Excess Free Time and Men's Mortality Risk," is the title of her paper with Dr. Gerard Kennedy. She considered the usual unhealthy lifestyle ingredients such as alcohol, tobacco, and sloth, and factored in the standard socio-demographic differences. Yet they didn't adequately explain a glaring disparity: all things being equal, why do men die younger than women?

Bloomfield looked at gender differences in housework and childcare and considered their implications later in life — and the differences were startling. Women who work outside the home may finish their jobs at the end of the workday but are often left with a household bursting with kids, cooking, cleaning, and the usual mayhem to sort out. Many women have had a lifetime of elusive leisure. Little has changed in the post-feminist world except, perhaps, greater guilt over not providing the Martha Stewart home.

Bloomfield took the traditional gender housework equation and turned it on its head: "The results of this study indicate that men's avoidance of, or their reluctance to spend more time in, housework and childcare might have multiple negative consequences for longevity," she and Kennedy wrote. Ironically, it is women who have the last laugh, after puffing through their work-filled lives. All the rhetoric of sharing the load hasn't changed women's lot. Yet the research of one woman just might. Bloomfield found that women live longer because of their extended family responsibilities.

Bloomfield later told Christine Jackman and Elizabeth Gosch of the *Australian*, "What is clear is that having more free time — and men already enjoy much more than women, because of gender inequalities in housework, childcare and other unpaid work — does not guarantee a leisure experience or better health for Australian men."[20] Bloomfield analyzed time-use diaries of 186 Australian men, and found that a leisure-filled life devoid of purpose appeared to pave a path to the graveyard.

"These findings highlight the importance of meaningful activity during free time," she and Kennedy wrote. "Research on unemployed people suggests that active pursuits such as hobbies, dancing, community involvement, voluntary and other work-like activities, study, home improvements, and domestic duties provide purpose, meaning, and structure to free time and these activities are associated with better health outcomes."

The scientists pointed to research showing that boredom causes anxiety and depression, which can then become lethal: "Anxiety and depression may increase the risk of mortality by interfering with the functioning of the human immune and neuroendocrine systems and increasing the likelihood of heart disease."

Stress and sleeplessness lurk more often within the lonely. These can kick-start hypertension and even, research suggests, cancer. "It may not be because free time is perceived as boring or lonely and television viewing relieves these negative states, but rather, a lack of meaningful and longer-term free time goals appeared to play a role in shaping men's leisure lifestyles," Bloomfield and Kennedy said.

Their research is persuasive and particularly relevant to the baby boomers waiting for the magic of an arbitrary number. The evidence supports seizing free time with vigour and purpose and finding meaning within each moment.

Loafing around, watching television, or doing nothing puts men at higher risk of gaining weight, becoming obese, and developing diabetes. Avoiding unpaid work like child care or community activities allows men excess free time that is usually filled with meaningless and unhealthy behaviours. These behaviours become ingrained over time, leaving men unwilling or unable to fill their spare time purposeful work. If they don't substitute something meaningful into their lives when they retire, such men become lost.

Idle men must learn to kill boredom instead of letting boredom kill them.

When Doc Seaman read a short news article about Bloomfield's study, he was intrigued. Finally, there was detailed research that proved what he intuitively believed: Boredom takes you down; a purpose-driven life moves you forward.

Correspondence with Bloomfield confirmed Doc's conviction.

"I agree with [Doc] about having a purpose-driven life and I believe this is what most people struggle with," said Bloomfield in an e-mail exchange. "We look through a very narrow meaning and purpose lens in Western countries … or, so many people believe. It is difficult for many people to think creatively about pursuing other long-term interests outside of their immediate jobs and families. As a writer and therapist, it is doubly difficult to generate strategies that enable people to tap into those aspects of their minds. Often they want a quick fix, an answer to be given to them … someone else to direct them on a path. It's all well and good to show the positive aspects of a meaningful life, but you 'simply cannot sit at a table and hand out purpose.'"

Doc's purpose was never handed out. It was learned through struggle, insight, conviction, and hard work. While he's always participated in community work, Doc hasn't always subscribed to complete gender parity. He chuckles when he considers some of his "politically incorrect" moments on the 1982 Macdonald Commission: "We went to a town hall meeting in Nova Scotia, and there were questions about women and the workforce. I was asked about my hiring attitude towards women versus men. I said that in a technical job, my preference would be to hire men because a lot of time and effort goes into training the person. With a man it's a life career, but with a woman she may be there for a few years and decide to have a family."

Doc's honest response twenty-five years ago made for a lively evening. "Boy, some lady got up and did she ever jump on me," laughs Doc. "I should have seen that one coming."

Doc's thinking has changed over the years, and he believes in hiring the best person for the job regardless of gender. He credits the influence of women such as his late secretary, Betty Fisher, his current executive assistant, Jean Brown, and his daughter, Diane Lefroy.

Doc is delighted with Bloomfield's research because it can help a new generation of men and women find balance and meaning as well as longer lives. He sees the research having particular relevance for anyone thinking that they should retire to gated communities of sun, sand, and golf. As they sink into a grey haze of meaningless leisure, these people often realize with horror that they've left behind the very things that matter most — friends, family, and community.

Too often the monotony of a purposeless life can lead to boredom, loneliness, and disease. A number of scientific articles on loneliness reveal a related increase in stress, high blood pressure, Alzheimer's disease, weaker immune systems, and even suicide.[21]

A *Washington Post* article points to the examination of 823 healthy participants by the Rush Alzheimer's Disease Centre in Chicago. The study concludes "that a rich social and intellectual life has a protective effect against Alzheimer's — besides the immediate benefit of simply making people happier."[22]

Another promising study on dementia reveals that an aging brain can build new cells and renew itself. "It has always been thought that dementia is an inexorable decline of mental impairment," says Dr. David Burke of Sydney, Australia. "In fact, the brain has a remarkable capacity to generate new brain cells. Basic lifestyle changes can reduce their risk of developing dementia and reduce the rate of deterioration." Furthermore, "mental, as well as physical exercise, helped the brain grow new cells."[23]

The research appears in the *British Journal of Psychiatry* and reinforces other studies that show "foods rich in fish oils, vitamin B12 and antioxidants aided the brain's cell-growth capacity. High blood pressure, smoking, diabetes and obesity impaired the brain's ability to grow."[24]

Dr. Elkhonon Goldberg, clinical professor of Neurology at New York University School of Medicine, advises people to stimulate their brains, but he is against the old adage "use it or lose it."

Instead, he says, be positive and build on your knowledge. "Use it and get more of it," Goldberg writes. "Well-directed mental exercise is a must for cognitive enhancement and healthy aging.... Research has shown that contrary to popular belief, the brain is constantly undergoing neurogenesis, the development of new neurons and dendrites." Goldberg is also co-founder of the Web site www.sharpbrains.com. "Learning and targeted mental exercise promotes neurogenesis ... just as muscle growth is promoted through physical exercise," he says.

Working should never stop at an arbitrary age. Staying active stimulates the body and mind and creates a healthier life. Fitness expert Pete Estabrooks, who trains people from every age group, believes fully in the "use it or lose it" philosophy. He also points out, however, "Fear not, it's not lost forever. With the proper amount of work, you can find it again. So don't be discouraged — because when you stop moving, you're just a target."

When the lifespan of industrial society was barely 65, then mandatory retirement at that age may have made sense. Today's average lifespan is between 77 and 82 for Western countries. In Canada, men can expect to live to 77.8 years and women to 82.6 years, according to Statistics Canada figures for 2006. These are average figures, and in 2006, there were 4,635 Canadians who had reached the age of 100. Indeed, the fastest growing age group is that between ages 55 and 64.

When Ponce de Leon searched for the mystical waters of the fountain of youth in 1513, he found Florida swampland instead. The fountain of youth may be elusive, even in the age of the facelift, but living longer is far more accessible. Over the twentieth century, nutrition and sanitation improved life expectancy in the West. Eating right, exercising the mind as well as the body, and engaging in community are the simple ingredients for a long life.

"I think Doc epitomizes that because he participates in business, industry, and community activities," says Bill Cochrane. "Then he goes on fishing trips with his pals and remains intellectually and socially stimulated. There's also the ranch and other travel. The balanced combination is key for anyone. There's a lot of information now suggesting that if you retire and do very little, then your chances of having health problems can occur more frequently than with someone who continues working."

One should recognize physical and intellectual limitations but not be paralyzed by them. Life in the Western world venerates the immortal and inexhaustible allure of youth. Yet drive and commitment needn't fail as the decades roll by.

Doc recharges his batteries through his work and his recreation. Participation and variety are the keys. He refuses to be bored and urges his friends to find a cause and purpose in life. He became particularly convinced after losing pals who had retired.

"It reinforced my own belief in not retiring," he says. "It's not that I don't have it somewhat easier today, but I am fully engaged."

His colleague at Dox Investments for the last seven years, Colin MacDonald, started out with Alcon Petroleums in the offices shared by Harley Hotchkiss, Boone Pickens, and Doc. Their paths continued to cross after MacDonald moved to Panarctic Oils. "You should never quit," says MacDonald, who has long embraced Doc's approach to work. "Because when you do, you die."

Sadly, MacDonald's stark remark rang too true for some of the Calgary Ratpack.

The storied Ratpack was a connected cluster of oil executives who often lunched at the Calgary Petroleum Club and occasionally played a mean game of poker or gin rummy. Together they golfed, skied, hunted, and fished everywhere, from scenic lodges to gritty cabins, from the Alberta badlands to the Scottish highlands to exotic locations in between.

"It was just an informal group, and we fancied up the name Ratpack. Maybe Frank Sinatra and his Ratpack picked up the name from us," jokes Doc.

The Ratpack included B.J. Seaman, Doc's brother and Bow Valley partner; Jack Sparks, CEO of Texaco Canada; Ron Coleman and Maury Paulson, senior VPs of Home Oil; Stan Paulson, venture capitalist and Maury's brother; Bob Phibbs, Bow Valley executive and former Canadian Olympic basketball captain; Rod McDaniel, founder of McDaniel and Associates, a petroleum engineering and consulting firm; Don Lougheed, Imperial Oil senior VP and brother of Peter Lougheed; Jack Harvie and John Poyen who also were senior executives with Imperial Oil; Dr. George Govier, chairman of the Alberta Energy Resources Conservation Board; Cliff Taylor, Baker Oil Tools executive; Louis Lebel, Chevron's senior lawyer; Frank Curley, drilling executive; Dick Hoy, haberdasher; Bruce Watson, CEO of Canadian Homestead Oils; Norm Gustavson, drilling entrepreneur and former Washington State ski team member; and Tubby Chapman, VP of Sun Oil (now Sunoco) working with its subsidiary, Great Canadian Oil Sands Company (which became the fully independent Suncor Energy).

"Tubby Chapman was in charge of purchasing and logistics for Sun Oil's Canadian subsidiary," says Doc. "J. Howard Pew, the head of Sun Oil, had a vision for transforming the vast northern Alberta oil sands into marketable production. That was in the 1960s, and Pew was way ahead of his time. But clearly he's been proved right. It took a lot of courage then to put the kind of money that he did into the oil sands. He used to come up from Pennsylvania for a month each summer and stay at the Jasper Park Lodge."

Chapman was convinced that the oil sands could be mined economically. He contracted Cardwell Supply Company, one of Bow Valley's subsidiaries, to bring German-manufactured bucket-wheel excavation technology to Alberta. Today's methods have evolved, but the persistence and ingenuity of oil sands pioneers like J. Howard Pew and Tubby Chapman set in motion Suncor's current successes.

The code of the Ratpack was simple. In the business world generally and in the oil business particularly, associations are important. Whether in the service or exploration and production end of the oil patch, making deals depends on the ability to work with people. And being a straight shooter is a big part of getting a deal done.

"It's the same today," adds Doc. "But especially in the early days when there weren't so many government forms involved, an awful lot of deals were done with handshakes. Your reputation for dealing honestly was very important."

The world of business consistently trumps recreation, so finding time to get the Ratpack together for sport was always a challenge. Their renowned trips were scheduled enough in advance to accommodate as many as possible.

"We usually discussed some business, but our main focus was recreation," says Doc. "We had a lot of good times. As a matter of fact, we had a crest designed for the Ratpack. I have it on one of my jackets at home. It was an eye-catching badge with a picture of a rat holding a shotgun in one hand and a golf club in the other."

The Ratpack's golf games were great fun and often involved complicated calculations to determine the winner. Several of the guys played golf at more competitive levels, too. Doc remembers the original Calgary Oilmen's golf tournament, which continues today at the Banff Springs or the Jasper Park Lodge. Invitations to the Oilmen's were, and still are, limited and highly prized.

"I played for close to thirty years," says Doc. "Then I decided to step aside and let some younger ones in. Very few of the original golfers are left. Most decided to give up their spot to younger players once they retired. It's a very successful tournament."

Doc remembers playing with some of Canada's top golfers, including Albertans Bob Wylie and Keith Alexander. Initially, the

Oilmen's Tournament was an open event, with no distinction between handicaps.

"Alexander and Wylie were winning tournaments everywhere, and they always shot under par. I could never get my handicap below two or three," says Doc, laughing, "but one year I shot a personal best of sixty-seven. I sure enjoyed playing against those guys, but I wasn't of their calibre."

Eventually, the Oilmen's rules were changed to allow for handicaps. "After that, I played in the championship final one time. The game was tied after eighteen, and I lost in an extra hole playoff." He chuckles. "But I did win the championship consolation." Doc can still shoot below his age on the golf course. And he still actively hunts game birds each year.

The Ratpack lives in memory, and a few of the rats are still thriving. While Doc encourages his friends, colleagues, and successors to never retire, that's not enough. Eating well, exercising regularly, engaging in life. If the mind doesn't keep challenged, the rest of the body goes," he says. "That thinking is pretty pervasive everywhere now."

Redefining age and work has also captured the imagination and zeal of Citytv co-founder Moses Znaimer, the media magnate who tapped into the youth market by creating MuchMusic. In January 2008, as the executive director of CARP (formerly the Canadian Association for Retired People), Znaimer created a new name — "Zoomer," meaning "boomer with zip" — for the boomer generation.

"Our new mission is to reevaluate what age and aging mean in 2008," he told the *Calgary Herald*'s Nancy Tousley on May 29, 2008. CARP's magazine was to be relaunched as *Zoomer*.

Doc Seaman's traditional conviction, learned over a lifetime, is becoming both modern science and mainstream thinking.

Grass Roots Hockey

Bill Hay, Ken Stiles, and Bob Nicholson
Ken Stiles Scholarship Awards
for young men and women referees

Funding provided to Hockey Canada
by Seaman Hotchkiss Hockey Foundation

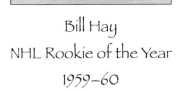

Bill Hay
NHL Rookie of the Year
1959–60

Scott Seaman
Age 14

Stanley Cup

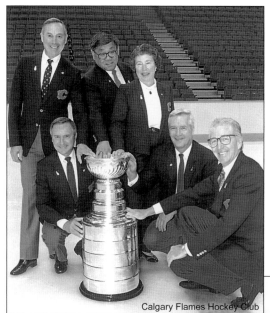

Calgary Flames Hockey Club

Calgary Flames Owners 1989
Stanley Cup Winners
Doc, B.J., Normie Kwong,
Sonia Scurfield,
Harley Hotchkiss,
and Norm Green

Doc, son Bob, and Al Murray
Cup day at the OH ~ 1989

Core Stability

Jarome Iginla

Robyn Regehr

Dion Phaneuf

Miikka Kiprusoff

Calgary Flames 2008

Calgary Olympics

Saddledome

Olympic Plaza

Fish & Game

Pheasant hunting in Scotland

Doc with 178 pound halibut
Queen Charlotte Islands
July 2008

Salmon fishing near
Prince Rupert ~ 2007

Community

Doc, B.J., and Harley Hotchkiss
Induction into Alberta Sports Hall of Fame ~ June 2007

Bud McCaig, Jim Gray, and Doc
Induction into Calgary Business Hall of Fame ~ October 2004

Medical Research

Dr. Garnette Sutherland and Doc ~ NeuroArm

Doc, Dr. Patch Adams, and Brett Wilson
Southern Alberta Institute of Urology ~ Promotional event ~ May 2008

Gamers

Peter Lougheed ~ 1982
Premier of Alberta (1971–1985)

Doc and Rev. Don McMahon ~ 2007

The Lieutenant Governor

Doc with Normie and Mary Kwong ~ Hawaii 1999

Normie Kwong
Edmonton Eskimos 1960

Honourable Norman L. Kwong
Lieutenant Governor of Alberta

Macdonald Commission

Commission Members (Doc, centre, in front of flag)

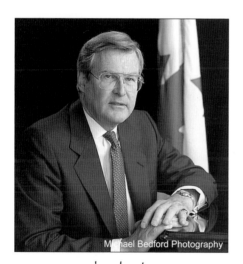

Michael Wilson
Finance Minister 1984-1991

Donald Macdonald
Commission Chair 1982 – 1985

Official Signing

Michael Bedford Photography

Doc on Parliament Hill ~ Ottawa 1985

Two Worlds

Doc, daughter Diane ~ Order of Canada reception ~ 1991
Governor General Raymond Hnatyshn and Mrs. Hnatyshn

Doc and Bud Maynard ~ Checking cattle at the OH

Cowboys

Branding crew ~ 1883

Robert Duvall, Paul Fuller, and Doc
On location for "Broken Trail" filmed at the OH ~ 2005

OH Ranch History

John Ware ~ Artwork by Robert Magee

Russell Moore Images

Replica of 1890 North West Mounted Police Cabin

Trail Ride

Doc

OH Ranch Annual Ride 2007
Don Taylor, Tood Snodgrass, Harold Milavsky, Fred Mannix, Doc, B.J.,
Paul Fuller, Peter Lougheed, Tom Bews

B.J.

Peter Lougheed

Remington

Doc on Remington at the OH

PART FOUR

~

And Now the Sports

CHAPTER EIGHT

The Sportsman

Where there's ice, it's never too cold to have a game of shinny. Find some friends, grab a stick, race to the rink, lace up the skates, and drop the puck. Scoring that goal or stopping that shot is all that counts, and freezing be damned.

During CBC's Hockey Day in Canada on February 9, 2008, kids of all ages, from Duncan, British Columbia, to New Glasgow, Nova Scotia, took to the rinks with their dreams, talent, and love of the game. In Black Diamond, Alberta, players and fans braved the weather's blast of -25°Celsius as they warmed to a dream realized — the official opening of the Scott Seaman Sports Rink. The honour to Scott, a hockey enthusiast who died tragically too young, is also the prototype for a rink that Hockey Canada hopes will be replicated across the country. Canada's hockey dominance as world champions and NHL leaders in the twenty-first century might depend on it.

"This is a fantastic opportunity for our young players to get more time on the ice to develop and improve their skills," says Hockey Canada president Bob Nicholson. "What we have in Black Diamond could be built across the country. For a project like this to be successful, the community involved must embrace it as Black Diamond has."

The rink's outdoor ice will be in play from November to March thanks to a refrigeration system that preserves the ice even in mild winter weather. During the warmer months, other sports such as lacrosse and ball hockey can command the turf.

The entire facility was built for about $1 million, a fraction of the cost of an indoor rink. From the outset, it was a community undertaking, kick-started with a gift of $500,000 from granddad Doc in Scott's memory and guided by Scott's father, Bob. The land was donated by the town of Black Diamond, and local residents contributed in countless ways. A matching grant of $500,000 was supplied by the Flames Project 75 Hockey Association.

"The bottom line is that we're going to provide more ice for hockey and other skating sports," says Doc. "There's a big shortage of ice all across Canada, and we think the Black Diamond model could provide a solution for other communities throughout the country."

Hockey is Canada's game. For the first part of the twentieth century, Canadian athletes dominated the sport in world competitions and the Olympics. By 1964, however, Canadian amateur hockey went into shock as championships were snatched by the Soviets. They were allowed to send their best "amateurs" — who happened to be paid by the Soviet government — to play in tournaments. Because the Canadians could not send professionals, the Soviets took their intriguing definition of amateur sport to the podium in many international competitions.

"The Soviets adopted our game and put more resources into it," notes Doc. "The Red Army team was the elite of Soviet society. They had great lifestyles. They were given nice apartments to live in. They were in effect professionals, whereas we had to have strictly amateur teams."

Canada wasn't allowed to use players from the National Hockey League's six teams: the Toronto Maple Leafs, Montreal Canadiens,

New York Rangers, Chicago Blackhawks, Boston Bruins, and Detroit Red Wings. Partly to tackle the international problem, a body that later became known as Hockey Canada was set up in 1968. Amateur hockey was still organized under the Canadian Amateur Hockey Association (CAHA).

Charlie Hay, president of Hockey Canada, and Joe Kryczka, president of the CAHA, later delivered an ultimatum to International Ice Hockey Federation (IIHF) head Bunny Ahearne and Andrei Starovoitov, general secretary of the USSR Ice Hockey Federation. It wasn't an easy mission; the Irish-born Ahearne's hostility to Canadian hockey was notorious among fans across the country. But the Canadians weren't bluffing. When Ahearne and Starovoitov refused to bend, Hay announced Canada's decision to withdraw from international competitions.

"At the IIHF," Doc recalls, "Charlie Hay said, 'If we're not allowed to play our best against your best in a series, we're going to withdraw from the Olympics, because it isn't right.' And that's how the 1972 Summit Series came about."

The hockey summit galvanized the country. Canada's best players from the NHL were picked to play against the Soviet national team. The Cold War whose shadow darkened the globe swooped onto the ice with ferocious intensity. A series of hockey games became a symbolic test not just of hockey skill but of geopolitical and cultural superiority.

"We played the first four games in Canada and didn't fare too well," recalls Doc. "Then we went into Russia, and our odds definitely didn't look good. But with typical Canadian spirit, we just rallied. All the marbles were on the line in the eighth and final game. It was like the seventh game of the Stanley Cup playoffs. The country's pride was at stake."

That game was marred first by a conflict over officiating, after the Soviets tried to change the officials at the last minute, and then by a near-brawl between Canadian players and Soviet soldiers after the goal judge failed to turn on the red light following a Canadian score. As time ran down with the score tied at five, the Canadian players were physically and emotionally exhausted. With only thirty-four seconds left, Paul Henderson scored a spectacular winning goal that remains the most famous single moment in the history of all Canadian sport. The country's pride as a world hockey leader was restored in that instant.

"Like every Canadian, I was ecstatic when we won," says Doc. "The refereeing was absolutely abysmal, but we managed to pull it off. The game was an electrifying event. That is the kind of thing that unifies people from all parts of Canada."

Not everyone shared the warm feelings about the value of all the regions in our country. During one of the Canada-Russia games, Doc recalls, he was introduced by Charlie Hay to Prime Minister Pierre Elliott Trudeau. "I was standing there at a cocktail party in Ottawa, and Trudeau said, 'Where are you from?' I said, 'I'm from out west, from Alberta.' 'Oh,' he said. 'I'd just as soon fly right over that place.'"

With the interest generated by the 1972 Summit Series, and Europe now acutely aware that international championships would be pale shadows without Canada, the IIHF reversed its earlier stance. In 1975, the IIHF Congress in Switzerland unanimously approved opening World Championships to all players, both amateur and professional. Canada had won both the hockey war and the equally rough political battle.

The Soviet Union collapsed in 1991, taking the Cold War with it but leaving Russia as the prominent competitor in hockey. Other nations, however, such as the United States, Sweden, Czechoslovakia, and Finland were also challenging Canada's hockey heritage. Many wondered if our country would continue to influence hockey, much less dominate the sport. Canada had given hockey to the world, and we were all proud of that; but Canadians still wanted our players to be better than the newcomers to the game.

While most of us simply watched and worried, Doc Seaman had long been searching for ways to improve Canadian skills and restore the nation's hockey superiority.

"We were having trouble in world hockey with the Russians and at the Olympics," notes Doc. "There was a feeling we were not as skilled as the Russians, and that we were falling behind. One brainchild Charlie Hay and I had in 1970 was to get back to the basics and develop the skills out in the community and put something back at the grassroots level." The vehicle that would propel Canadian hockey into world renown once more was the Flames Project 75 Hockey Association. Named for Alberta's seventy-fifth birthday as a province in 1980, the innovative concept had never been tried before in Canada.

Doc asked an independent auditing firm if there was any business in which he and his partners could invest where the revenues, if used for sport development, would not be taxable. They discovered that a Canadian-registered amateur athletic association could own oil and gas properties so long as the profits were dedicated to development of amateur sport in Canada. "We thought this would be a good way to generate tax-exempt funds for amateur hockey. So we went through the proper registration process, and then we bought some oil and gas properties and donated them to Project 75," recalls Doc.

"Project 75 was really Doc and B.J.'s idea, with Doc taking the lead," says Harley Hotchkiss, who, with the Seamans, is an original and current Calgary Flames co-owner. "We had a feeling that Canadian hockey was maybe slipping in a couple of key areas compared to the Russians, who were coming on strong. I'm talking about the basics of skating and shooting and passing and coaching. We made a commitment to support grassroots hockey," he adds.

"Doc takes a scientific approach to everything," says Bill Hay, chairman and CEO of the Hockey Hall of Fame and son of the late Charlie Hay. "I remember Doc telling me, 'Every good business invests in research and development.' He believed that Canada should make an investment into research and development for its national game."

This plan, developed in one city by a group of hockey-mad businessmen, is a major reason Canada now rules men's junior hockey and women's hockey and competes every time for world championships and Olympic gold.

Doc also had another dream he'd been thinking about for a long time: to bring an NHL team to Calgary. Edmonton already had the proud Oilers franchise. It was time for Calgary to have one too.

Doc didn't have to go far for advice. Bill Hay, then in his mid-forties, was a vice-president in a subsidiary of Doc's flagship company, Bow Valley Industries. Charlie's son certainly knew hockey. After graduating from Colorado College, he became the first college player ever to break into the NHL. In his first season, he won the Calder Memorial Trophy as rookie of the year, while centring Bobby Hull and Murray Balfour on Chicago's Million Dollar Line. The following season, 1960–61, Hay and his linemates helped the Blackhawks win the Stanley Cup.

From Doc's boardroom, Bill Hay called NHL President John Ziegler. Ziegler suggested taking a look at the Atlanta Flames, who were in bankruptcy at the time. He offered to make a call to Tom Cousins, a Georgia real estate developer who led the Atlanta ownership group. Cousins soon phoned Edmonton Oilers' owner Peter Pocklington to get whatever information he could about "that guy from Calgary named Doc Seaman."

Doc and Cousins then began the long and laborious slog that would bring the Flames from Atlanta to Calgary. This was not the oil patch, where a handshake sealed the deal. Invisible chefs stirred the stew, and the ingredients often changed without notice. So did the price. Negotiations were intense and lasted for nearly a year, with Doc and B.J. flying occasionally to Atlanta after telephone talks.

"Usually, when you sat down to do a deal with people in the oil patch, you had your idea of what the prospect would be worth and they had their idea," says Doc. "Things would either make sense, in which case you negotiated a little, or, if you were way off the mark, you'd go somewhere else. But there generally weren't any protracted negotiations that I remember. In the oil patch, we'd normally do a deal in short order and share the spoils if it worked out. But I wasn't used to drawn-out sports deals like this."

In the end, the deal wouldn't cost Doc much more than he had initially been willing to pay, although the road was dark and winding and the price kept rising. At first he was told the franchise could be Calgary's for between $10 and $11 million. But was that American or Canadian currency? They agreed on American. Then Coca-Cola, headquartered in Atlanta, balked at the team leaving, and suddenly the price popped up to US$12 million.

"It sounded logical," says Doc. "Coca-Cola had their main office in Atlanta and didn't want to see a major sports franchise head out of there. So we thought about it for a month and then said, 'Okay, we'll meet the price.'"

It looked like a deal was done, until Jack Kent Cooke stepped in. Cooke owned the Los Angeles Lakers basketball team and the L.A. Kings hockey franchise and sold both in 1979 for the record-breaking price of US$67.5 million. He kept his Washington Redskins football franchise. The Hamilton, Ontario–born tycoon wanted the Atlanta team to stay put; he offered $14 million.

"Again, it seemed logical, especially since he had owned a hockey team, had even been Canadian and was now American," continues Doc. "So, I said, 'Okay, we'll meet that too.'"

Doc wonders whether if he had put his foot down at the $14 million mark and said 'That's it — that's all we'll do' the deal could have been completed right there. Likely not, as Cousins seemed determined to get the top price and continued to talk to other prospective buyers.

"He just kept pulling us along," says Doc. "Finally, right before the 1979 hockey season starts, Cousins comes up to Calgary and says, 'I've dealt with you guys for quite a while. I like you. I'd like you to have first crack at it.' But he says there's another fellow interested, and for $16 million the team is ours. This seemed peculiar, and I finally said no. Then lo and behold if Nelson Skalbania doesn't jump in."

Brother B.J. adds, "We thought that we had struck a deal with Cousins and then Skalbania came along and said to him, 'You can get more money.'"

Vancouver-based Skalbania had once owned the Edmonton Oilers and had sold half his interest to Peter Pocklington in 1976. The two entrepreneurs were colourful and controversial business figures who basked in the public lights. They brokered their Oilers deal in the middle of a well-known Edmonton steakhouse as Pocklington dined with his wife, Eva. Skalbania blew in with a squad of reporters and ended the evening owning an exquisite art canvas, an exceptional diamond ring that Eva was wearing one last time, and a vintage Rolls-Royce. In 1977, Skalbania relinquished his remaining half of the Oilers to Pocklington.

It was Skalbania who initially signed Wayne Gretzky at age seventeen into a binding personal services contract to play for his Indianapolis franchise of the World Hockey Association. Many saw Gretzky as an exceptionally gifted kid, but it was Skalbania who swooped in and signed him up as an underage player.

In less than a year, Skalbania sold Gretzky's contract to Pocklington, who, when Gretzky turned eighteen on January 26, 1979, offered the young player a twenty-one-year deal — the longest personal services contract in hockey history.

Skalbania then focused on grabbing the Atlanta Flames from Cousins. To raise funds, he sold the Flames' television rights for the next ten years to Molson brewers for $6 million. "Skalbania borrowed enough money to get the bank to put up the rest of the funds and was able to satisfy Cousins," adds Doc.

The setback didn't deter Doc for long. He quickly contacted B.J., Harley Hotchkiss, and Ralph Scurfield, the group that had initially pulled together the Flames bid. They met with Skalbania, entrepreneur Norm Green, and football great Norman Kwong (enormously popular in Alberta since his days as a star running back for the Calgary Stampeders and then the Edmonton Eskimos, Norman Kwong was appointed lieutenant-governor of Alberta on January 20, 2005; his pals still call him Normie). The deal was struck, and on May 21, 1980, the group told the world the Flames were heading to Calgary.

"We made a deal to take 50 percent of the ownership while Skalbania kept 50 percent at first," recalls Doc. "And then he realized what we were doing in co-operation with the province. We had agreed to put money back into amateur hockey and into the community."

Doc's plan was always to structure the Flames as a community venture. He and his Calgary partners agreed to donate a share of their revenues to amateur sports. Skalbania's interests were seldom aligned with those of the Calgarians. At first, he agreed to contribute a share of his profits to community hockey, but by August 1981 he decided to sell his stake, making between $1 and $2 million profit from the venture. The ownership remained firmly in the hands of the initial Calgary six until Norm Green sold his interest on June 15, 1990, in order to buy the Minnesota North Stars (the Dallas Stars today). Four years later, on August 8, 1994, Norman Kwong and Ralph Scurfield's widow, Sonia, sold their stakes.

"I knew Doc by reputation but hadn't met him until our partnership in the hockey business," says Kwong. "I had heard wonderful things, and when I met him, all of it was true. He's a great guy, a smart, level-headed businessman, and when things came up, he always seemed to have the right answer. Through the partnership, we became good friends, and that has continued."

Before entering into the topsy-turvy talks with Tom Cousins to bring the Flames to Calgary, Doc knew he would eventually need a new arena for the NHL team. Calgary's largest hockey arena was the Stampede Corral. Built in 1950, the Corral was a magnificent building in its day and still a serviceable hockey venue, but with only enough space — including jam-packed standing room — for fewer than nine thousand spectators.

Calgary had made a bid to host the Winter Olympics in 1964 and again in 1968, both times without success. By the late 1970s, the city and the province were determined to try again. Doc had visited earlier Olympics and seen that most had a showcase facility that helped convince the International Olympic Committee to support their bids.

"I realized we might be able to combine our vision with that of the Calgary Olympics bid committee," says Doc. "So I went to visit Premier Peter Lougheed at his office in Edmonton and said, 'If you can support putting a showcase building in Calgary for the Olympics, I will do my best to get an NHL franchise and we'll pay the rent as a long-term tenant.'"

Lougheed and Doc weren't strangers to bold initiatives; they hadn't reached the pinnacles of success without daring and dreaming. Lougheed was intrigued, and the drive for the Saddledome was launched.

"In my experience, this was one of the most remarkable coincidences of common interests," says the former premier. "I can recall well Doc coming to see me in Edmonton. I didn't know what he was going to raise with me, but I had such high regard for him that I was interested in seeing him and finding out what was on his mind. It was one of those incredible meetings where Doc said, 'Is there any way, with Edmonton having their Coliseum, the province could take the lead in constructing a similar facility in Calgary?' I just beamed. I said, 'This is an amazing experience. I'm not sure I've had very many, where you're just coming forward to solve a problem and we're responding in a constructive way to your challenge.' It was a made-in-heaven meeting where we agreed to take the lead with what became the Saddledome, and Doc had a home for the Calgary Flames. It all happened inside of a week."

Doc now knew that if he could secure the Flames franchise, he could confidently continue his push for some provincial support, since the Saddledome would have a permanent tenant. For his part, Lougheed knew exactly whom he was dealing with, as Doc had talked with him in the past about energy issues. Over the years they had grown to respect each other; but Doc was aware that before he climbed those solid legislature steps again, he had to have an equally solid case for the premier. And he was determined that his proposal to the premier would become a promise fulfilled.

Premier Lougheed knew through discussions with Frank King, Bob Niven, and Bill Warren, who led Calgary's 1988 Olympic bid, that success depended in part on a showcase venue for the hockey and other ice-skating events. Edmonton was given its Coliseum, which had solidified that city's proposal for the 1983 World University Games.

"We were in a fortunate position politically in that we had already, with the city of Edmonton, taken the lead with the world student games in providing the Coliseum as a provincial initiative," says Lougheed.

The city of Calgary had already endorsed a report in principle, written in April 1980, calling for a coliseum to be constructed. Yet they were confronted with a catch-22, as outlined in a report called "Olympic Saddledome Foundation, The First Five Years 1983–1988."

"A major facility built just for the Olympics would be a white elephant," the report states. "An NHL franchise would help meet operating expenses, but the city stood little chance of attracting a franchise without a new facility that the city couldn't afford to build on its own."

Doc wanted the franchise in Calgary but knew the Stampede Corral wouldn't cut it as a long-term home for an NHL team. A new coliseum was critical.

Lougheed firmly believed that a designated showcase building would bolster the bid for the 1988 Winter Olympics. He wrote to Calgary mayor Ross Alger that the province would support the construction of a coliseum with the Calgary Flames as principal tenant.

On July 3, 1980, the premier wrote, "Such a facility would substantially strengthen the bid by the Calgary Olympic Development Association for the 1988 Winter Games. Acquiring these games will enhance Alberta's reputation worldwide and provide excellent winter sports facilities for all of southern Alberta in the future. Such a coliseum would provide a permanent home for Hockey Canada, the Olympic Hockey Team, and give a much needed impetus to amateur hockey for the whole country. It is hoped that Canada's national sport can be returned to the 'world stature it once had,' as stated in the report of the Calgary Sports Facilities Advisory Committee."

The premier also proposed a funding formula for the coliseum. Federal, provincial, and municipal governments would share the cost equally. When construction began in the summer of 1981, the province guaranteed a loan for Ottawa's share. On October 15, 1983, the Saddledome officially opened, managed by the non-profit Olympic Saddledome Foundation.

"It was really significant," says Lougheed. "By the time Frank King and his team made the bid in 1981 — and I was with them in Baden-Baden, Germany — the Saddledome was already under construction. It wasn't something we were promising to do; it was something that was already in progress. So it was more tangible in our bid to get the '88 winter games. From the public point of view, on the other hand, I was able to say that we'd have the best possible tenant for our building — the Calgary Flames." The political endorsement was strengthened by Doc and his colleagues' commitment to channel a portion of their revenues back into the community. "You couldn't have a better coming together of interests," adds Lougheed. "It was really remarkable."

The federal government had written that it was delighted "a growing share of the money generated from the operations of the Saddledome will be used to support amateur sport in Canada," notes the Saddledome Foundation report.

"To say that they had the provincial and federal government behind them, plus a major showpiece in the Saddledome, I'm sure substantially benefited the bid," says Doc. "The crucial point, though, is that Frank King and his team did an outstanding job."

King became the chairman and CEO of the XV Olympic Winter Games in Calgary. "We went to Baden-Baden and presented drawings and a model of the Saddledome," he says. "We said it was to be finished in 1983. That became a pledge, and we used it." King guaranteed that all the buildings for Olympic events would be constructed to the same standard. This too was crucial, as there were no facilities in Calgary or the surrounding area that the Olympic Games could use. "We had nothing else," continues King, "so the Saddledome was an absolutely essential ingredient in the bid and in the success of the Games ultimately. Doc Seaman was a key part of that success."

Doc was also a governor of the Olympic trust of Canada and chairman of its Alberta division. With Harley Hotchkiss, he co-chaired the Team Petroleum Olympics Fund, which encouraged oil and gas producers to buy tickets and support the Games financially.

The Olympic Saddledome Foundation was governed by a nine-member board of appointees from the city of Calgary, the province of Alberta, the Calgary Olympic Development Association, the Calgary Exhibition & Stampede, and Hockey Canada. Bill Hay was selected as the first chairman.

Revenue shares from the Flames' owners were paid into the Saddledome Foundation and then divided equally among the Calgary Parks Foundation; the Calgary Olympic Development Association; and Hockey Canada. As original investors, the city, provincial, and federal governments still receive a percentage of Flames' revenues for their projects, whether the Flames' owners make a profit or not. In the twenty-five years following the Saddledome's opening in late 1983, Flames' owners distributed some $23 million to amateur sports and community projects.

With the Saddledome as a venue for the Olympics, NHL hockey, and other events, Doc was determined to build a professional franchise that would become a unique community venture.

On a parallel track, he wanted Project 75 to promote amateur hockey and create a sports environment where players could learn, train, compete, and excel nationally and globally. He saw it as a vehicle for reestablishing Canada's dominance in world hockey.

Doc wanted Project 75 to be self-sustaining from the start, so the he and the original owners of the Flames dug into their pockets and donated $3 million to purchase producing oil and gas wells in eastern Alberta.

"When we made that decision, Doc was the leader, and it was his idea to set it up the way we did," says Harley Hotchkiss. "We got it incorporated and registered so that donations to it were tax-deductible. We funded it from our own resources, as the Flames certainly didn't make any money in the early years. The concept of oil and gas properties was Doc's idea, and I played a role there because that is my background. Eventually, we sold the oil and gas properties, and the proceeds went into an investment fund. We've done a pretty good job of investing with that fund and the profits we're generating go directly to Hockey Canada development initiatives. There is a bit of pride in that. Doc, B.J., and I have continued with it and expanded it and helped it to grow to where it is today."

Since its inception, Project 75 has grown to hold more than $8 million in cash and securities and put $4.7 million back into scholarships and the research and development of hockey programs across Canada. Ken Stiles was the chairman and the money maestro who invested brilliantly and took the lead role in the day-to-day operations of Project 75. The others were John Poetker, lawyer with Borden Ladner Gervais LLP, and Clare Rhyasen, CFO for Max Pasley Enterprises and current president of Project 75. Rob Moffat, CEO of Bow Valley Energy, later joined as a director.

Project 75's early initiatives included creating a hockey research institute overseen by the University of Calgary and the University of Alberta, with a focus on physiological and psychological sports expertise. It also established hockey bursaries and helped the Canadian Amateur Hockey Association sponsor sports clinics. Once the winning 1988 bid was announced, Project 75 co-funded a training base in Calgary for the Canadian Olympic Hockey Team.

Charlie Hay died just one year after the 1972 Summit Series, and his son, Bill, became a director on Hockey Canada's board. By the early 1980s, Hockey Canada had firmly established itself as a leader in promoting top-level international competitions. Influential board members included president Ron Robison, Montreal Canadiens general manager Sam Pollock, CAHA president Murray Costello, Supreme Court Justice William Estey, Ottawa columnist and former MP Doug Fisher, marketing consultant Chris Lang, and NHL Players' Association executive director Alan Eagleson. Winning gold medals was the key goal; but at this point little progress was being made on the second part of Hockey Canada's mandate — improving hockey at a grassroots level.

Meanwhile in Calgary, preparations for the 1988 Olympics were in full swing, and Project 75 was providing funding for Hockey Canada's developmental and training programs for amateur hockey. Co-operation between the two organizations was facilitated by Bill Hay's relationships and his participation on Hockey Canada's board.

In 1984, this co-operation was formalized through a joint Research and Development Committee that had seasoned pros to make it work: Bill Hay (as chair), Project 75's Ken Stiles, Western Canadian Hockey League president Ed Chynoweth, and Hockey Canada's Norm Robertson. Within a year, they saw the first Centre of Excellence open in Calgary. This was the catalyst for setting up similar centres later in Montreal, Vancouver, and Saint John. Vision and tenacity were taking amateur hockey in Canada to another level.

Having the Canadian national hockey team based in Calgary, training for the upcoming Olympics, provided an added bonus. Coach Dave King volunteered countless hours to work with the Research and Development Committee.

Clearly there was growing support for Project 75. Yet there was also a good deal of bemused wonder at Doc's initiatives: they were bold and innovative, very much in the mould of an entrepreneur who went against the grain and looked for solutions beyond the staid corridors of wood-panelled power. Doc and his colleagues were committed to grassroots hockey throughout the country, whether the young athletes played on community teams or just grabbed sticks and a puck for a game of pond hockey.

In hindsight, it's clear that when Canada's hockey dominance was severely threatened, three men significantly revived amateur hockey and restored dominance and dignity to our national sport.

"It was unbelievable — really unbelievable. Doc, Harley, and B.J. helped to make amateur hockey the way it is today. They're a huge, huge part in that," says Bob Nicholson, CEO of Hockey Canada, the body that now governs national ice hockey. "Project 75 was something special to sport — it had never been done. It's a huge emphasis on hockey and close to $5 million to programs that would never have happened in this country. No one did it before and no one has since."

Hockey Canada, through Project 75, produces a range of hockey skills videos for players and coaches. Fitting into Project 75's research and development mandate, the Charles Hay Memorial Library hosts the world's largest collection of hockey educational resources. In addition, Hockey Canada's popular Web site (www. HockeyCanada.ca) offers players and parents videos to download, as well as offering coaches on-line chats through its Coaches Club.

"Dave King, who was coach of the Olympic hockey team, did much of the initial work on this with the help of Ron Robison," says Doc. "They developed the videos and other instructional material for the coaches and the young hockey players." King has coached around the world and in Canada for the Calgary Flames. Robison is now the commissioner of the Western Hockey League (WHL).

Project 75 also helps fund cutting-edge research into prevention and treatment of hockey injuries. This feeds into a national reporting system that regularly adjusts policies and playing rules. The research ties into hockey safety and injury prevention programs as well as bodychecking education seminars.

"We have instructional videos that coaches across Canada or anywhere else can access and clinics where coaches can come for training," says Hotchkiss. "We get big attendance from coaches around the world. We set up scholarships and financed research on injuries. We are doing some work on officiating now."

Adds Doc, "We get together at least once a year to see where we are with Project 75. And Hockey Canada comes to us with projects that meet our mandate of putting support back into the grassroots level of the game."

The partnership between Project 75 and Hockey Canada produced its initial coaching venture, the very first of its kind in Canada. The National Program of Excellence High Performance Coaching Seminar had a long name but proved to be an even longer running hit. These popular coaches' conferences, hosted at the Centres of Excellence, attract participants from Flin Flon to Finland. In the beginning, fourteen coaches came for the course. More than twenty years later, the international coaching conferences across Canada often draw five hundred delegates from ten countries.

"They're held every two years, and coaches come from the NHL and national teams from other countries," says Nicholson. "The program flourishes. They were part of Doc's vision and were successful because of Project 75's research and development initiatives. They've really had an impact on people's lives. With all the aids now available from Project 75, the program has affected hundreds of thousands of people in Canada and that many more again in other countries combined. There's an initiation program for players under ten that runs in more than twenty countries around the world."

Opening the program to other countries has also created tremendous goodwill around the world by showing that Canada cares about creating quality hockey as much as winning medals.

"The interesting thing is that people don't know about Project 75," Nicholson says. "Doc, B.J., and Harley were inducted into the Alberta Sports Hall of Fame, and the stories are finally being told. They always want to do it quietly. Doc is a humble person, but you can see a big smile come across his face when something is accomplished — that's all he really wants."

Hockey is once again Canada's game. For a while in the late twentieth century, Russia ruled. Today, Canada's junior and senior men and women's teams roar and score, making the country proud. Project 75 has armed a generation of hockey players with the skills, expertise, and energy to play, compete, and win.

On a related front, Bill Hay's perseverance at Hockey Canada's board meetings paid off. In 1994, with the unflagging support of Ken Stiles, he secured approval to merge Hockey Canada and the Canadian Amateur Hockey Association. With a $400,000 grant from Project 75, Calgary's Father David Bauer Olympic Arena was upgraded and office space was added. Together with the hockey research and development initiatives provided by Project 75, the merger of the two governing bodies was a major step forward for hockey in Canada.

When the merged entity moved from Ottawa to Calgary, Bob Nicholson moved too. "Doc and Ken Stiles made the whole transition easier for my family, but not so easy for me," laughs Nicholson.

"They wanted to change how the CAHA worked so it didn't rely on government funding. This involved a major mind-set change. It was really tough — no one was sure if we could do it."

Doc knew. He counted on Bill Hay, who understood hockey as an elite player and business as a vice-president with Bow Valley. He had been president of Hockey Canada before moving to the Calgary Flames as CEO. Later, Hay became the planning advisor for Hockey Canada's Centres of Excellence. "He was a key person," notes Nicholson. "Bill Hay is just phenomenal in building those bridges to start a relationship. Today, we are self-sufficient, thanks also to our volunteers."

In 1998, Hockey Canada boasted a budget of $5 million with a staff of thirty-two. By 2008, the budget jumped more than tenfold to $56 million, while the staff nearly tripled to ninety-two.

"It's changed the culture of how we work," adds Nicholson. "We make sure there is a business plan to everything we do. Any time Doc and Project 75 gave us seed money to get a program going, I had to have a business plan to show how it would work in the succeeding years after the initial grant. We needed to operate with new revenue sources by the second or third year."

When Nicholson went to his very first meeting in Calgary, held at the Petroleum Club, he was more than a little nervous. Standing tall before the advisory board, he enthusiastically presented his plans, sat down, and waited for the funds to start flowing.

"I thought I would have the money and simply go spend it," says Nicholson. "Instead, I was told I had to change my structure and how I work. I thought, 'So this is how they make things work in Calgary — that should be interesting.'"

That was not the way it was done in Ottawa, where money came mainly through government grants and the key skill was filling out an application form. The Project 75 board wanted Nicholson to reorganize. The newcomer was faced with a huge culture shock as he faced the verdict: Hockey Canada had too many committees; he must develop a business model for the organization rather than relying on government grants and funding.

"This is going to be run as a business. We don't want to be dependent on government grants. We'll generate our own revenues," Bill Hay recalls Ken Stiles saying. Nicholson had no thought of backing out. He got on board and did the work. It took him six months to develop a plan and cut the bureaucracy, but the goal was worth the effort. "The board wants to make sure money goes directly to kids, players, and officials," he says. "They want the end-users rather than administration to get the funds."

Nicholson now embraces marketing, with its constant challenges and opportunities. A big part of the business is licensing and sponsorship sales, which have risen dramatically since the 1998 Nagano Olympics. For all hockey products combined, gross sales that year amounted to under $1 million. By 2006, combined licensing of apparel soared to $52 million in gross sales. The royalty take was 10 percent. As Doc says, "The long and short of it is that Hockey Canada today is pretty much independent of any government assistance."

Nicholson has learned to love the way of the West, where the handshake seals the deal. "It's a great way to work. If you have those kinds of relationships, there's no better way," he says. "I remember Bill Hay telling me that if you shake someone's hand, you make sure you deliver. That is the Calgary mentality, and that's why it's a great home for Hockey Canada. The staff learns a lot from this environment. Every Centre of Excellence is unique, but Calgary is great. And Doc is instrumental. He doesn't say a lot, but he asks very direct questions and never in a negative way. He doesn't raise his voice, and I've never seen him explode. He's a fair and generous person, and there's a feeling of support when he's around."

The Project 75 programs are extensive, educational, inclusive, and innovative. They dip into every corner of Canada and offer girls and boys of all ages the chance to put their dreams behind that slapshot. They provide four scholarships to the University of Calgary: three in the names of Doc Seaman, B.J. Seaman, and Harley Hotchkiss, and the Lanny McDonald Hockey Award to a men's hockey player.

In early 2008, Project 75's directors voted to officially change the body's name to the Seaman Hotchkiss Hockey Foundation in honour of the contributions Doc and B.J. Seaman and Harley Hotchkiss have made to hockey development in Canada. Among the first funds distributed under the new name will be $1 million toward a state-of-the-art hockey centre in Mississauga, Ontario. Scheduled to open in the fall of 2009, this complex will house the largest Centre of Excellence in Canada, incorporating theatres, auditoriums, four ice pads, and the Hockey Hall of Fame Resource Centre. The Toronto Maple Leafs made a major investment in the new complex. Along with the Toronto Marlies, the Leafs will use it as their permanent training and practice facility.

Hockey Canada now has 13 branches with more than 31,000 teams and 530,000 players stretched across the country. More than 4.5 million Canadians are absorbed by the game as players, coaches, trainers, officials, administrators, and, crucially, volunteers. Add the parents and the fans and the numbers boggle the mind, as well as clog the rinks. The pressure on ice time is a problem caused in part by the success of Hockey Canada.

But Doc, as always, has his plan for that, too — outdoor rinks like the one he co-funded in Black Diamond, Alberta.

CHAPTER NINE

The Fan

In the whole history of the National Hockey League, and perhaps all North American sport, there has never been anything quite like the party that spontaneously erupted when the Calgary Flames made their run for the Stanley Cup in the spring of 2004.

It started small, when the team won the first games in the early elimination rounds: a few thousand people began trailing down 17th Avenue west from the Saddledome, hitting the restaurants and bars after the game, generally having a good time. As the victories mounted and the Flames won their way through one series after another, the crowds grew enormous. When the Flames faced the Tampa Bay Lightning in the final series in early June, as many as sixty thousand people were jamming the avenue on game nights. Dubbed the Red Mile, the amazing outpouring of fan affection drew media attention across North America. Viewers were fascinated by CBC-TV coverage of the heaving, surging masses of fans who partied for weeks without any major incidents of crime.

The Flames had become enormously important to the psyche of Calgary and all of southern Alberta. A team that had won only one Stanley Cup, in 1989, gradually became the symbol of the city's co-operative, volunteer ethic. In a way seldom recognized, the Flames carried the spirit of the 1988 Olympic Winter Games, when thousands of Calgarians volunteered on a scale that awed the International Olympic Committee. It's no accident that both the Olympics and the Flames were forged in the community vision of men like Doc Seaman and Peter Lougheed. Young Calgarians flooded the Red Mile because it was one of the great Canadian parties of all time; but on another level, they were revealing the rewards of solid community planning and leadership. The Flames today are far from the most successful on-ice franchise in the NHL; the Montreal Canadiens will probably always hold that honour. But this team is unique in its deep bond with the community.

Even the loss of the series in the seventh game to the Lightning didn't cool the ardour, despite the conviction of many fans that the series had been stolen in game six when officials disallowed what appeared to be a Flames goal. The following year became a nightmare that threatened the whole league, as a labour dispute halted play for the season. But when the Flames took the ice again in the fall of 2005, the fans were back in their legions, as fervent as ever.

Doc says, "Our fans are tremendous. Look at the number that wear our red jerseys. You don't see fans in other buildings displaying that kind of identity with their team."

Even during the team's darkest days in the 1990s, fans always knew that the franchise was born in a spirit of giving, spinning off proceeds to both charity and hockey development. The resulting goodwill toward the owners probably saved the team from collapse. For seven straight years after they won the Stanley Cup in 1989, the Flames failed to make the playoffs. Gradually the fans became disenchanted and began to fade away. Season ticket sales drifted downward.

But when co-owner Harley Hotchkiss made a personal appeal to the fans to buy season tickets in 1999 and 2000, or face losing the team, they believed him and responded with thousands of purchases. Everyone knew the owners personally lost millions when the team did badly. Had the Flames been a standard profit-making venture, they probably would have been lost to the United States by 2002. The fans were willing to give them another chance in the hope that play would improve, as it soon did.

There was some ill will in the mid-1990s, too, when the owners had to ask the city and province for help renovating the Saddledome. Outdated seating arrangements and the owners' lack of control over the building were making it difficult to break even. Losses mounted even as the team continued to pay its charity and hockey development money. Many Calgary aldermen, playing politics, lamented the demand on the public treasury, but finally struck a deal because they knew the alternative — the loss of both the team and a great deal of community funding. Not all the fans were happy, but the owners always had a counter-argument; they weren't making a personal penny out of this.

Doc and B.J. Seaman stayed in the background of all these disputes. They always remained team players with the other owners, while freely offering advice and helping reach consensus in some difficult dilemmas. Indeed, Doc has been so quiet about his part in all these events that it's often assumed Nelson Skalbania brought the Flames to Calgary in the first place. Skalbania certainly was involved, but Doc Seaman was grinding out the Atlanta deal long before the high roller from the West Coast blew through town.

Doc hopes the team has been important to the city at crucial moments. In 1986, for instance, oil prices crashed and many Calgarians faced dire economic times, even personal ruin. But although the general mood was bleak, the hockey team provided a huge lift, going to the Stanley Cup final series against Montreal.

"That was a tough year in the oil patch, but we had a particularly good run with the hockey team in '86," says Doc. "At the end, Montreal beat us in five games, with the last game in Calgary. The whole crowd stood up and started singing 'Thank You Flames.' It was a lift for the entire community. It was a bit like the Red Mile in 2004."

Calgarians still wanted the big prize, though — the Stanley Cup itself.

"We had some great teams in the 1980s," Doc continues. "Unfortunately, we were usually stymied by the juggernaut Edmonton had in those days."

Led by a record-shattering Wayne Gretzky, the Oilers won an incredible four Stanley Cups in five years. In 1989–90, they added a fifth, just one season after Gretzky had been traded to Los Angeles.

"Some of our league games against the Oilers were more exciting than the Stanley Cup finals," Doc recalls.

The Battle of Alberta has never been more intense than during the Flames-Oilers matchups of the 1980s. Rivalries between the fans over bragging rights were almost as heated as the battles on the ice to claim hockey's biggest prize. Both teams played wide open hockey with plenty of goals scored and even more bodychecks thrown.

In the summer of 1987, coach Bob Johnson left to head up the American amateur hockey program, and his position was filled by Terry Crisp. The Flames finished first overall in league play in 1987–88, winning the Presidents' Trophy for the first time in team history. Disappointingly, they were swept in four straight games by the Oilers in the second round of the playoffs.

General Manager Cliff Fletcher was convinced that a few key changes would be needed to take the Flames to the next level. In one of his shrewdest moves in Calgary, Fletcher acquired Doug Gilmour and Mark Hunter from St. Louis in a multi-player trade. Gilmour was a perfect fit for the Flames, a skilled and gritty forward. When he first broke into the league, Blues' Captain Brian Sutter tagged him with the nickname "Killer." The name stuck.

Fletcher's other big trade that year had been completed a few months earlier and was more controversial. Near the end of the 1987–88 season, he sent twenty-three-year-old Brett Hull to St.

Louis as part of a package deal in exchange for defenceman Rob Ramage and goaltender Rick Wamsley.

"I hated to give up Brett," Doc recalls. "He could really shoot the puck, and he had a pretty good pedigree. But the consensus among our guys was that we had plenty of scoring, and we really needed another high-quality veteran defenceman and a proven back-up goalie."

The Flames were also concerned about being able to keep all their talented young players with free agency looming. They knew they were giving up a potential star in Brett Hull but felt they needed veteran talent to make a run at the Stanley Cup. It was a calculated risk.

Fletcher's wheeling and dealing paid immediate dividends. The Flames had a terrific season in 1988–89, winning the Presidents' Trophy for a second straight year with an even higher point total.

"I think overall our team in 1988–89 was probably our best ever," Doc says. "We had eight players that year with over twenty goals. Some of our guys had the best year of their careers. And I guess we had a few lucky breaks, too. We didn't have much problem with injuries that season. That's often an important factor, as the long playoff rounds become a survival test."

Joe Mullen had a fabulous year, putting up career-high numbers with 51 goals and 110 total points. A native New Yorker, and one of three American-born regulars on the team, Mullen was named a First Team All-Star and winner of the Lady Byng Memorial Trophy, the award based on playing ability, sportsmanship, and gentlemanly conduct. St. Louis Blues General Manager Emile Francis, one of Doc's rivals from senior baseball in Saskatchewan in the 1940s, described Mullen as "not the biggest guy in the world, but he's strong and he's got great balance."

Joe Nieuwendyk had been drafted by the Flames in 1985 and joined the team for the 1987–88 season. He made an immediate impact, scoring an astounding fifty-one goals as a rookie, and was awarded the Calder Trophy. The following year, Nieuwendyk again scored fifty-one goals, matching Joe Mullen's team-leading total.

Nieuwendyk had earlier been an exceptional lacrosse player, starring on a team from Whitby, Ontario, that won the Minto Cup in 1984. One of his teammates in Whitby, Gary Roberts, was drafted by the Flames that same year. A rugged and aggressive power forward with an ability to score goals, Roberts was delighted to team up again with his friend in Calgary.

The Flames' best European-born player during the late 1980s was Hakken Loob. In 1987–88, Loob scored fifty goals, the most ever for a Swedish-born player in the NHL — more even than the Flames' better known Swede, Kent Nilsson, "the Magic Man," who came with the team from Atlanta. An incredibly talented player in the late 1970s and early 1980s, Nilsson's highest goal total for a single season was forty-nine. Loob was named as a First Team All-Star in 1987–88, and although his scoring dropped off the following season, his last in the NHL, he still tallied an impressive twenty-seven goals.

Cliff Fletcher's trades for Gilmour and Ramage were the most notable and might have had the biggest impact, but two other deals he brokered in 1988 also proved invaluable.

Jiri Hrdina joined the Flames late in the 1987–88 season after playing with the Czech national team in the 1988 Olympics in Calgary. Although he later skated on two Stanley Cup teams in Pittsburgh along with Mario Lemieux and countryman Jaromir Jagr, Hrdina's twenty-two goals with the Flames in 1988–89 was his personal best in the NHL.

Earlier that same year, Fletcher had acquired Dana Murzyn in a trade with the Hartford Whalers. A standout with his hometown Calgary Wranglers of the WHL, Murzyn had been chosen fifth overall by Hartford in the 1985 NHL entry draft and immediately fit in with the Flames' defensive pairings.

For a span of more than ten years, another Calgary native, Tim Hunter, was the Flames' enforcer and could always be counted on to answer the bell against opposing heavyweights. The Flames' all-time leader in penalty minutes, Hunter is best remembered for his epic slugfests with Dave Semenko, the Oilers' tough guy, whom fans around the league loved to hate in his role as Wayne Gretzky's bodyguard.

Colin Patterson grew up as a lacrosse player and competed internationally on Canada's national team. Signed by the Flames as a free agent, he adapted his lacrosse skills to the role of a checking forward. In 1988–89, Patterson's plus-minus rating on the team was bettered only by Doug Gilmour's and the league-leading figure of plus fifty-one, posted by Joe Mullen.

Another solid role player, Perry Berezan, was traded to Minnesota in March 1989 for veteran power forward Brian MacLellan. The Edmonton-born Berezan is fondly remembered in Calgary as the player credited with the winning goal that propelled the Flames into the Stanley Cup final in 1986. In fact, Oiler defenceman Steve Smith inadvertently put the puck into his own net, but Berezan's name is in the record books in that shocking upset of the highly favoured Edmonton team.

Co-captain Jim Peplinski was drafted by the Flames in 1979 before they left Atlanta and went on to play his entire career in Calgary. Tough and scrappy, he was a dependable and versatile two-way forward. Originally from Ontario, Peplinski adopted Alberta as his new home and has become a fixture in Calgary business circles and a mainstay with the Calgary Flames Alumni organization.

At 6', 4" and 220 pounds, centreman Joel Otto was the Flames' biggest player. From Minnesota, Otto had quick hands along with size and strength and was one of the NHL's top faceoff specialists. Against the Oilers, he was regularly called upon to go head to head with Mark "Moose" Messier. As one of the few players in the league who matched up well against Messier in the faceoff circle, along the boards, and in front of the net, Otto was a key figure in every Battle of Alberta.

"I remember watching a game in Toronto," Doc says. "One of the Maple Leafs fans sitting near me blurted out, 'That Otto is like a big oak tree. You can't move him.'" He also contributed on the scoresheet; in 1988–89, Otto scored twenty-three goals.

Calgary's blue line that year featured two mobile defencemen who regularly put up big offensive numbers: Al MacInnis and Gary Suter.

Al MacInnis grew up in Nova Scotia. Drafted in the first round by the Flames in 1981, he joined the team two years later and developed into one of the premier defencemen of all time. With his lethal slapshot, MacInnis won the hardest shot competition at the NHL All-Star game seven times.

Gary Suter, picked 180th overall in the 1984 NHL Entry Draft, proved to be one of the Flames' best late round selections ever. An alumnus of the University of Wisconsin Badgers in his hometown of Madison, Suter was a fast, effortless skater. In his rookie season with the Flames, 1985–86, he won the Calder Trophy. Two years later, Suter led the team in assists, with seventy, and also set a career high with ninety-one total points.

Along with Ramage and Murzyn, Calgary's rock-solid defence was anchored by stay-at-home defencemen Brad McCrimmon, Jamie Macoun, and Ric Nattress.

Veteran Brad McCrimmon from Dodsland, Saskatchewan, had been a Second Team All-Star in 1987–88 and regularly put up the best plus-minus ratings among Flames defencemen.

From Newmarket, Ontario, Jamie Macoun went on to play at Ohio State University and signed with Calgary as a free agent in 1983. A steady positional defenceman, Macoun became a fixture with the Flames until a car accident severely damaged his arm and forced him to sit out the entire 1987–88 season. Courage and hard work got him back onto the ice, and Macoun had one of his finest years ever in 1988–89.

Calgary added another weapon midway through the 1988–89

season, and it arrived in an unconventional package. Theoren Fleury grew up tough in Russell, Manitoba, and played junior with the Moose Jaw Warriors. At 5′, 6″, Fleury was widely considered too small to play in the NHL, but with strong lobbying from scout Ian MacKenzie, Calgary decided to take a chance on him. In the ninth and final round of the 1987 Entry Draft, the Flames selected him 166th overall. That same year, Joe Sakic had been grabbed quickly in the first round with the fifteenth pick. The following season, 1987–88, his last in the Western Hockey League, Fleury tied Sakic for the league scoring title, but the Flames were still not convinced and posted him to their International Hockey League affiliate in Salt Lake City. Given his chance as a pro, Fleury tore up the league, scoring thirty-seven goals in just forty games. Cliff Fletcher became a believer.

Joining the Flames at mid-season, Fleury immediately added energy and attitude. Opponents soon learned he was surprisingly strong for his size — and absolutely fearless. With his trademark crooked grin and missing front tooth, the "little guy" was ready to take on all comers. And with his speed and his puck handling skill, he chipped in with fourteen goals in thirty-six games.

With the Flames' unprecedented success in the regular season, Calgary was abuzz in the spring of 1989 with the hint of a Cup. Tensions ramped up quickly. In the opening round of the playoffs, Calgary ran into a surprisingly resilient Vancouver squad, and the dream machine almost went off the rails early. The Canucks, who had finished far below the Flames in the league standings, pushed the series to seven games. Joel Otto finally ended it with the winning goal in overtime.

The most talked about play of the series, though, was goalie Mike Vernon's unbelievable glove save, robbing Stan Smyl on a clear breakaway in sudden death overtime. A local hero, Vernon was outstanding throughout the 1989 playoff run. After playing junior hockey with the Calgary Wranglers of the WHL, he had been drafted by the Flames in 1981 and took over as their starting goalie late in the 1985–86 season.

Following the scare by Vancouver, the Flames steamed through the second round. Their nemesis, Wayne Gretzky, now in Los Angeles, had led the Kings to a dramatic come-from-behind series victory over his former teammates from Edmonton. Trailing three games to one, Gretzky rallied his troops and knocked off the Oilers with three straight wins.

Calgary's first game against Los Angeles went to overtime. The Flames won. After that, it wasn't close. Some pundits said Los Angeles didn't have enough left in the tank after the heroics against Edmonton. Perhaps, but Gretzky had never run out of gas against Calgary in the past. A better explanation was that the Flames were the best team in the West that year; and now they were brimming with confidence, playing outstanding hockey.

In the Conference final, Calgary faced off against Chicago. The Blackhawks had taken out their more highly ranked division rivals, the Detroit Red Wings and the St. Louis Blues, but they couldn't handle the Flames. Calgary won the series in five games.

Meanwhile in the East, Montreal had annihilated the competition. The Canadiens had finished the regular season with 115 points, just two fewer than the Flames' league-leading total. Now it was showtime: Calgary had its Stanley Cup rematch with Montreal.

Starting off in Calgary, the teams split the first two games. Then in Montreal, they split again. The Flames had pushed the Canadiens to double overtime before losing game three and then came back strongly to take game four. Back at home for game five, Calgary won 3–2 and now led the series by the same margin. As they returned to Montreal for game six, the Flames knew tradition was against them; the Canadiens had never lost a Stanley Cup on Forum ice.

This year was different. The score was tied at one goal apiece after the first period. Then in the second, Lanny McDonald swooped in off the right wing and snapped a shot under the crossbar. The image of McDonald skating behind the Montreal net with his arms raised in celebration became one of the most widely circulated sports photos of the year. The Canadiens answered with a goal of their own, but it wasn't enough. Doug Gilmour scored the game winner in the final period and later added an empty netter.

It was magical. As Flames players made the traditional victory laps around the ice, each taking a turn hoisting Lord Stanley's Cup, the crowd stood and cheered. Hardened columnists described it as a display of sportsmanship rarely seen in professional events. It was that and more — a spontaneous outpouring of appreciation for Canada's game mixed with a sense of national pride. And Montrealers had not forgotten the way Calgary fans had applauded their Canadiens when they won the Cup in the Saddledome in 1986.

"I've always had good experiences at hockey games in Montreal," Doc says. "I think their fans are among the best-mannered anywhere. They know the game and really appreciate the technical skills involved, including those of opposing players. And they don't take exception if you cheer for the visiting team."

In addition to the Flames winning the Stanley Cup, Al MacInnis won the Conn Smythe Trophy as the most valuable player of the playoffs. He led all players in assists and total points. Joe Mullen had the most playoff goals. And Mike Vernon had the most wins among goalies.

On a team packed with talent and energy, it was still the veteran Lanny McDonald, with his huge handlebar moustache and charisma both on and off the ice, who was seen as the soul of the Flames. He retired after winning the Stanley Cup, putting a storybook ending on a magnificent career. In addition to his memorable goal in the Cup final, McDonald had scored in his final game of the regular season, giving him exactly five hundred goals in an NHL career that spanned sixteen years.

McDonald grew up on a ranch near Hanna in eastern Alberta. He starred with the Medicine Hat Tigers of the WHL and in 1973 was drafted fourth overall by his favourite NHL team, the Toronto Maple Leafs. A grinding forward with a terrific shot, McDonald made an impact immediately and went on to become captain of the Maple Leafs and later of the Colorado Rockies.

Early in the 1981–82 season, Cliff Fletcher engineered a multi-player deal to bring McDonald back to Alberta.

"I felt a lot of pressure coming back so close to home and family and friends," McDonald was later quoted as saying. "It really turned out to be a blessing, and it was the best thing that ever happened for my career."

The following year, McDonald netted his highest goal total ever, sixty-six, a single season record that still stands among Flames.

Three of Calgary's 1988–89 Stanley Cup winners are now in the Hockey Hall of Fame: Lanny McDonald, Joe Mullen, and Al MacInnis. They are joined by goalie Grant Fuhr, who is best known for shutting down Calgary shooters during the Battles of Alberta of the 1980s. The former Edmonton Oilers star played just one season in Calgary, 1999–2000, during which time he recorded his four hundredth career win.

In the Builder class, the Hockey Hall of Fame includes former Flames head coach Bob Johnson, who took the team to 193 wins from 1982 to 1987, a record that has yet to be broken; Cliff Fletcher, the general manager from the team's start in 1972 to 1991, who led the Flames to sixteen consecutive playoffs starting in 1976; and Harley Hotchkiss, Flames co-owner, who was instrumental in ending the NHL lockout in 2004–05.

For every Flames fan, there is one unmistakable voice that brings them the game. If they've somehow missed a play, Peter Maher is there with the goods. Since 1981, Maher has broadcast the play with adrenaline-boosting bravado. In 2006, he won the Foster Hewitt Memorial Award for long-time service and expertise as the

Flames broadcaster. The following year, Maher was honoured in the media category of the Hockey Hall of Fame.

After the Flames won the big one in 1989, Doc's office was open for all employees who wanted to see and have their photos taken with the Seamans and the Stanley Cup. The Cup symbolized the hard run not just to win but to get the franchise in the first place. It also represented what the Flames family has given back to Calgary.

In addition to the owners' revenue contributions through the Saddledome Foundation and the efforts of the Seaman Hotchkiss Hockey Foundation (formerly Project 75), other community initiatives have been undertaken by the Flames Foundation for Life and the Calgary Flames Alumni Association.

"The Calgary Flames and the Calgary Flames Foundation do a whole myriad of things in our community that have raised millions of dollars," says Doc. "The players and their wives, the alumni, the management and staff — they all do a lot of things that no one hears about. Just think of the countless autographs and the visits to the schools and the visits to the hospitals. We're especially proud of our players and our alumni association, which is one of the strongest in the National Hockey League."

The Flames Foundation for Life was set up during the 2005–06 season in conjunction with the twenty-fifth anniversary of NHL hockey in Calgary. Long-standing team relationships with the Alberta Children's Hospital and the University of Calgary are now being expanded through a partnership between the Flames Foundation for Life and the Rotary Club to advance education, health, and medical research in southern Alberta. One outstanding result of this partnership will be the Rotary/Flames House, a pediatric hospice centre scheduled to open in spring 2009, a first for Alberta and only the sixth one in North America.

In his eight years with the Flames, Lanny McDonald became deeply involved in many community endeavours. He was a perfect match with the spirit of the Flames owners.

"When the Flames came to Calgary, the six original owners, and especially Doc, Harley, and B.J., stayed constant," says McDonald. "They have been tremendous supporters. It was all about the Flames family and putting something back. Their whole philosophy was to do something great for the community in bringing the team here and leaving a legacy, both on and off the ice."

McDonald points out that during an era when hockey changed from sport for sport's sake to big business, the Flames owners never lost their resolve to contribute to community with little fanfare. After his playing career ended, McDonald became a steadfast hockey volunteer and understands what Project 75 has done for the game.

"Hockey in Canada would not be where it is today if not for the brilliance of people like Doc, Harley, and B.J.," he says. "Look at what this has meant for minor hockey in the country and where Canada now stands internationally in hockey."

McDonald is passionate about the power of sports to change lives and bring a balance so people can feel good about themselves. "I'm a firm believer in team sports helping to mould people for the rest of their lives," he adds. "Finding where they fit into the team helps them find themselves in work and in other areas. The friendships it creates last a lifetime. That's all thanks to people like Doc."

Bill Hay agrees. "Calgary is fortunate to have owners who love hockey and are determined to make an NHL team survive in a small market. They are smart businessmen and community leaders who enjoy success and the growth of the NHL."

Jim Peplinski knows Doc well as an original Flames player and former team captain. Today, he's a businessman, community organizer, and president of the Flames Alumni Association; in the latter role, he led the Scott Seaman Sports Rink project. The Flames Alumni raise over $350,000 a year. All the money goes back into the community through the Flames Foundation.

"The relationship between the owners and players is different in Calgary," says Peplinski. "We would speak with players in other teams and they would say, 'You think our owners treat players the way these guys do? It's not the way it is.'"

Doc and Harley Hotchkiss have toiled together for the Calgary Flames for twenty-eight years. Hotchkiss has been the Flames' designated governor to the NHL for sixteen years and in 2008 was completing his twelfth year as chairman of the NHL Board of Governors — a role that put him front and centre, often to his discomfort, during the lockout of 2004–05.

"I've been involved in a number of ventures with Doc, but our longest relationship is through the Flames," says Hotchkiss. "It has been at times the most difficult and at other times the most rewarding experience. Through all of that time and through some of the most difficult business times of any kind in my whole career, one of the strengths is that Doc Seaman was there as a partner, in his quiet and solid way. I couldn't have done it without him, really. It sounds kind of overdone, but that's the simple truth."

The tremendous respect that the two have for each other is obvious as they describe each other's characters and accomplishments. When Hotchkiss won his place in the Hockey Hall of Fame, Doc beamed at the tribute to his friend. "He's being recognized for the work he did in keeping the NHL together during the labour dispute," notes Doc. "It's a well-deserved honour for him."

Hotchkiss was as committed as Doc to developing the Flames' culture of community. When the franchise was a money pit, they did everything they could to avoid selling the team. That would have been selling out Calgary and grassroots hockey. They went against the financial grain for the good of the game and held to their ideal of giving back. The Flames were heroes to those who wanted to play and to those who simply wanted to watch. Owning the Flames was a way to provide opportunities for kids who wanted to be part of the game. But it came with all kinds of costs.

"Doc and I have weathered some storms," adds Hotchkiss. "Maybe the prime example of that, and probably the toughest time for me in my business-sporting career, was keeping the Calgary Flames in Calgary."

Above all, the owners envisioned the team as part of the community rather than an extension of their own egos, full of privileges and profits — a model all too common in other cities.

"The Flames have always been part of the community. That was one of our objectives, one of our priorities. We felt that Calgary would support it, and we have had great support from our fans," notes Hotchkiss. "It drifted for a while during a period from 1994. Then in 2004 we had that one-year lockout. We made some mistakes when we renovated the Saddledome. We shortened the lower bowl from nine thousand seats to fewer than five thousand because we put in that row of suites. The suites are wonderful, but some people that had been in the lower bowl thought we had disenfranchised them. We had all kinds of expert advice, but we've paid a huge price for doing that. In retrospect, it was a serious error."

Doc heartily agrees with Hotchkiss. The larger challenges, however, were always financial. The Canadian dollar fell sharply against American currency during the technology boom of the 1990s. Although the loonie nearly topped US$.90 in 1992, it drifted ever downward to just under US$.62 by January 2002. Throughout the dollar doldrums, the Flames' owners paid their players in American currency.

"Before we even dropped the puck, the Canadian dollar was costing us about $18 million a year at its nastiest time," says Doc. "The reason was that our single biggest cost was players' salaries, which were in U.S. dollars." In effect, the Flames' owners were being cash-called for millions each year.

The performance of the team drifted downward too. By 1995, only Joe Nieuwendyk, Gary Roberts, and Theoren Fleury remained from the Stanley Cup team. Al Coates was appointed general manager that year and was burdened with reducing expenses.

Nieuwendyk had developed knee problems and was unable to

start the 1995–96 season, but he still commanded a high salary. In December, Coates traded him to the Dallas Stars for Corey Millen and an eighteen-year-old junior prospect, Jarome Iginla. Today, it's often forgotten how controversial that trade was; even though he had led the Kamloops Blazers to two Memorial Cups, few of the angry fans realized what they were getting in Iginla. Calgary fans had grown accustomed to their team making the playoffs every year, but the Flames fell short in 1996–97, and their fortunes on the ice weren't about to improve soon.

Faced with mounting budget pressures, Coates traded the team's top scorer, Theoren Fleury, to Colorado in early 1999. During his ten years in Calgary, Fleury had tallied 364 goals, the most ever by a player skating as a Flame — a record that would stand until 2008. As part of the package deal for Fleury, the Flames received another highly ranked junior prospect, Robyn Regehr.

Marketed to fans as the "young guns," the Flames clearly didn't have enough bullets. As they continued to miss the playoffs year after year, attendance dwindled and the owners' losses mounted.

Even through the most discouraging seasons, though, there were flashes of hope. Iginla was developing into one of the top players in hockey. His breakout year came in 2001–02, when he scored a league-leading fifty-two goals and was voted by fellow NHL players as the league's most outstanding player and winner of the Lester B. Pearson Trophy. An even bigger thrill for Iginla that year was helping Canada win a gold medal at the Olympics in Salt Lake City.

While 2001–02 was a high-water mark for Iginla, the following season was to produce a turning point for the whole team: Darryl Sutter came home to Alberta. With one of the most successful records among all active coaches in the NHL, Sutter was seen by Flames' owners as a prize catch and was signed to a long-term contract in December 2002. Taking charge behind the bench, Sutter replaced Al MacNeil, who had filled in admirably as interim coach. MacNeil took on many roles for the Flames over the years; he had come with the team from Atlanta and continued as the Flames' head coach during their first two seasons in Calgary.

By April 2003, Sutter signed a second contract, making him general manager as well as head coach. In the months ahead, he would transform a team that had finished out of the playoffs for a sixth consecutive year to a Stanley Cup contender in the spring of 2004.

Of the original ownership group, only Doc, B.J., and Hotchkiss remain. After the departures in the 1990s of Norm Green, Norman Kwong, and Sonia Scurfield, six new owners joined: Grant Bartlett, Murray Edwards, Ron Joyce, Alvin Libin, Allan Markin, and Bud McCaig. In 2001, Bartlett and Joyce sold their interests to the remaining leadership group. In 2003, Clayton (Clay) Riddell bought in. After Bud McCaig passed away in early 2005, his son Jeff McCaig continued his father's dream as a Flames owner. Today the owners' roster is a solid group of outstanding community givers: Doc, B.J., Hotchkiss, Edwards, Libin, Markin, McCaig, and Riddell.

For the veterans it has been an interesting ride, and sometimes a rough one. "We had a substantial change in ownership in 1994," says Hotchkiss. "While Doc and B.J. and I had been around for some good years, at other times the business was not very good. We had some of the new owners kind of wondering what they had gotten into, and by 2001, two of them said they weren't prepared to stay. I'm not critical of them. It was their money and their decision. So we bought them out."

Over the years, Hotchkiss became the owners' public spokesman, a job he didn't care for. "I didn't like the role of being out there speaking to the fans, telling them we needed to have their support to survive. Finally we had that year-long lockout. I guess some sanity came back in after that. We got an agreement that works. It is not perfect, but it's good for everyone in the game, particularly the players. We put a so-called hard salary cap on. That made the league substantially healthier and more competitive," he says.

"We have pretty good parity in the league now," adds Doc. "Just look at the resurgence of teams like Pittsburgh and Chicago with their young stars. And the teams that were in the Stanley Cup finals two years before didn't even make the playoffs in 2008."

Hotchkiss says, "We made some changes in the game. We set up a competition committee that consisted of players, management representatives, officials, and an owner's representative with the idea that they would make some changes in the game. They opened the game up with penalties for what you would call obstruction — hooking, holding, and high sticking. So the skill players got a little more room to move."

Doc notes that speed is now a more important factor in the game. "I'm amazed by how fast some of the young guys are. And their physical conditioning is incredible."

The competition committee also added the shootout. "I was kind of opposed to the shootout, but the fans love it. They stay in the seats. The fans ultimately pay the bills, and you have to pay attention to that," Hotchkiss says.

"So where are we today?" he continues. "I think our ownership group is solid. We are totally committed to this community. We've got a very strong management organization. Our fans have come back, and we are sold out. I think the Calgary Flames are here for way beyond my time. There will always be challenges. We'll have future negotiations when collective bargaining comes up again with the players' association. I expect there will be hard bargaining. I'd hate to see an atmosphere where we aren't dealing with each other with respect on both sides. We just need a fundamental focus on what is right. I would never want to see us go back to lack of co-operation and not working together. I understand hard bargaining, but we all need to work together to make the game better."

Having gone through such a difficult time, Doc points out that he doesn't want to "ever see us go back to that again. You can't accomplish things in life and make things better if you can't work together as partners."

Even as they struggled, Doc remembered the fun of the first few years of the Calgary Flames. They played in the Stampede Corral with everyone having a great time even as the owners were losing money. "It was a riotous atmosphere in the old Corral," Doc recalls fondly. "The fans were hanging from the rafters. There weren't many seats, and we packed them in to standing room only. We lost money all through that period while the Saddledome was being built, but the fans had fun."

Doc played amateur hockey for the legendary Père Athol Murray of Notre Dame College in Wilcox, Saskatchewan, and later for the Moose Jaw Canucks. He loved the spirit of the game and the adrenaline rush.

"Hockey is a passion," he says. "Even in my hometown of Rouleau, we couldn't wait to hear Foster Hewitt on the radio every Saturday before we headed to the rink. At the time, I was a Maple Leaf fan. I eventually switched and liked the Montreal style of play for a long time. Then we got the Flames here."

Doc recalls all the early challenges vividly, but he never lost the thrill of being involved in hockey at the highest level. Today, as often as not, he can just sit back and enjoy the games. He loves being in the Saddledome with his friends watching his Flames. While he has a great and abiding passion for the sport, Doc is an analytical fan.

"He looks at the game through technical eyes, in contrast to B.J., who is a more emotional fan," says Flames CEO Ken King. "Doc knows who the players are and is interested in how each performs on a given night: who's winning the faceoffs, who's playing with attitude and energy. He has tremendous respect for players who exhibit the kind of will and fortitude you want."

Very much a fan as well as an owner, Doc is interested in recruiting and developing talent. He asks about the farm team, the top prospects, and the scouting system. Doc goes for fundamentals rather than glitz and appreciates talent, skill, and hard work. His style is thoughtful, sometimes introspective, and always professional.

"Doc's leadership skills are deep and intellectually oriented as opposed to bombastic or loud," says King. "He takes the time. He'll come and sit with me and explain the issues and concerns. It's done in a logical, sequential, thoughtful manner. Doc is not given to fits of pique. When he goes down to the dressing room, which he only does sometimes, he always has a big smile and pat on the back. He's always encouraging to anyone that he talks to."

Doc is also a huge supporter of King, a public relations wizard who was publisher, successively, of both the *Calgary Sun* and the *Calgary Herald*. "Ken King does a great job," Doc says. "We've got a very good bunch of people now. Look at Darryl Sutter."

Today, nobody represents the Flames' tenacious identity better than general manager Sutter, who comes from Alberta's best known hockey clan. Incredibly, in a family of seven brothers, six played in the NHL. Sutter was captain of the Chicago Blackhawks and still holds the team record for most goals in one playoff year. After his career was cut short due to injuries, he went on to coach the Blackhawks and later the San Jose Sharks before coming to Calgary.

"One thing I've learned about Doc is that he's a great visionary about the game and everything that applies to sport and to life," says Sutter. "He knows and appreciates the Canadian value of hockey, the tradition of the game, and what's important. We have to develop the young Canadian players. Doc is firmly committed to that."

Small-town roots play a huge role in Doc's character, as they do for many of the Flames' owners, players, and alumni. "They are the core of who he is, and Doc understands those values," says Sutter, who grew up near Viking, Alberta.

In a small Alberta town, there are three things to rally around: religion, education, and hockey. For most kids, there isn't much competition from the first two. "If you really have a choice, it's the arena," Sutter says. "It can be thirty below outside and inside those rinks, it feels like forty below. But you still play."

The kid from the Rouleau rink understands as well as anyone the role of hockey in the Canadian psyche. Increasingly, girls as well as boys take the game as a rite of passage to being Canadian. Hockey is our tradition and our history. Doc wants to ensure it continues in our future by promoting hockey through the Seaman-Hotchkiss Foundation and other ventures.

"Doc doesn't just show it in grassroots financial support and Hockey Canada," notes Sutter. "He reveals it in how he speaks and feels about the game. You can talk about the players, team concepts, and skill, and Doc understands all that like a player and coach. You can go to Doc and ask what he thinks and he answers immediately — he tells you — he knows exactly what's going on."

When Doc talks to the players, he "looks them in the eye, shakes their hands with that firm grip, and calls a spade a spade. The players have tremendous respect for our ownership, starting with Doc and Harley," says Sutter. "He's very competitive. Oh, and don't be surprised when you shake hands — he tries to crunch you. He's like a seventeen- or eighteen-year-old kid, trying to squeeze you down. Shake Doc's hand and you have a deal. He's a man of his word, and when he tells you something, that's good. That's why, when you need advice or an opinion, you can get it from him."

Sutter admires the owners who fought for the team when it would have been easy to sell out and move on. "They could have just given up. At the end of the day, the original owners' goal was to keep the Flames because the city and the players need it."

Sutter finds an echo of his own close-knit but competitive family in the Seaman brothers. "My brothers and I come from a big family, and we're as close as little boys. We went and did things all over the world," he says. "We're closer to each other than to anybody else; and when you look at Doc, Don, and B.J. it's the same. They're so much alike, yet they have their own personalities and their own deals. Doc is clearly the guy at the end of day, and he's the leader of the group. There's another reason they're so close, and that's because I bet he kept it close. It's not easy to do when you're in business with siblings. There's room and cause for friction, and someone has to keep it together. I know it's him."

Doc learned about leadership, teamwork, and working together at home in Rouleau.

"Don and B.J. and Doc were very close probably because they grew up together in the Depression and worked very hard," says Norman Kwong. "It breeds strong family relationships others don't have, because things were so tough."

He recalls the road trips he took as a Flames co-owner with Doc and B.J. playing gin rummy on the airplane. "Doc used to delight in beating his brother. We could always hear them when he or B.J. let out a victory yelp, and then we knew who won."

At a 2007 fundraising tribute dinner for Doc and B.J., Bill Hay kidded Doc about not getting a raise when he worked for him. Not missing a beat, B.J. chortled, "Doc hasn't given me a raise either." The room erupted, and Doc quietly chuckled.

"You can say things about your brothers, but nobody else can," notes Sutter. "Doc can probably critique his family very well, but let somebody else try it and they're in trouble." With those six brothers, Sutter knows the territory.

Doc, B.J., and Hotchkiss were inducted into the Alberta Sports Hall of Fame on June 1, 2007, along with the Edmonton Eskimos team that won the Grey Cup from 1954 to 1956. "You could see that Doc was really appreciative," says Sutter, who was sitting beside him. As one of the Edmonton Eskimo veterans talked about living in Alberta, Doc tapped Sutter on the knee and declared, "Alberta is the best place to live in the world."

The theme that ties each Flames owner to the next is community. The owners are some of the country's most philanthropic leaders, who take their good fortune as a personal obligation to make their community and country a better place. Through foundations for medical research, cultural enrichment, social progress, and educational enlightenment, each is renowned for humanity and generosity.

When Murray Edwards joined the Flames as an owner, he told the *Calgary Herald*'s Gordon Jaremko on October 22, 1994: "Business is responsible to much more than just shareholders. It has responsibilities to employees, governments and the community."

When asked about buying into the Flames, Edwards added, "It was an opportunity to make an investment that is more than an investment." Today, Edwards says the franchise has been at times a financial challenge, but "the great thing about the Flames is that the ownership group is fairly tight in terms of working together." He says there's a good mix of different personalities, and Doc is "always the more patient one. He focuses on development. Doc has the greatest interest in the game of hockey and real encouragement of young players."

Edwards also poses an intriguing question: "What if Calgary had not had the Olympics — would we not have a hockey team?" In the event of that unimaginable misfortune, Calgarians would have missed not only the investment in community but also the thrill of the Flames becoming an integral part of the fabric of Calgary, and playing some pretty good hockey while they're at it.

Despite the Flames' loss to San Jose in the first round of the 2008 playoffs, the lineup for 2008–09 still hearkens back to the exciting team that took the 1989 Stanley Cup. Led by the four elite Calgary players who've been signed to long-term contracts, Doc thinks the current Flames have what it takes for another Cup run.

"I like our guys a lot, and I like our chances," Doc says. "But you never know how things will work out. The league is really competitive. Our philosophy is about selecting talented young players with good character and then trying to develop them into professionals for the long haul."

Darryl Sutter shares this philosophy. Upon being appointed general manager, Sutter's highest priority was to prepare the Flames organization for the 2003 NHL entry draft. The Flames had a high pick, ninth overall. Sutter knew what he wanted. Faced with the unpredictability of the draft, he sweated through the first eight picks; but when his number was finally called and he walked to the podium, he felt like he had hit the jackpot. He selected Dion Phaneuf from his brother Brent's Red Deer Rebels.

Phaneuf soon established himself as one of the game's top defencemen. Best known for his devastating open ice checks and blistering one-timers from the point, Phaneuf is already a Norris Trophy candidate after only three seasons in the NHL. In early 2008, the Flames signed him to a six-year contract.

Sutter's next major move came shortly after the start of the 2003–04 season when he traded a second round draft pick to San Jose for Miikka Kiprusoff, a little known Finnish goaltender. Kiprusoff was third on the Sharks depth chart, but Sutter, while still in San Jose, had spotted his potential. It proved to be a brilliant transaction. Given the chance to be a starting goaltender in Calgary, Kiprusoff backstopped the Flames to within one game of winning the Stanley Cup. With his unflappable temperament and tremendous athleticism, Kiprusoff won the Vezina Trophy as the NHL's best goalie in the 2005–06 season. Widely recognized as one of the top netminders in the world, and a fan favourite in Calgary, Kipper signed a six-year contract extension with the Flames in late 2007.

Earlier, in the summer of 2007, the Flames locked up both Jarome Iginla and Robyn Regehr with five-year contract extensions that came into effect following the 2007–08 season. The similarities don't end there: both had been first round draft picks; both were acquired by the Flames as junior prospects in exchange for established stars; and both had played major junior hockey with the Kamloops Blazers of the WHL.

Regehr is a rugged, positional player and is recognized in NHL circles one of the top shut-down defencemen in the league. Iginla became the Flames' all-time leading goal-scorer when he topped Theoren Fleury with goal 365 on March 10, 2008. Pierre Page, who now coaches in Europe, remembers Iginla as a dream player. "I only coached him a year, really, but you could tell right away this was going to be a special player," Page told George Johnson of the *Calgary Herald* after Iginla scored the record-breaker. "Everybody always says that about great players in retrospect, but in this case it happens to be true. You could see. You knew."

Now one of Hockey's best ambassadors, Jarome Iginla is also the quintessential Calgary Flame. A unique package of skill and toughness, combined with humility, decency, and community spirit, Iginla epitomizes what Doc Seaman had in mind when he set out to buy an NHL team for all southern Albertans to enjoy.

"Continuity is crucial to the future of the Flames," notes Doc. "Having four elite players signed long-term gives us a great core to work with."

Certainly these star players could command greater salaries if they were free agents. But taking a home team discount does have its rewards. "Calgary is a preferred place for players to go," states Doc. "They like the fans here, and they like to be appreciated."

And they are, by both the fans and the owners. One day they could be joined by a young defenceman named Keith Aulie, who, as a top Grade 12 student and a promising member of the Brandon Wheat Kings, was awarded the Doc Seaman Scholastic Player of the Year Trophy in May 2007. The Western Hockey League named this award in honour of Doc's efforts to ensure that all league players are able to combine education with hockey. Aulie also happens to hail from Doc's hometown of Rouleau.

Aulie was drafted by the Flames and is now working his way up to the big time. He might make it, or maybe not; but his future is his own to forge. It's a story familiar to Iginla, the Sutters, the Seaman brothers, and all the others who built the Calgary Flames.

PART FIVE

~

Civic Duty

CHAPTER TEN

The Giver

"AGE IS ONLY A NUMBER, A CIPHER FOR THE RECORDS.
A MAN CAN'T RETIRE HIS EXPERIENCE. HE MUST USE IT."
— BERNARD BARUCH

The Starship *Enterprise* landed in Doc Seaman's office and he jumped aboard. While Dr. Garnette Sutherland didn't look like Dr. Spock, his request was ambitiously futuristic. It was 2001, and his dream was to build a robotic arm to perform intricate neurosurgery. The vision belonged more in the sealed fantasy of a *Star Trek* spaceship than in the halls of medical academia at the University of Calgary. Yet Sutherland needed funds for robotic brain surgery and knew he had found a kindred spirit. Doc Seaman's fondness for pioneering and engineering feats has guided him to the edge of the frontier where risk and imagination are fraternal twins. His philanthropic dreams start locally, but they travel globally.

"In his characteristic quiet way, Doc listens to you and asks few questions," says Sutherland. "He and his brothers were at the meeting. Normally, someone hearing about this high-tech idea and what it could do would probably ask, 'What has that guy been smoking?' But Doc's able to see to the heart of those kinds of things. He lends support to projects others might not understand."

Doc and his brothers, B.J. and Don, donated the crucial seed funding, giving the project, in Sutherland's words, "leverage that led to more money." Seven years later, in 2008, the $30-million neuroArm made medical history and became the world's first MRI-compatible surgical robot in neurosurgery.

"Doctors at Foothills Hospital used remote controls and an imaging screen, similar to a video game, to guide the two-armed robot through Paige Nickason's brain during the nine-hour surgery," wrote Michelle Butterfield on the front page of the *Calgary Herald* on May 17, 2008. "Surgical instruments acting as the hands of the robot — called neuroArm — provided surgeons with precision tools to remove the egg-shaped tumour, about the size of a loonie."

The groundbreaking surgery brought the future squarely into the present for a waiting list of patients. Sutherland's vision never wavered, nor did Doc's support.

"Doc doesn't just give a large sum of money — he keeps engaged," notes Sutherland. "He set up a number of breakfast meetings over a period of several years, invited a few of his friends, and we'd present the idea. Over the years, there were bumps along the way, but he was always there to help."

Doc developed an advisory board for the neuroArm project that met every few months with Sutherland. Given the intricate technology and highly sophisticated work, Doc's choice of expertise for the board gave Sutherland a degree of comfort as well as guidance.

"Brain surgery by robots seems a little far-fetched. But that's the genius of it," says Doc. "When a man of the calibre of Dr. Sutherland gets to work, it's all possible. He's an exceptional scientist working way beyond the normal scope of most of us. Surgeons tell me that one of the biggest problems with removing brain tumours is striking a delicate balance between excising too much or too little. I understand it's often difficult to visually distinguish normal brain tissue from a tumor. Rather than risk damaging healthy brain tissue, neurosurgeons sometimes err on the side of caution and leave a small portion of the tumour in place. When this occurs, a follow-up surgery is usually required. Using an intraoperative MRI to provide images of the patient's brain while conducting surgery with a neuroArm allows the medical team to ensure every trace of a tumour is removed before the incision is closed."

Doc, the mechanical engineer, continues: "A major advantage of the neuroArm is precision. The best surgeons in the world can work to within tolerances of an eighth of an inch. NeuroArm makes it possible for surgeons to work accurately within a few microns. And, of course, with the miniaturization of the remotely controlled surgical tools, the entire process is much less invasive."

He adds, "I had a good laugh with Garnette Sutherland after the neuroArm was successfully tested. I told him I was glad to see that neurosurgery was finally catching up to our technology in the oil drilling business!"

Doc was able to convince his brothers, who are also engineers, of the worth of Sutherland's plans, even if the technical understanding sometimes left them all in the dust. "I can't keep up with him, and I'm a pretty technical person," says Doc. "We knew this project, when completed, would put Calgary on the world stage of medical science."

Sutherland's team of scientists worked with MacDonald, Dettwiler and Associates (MDA), who founded the world-renowned Canadarm, used on American space shuttles. As an established company in robotic technology, MDA brought its skill and experience to Sutherland's neuroArm creation. The neuroArm was developed at the University of Calgary's Seaman Family MR Research Centre, whose program for stroke research has become a leader worldwide. Named in honour of the brothers' parents, the Seaman Centre had earlier masterminded the first intraoperative MRI scanner with a moveable high-intensity magnet. Since this specialized MRI allows neurosurgeons to scan the patient's brain even while they operate, it dovetails beautifully with the neuroArm.

The Reverend Don MacMahon recalls the day Doc phoned and said, "Can you come up to the university this afternoon?" That was it — nothing more. MacMahon arrived to see the Seaman brothers at the centre of a ceremony. They were making a large donation, including the MRI machine, to the Seaman Centre. MacMahon had no idea: "Here they give millions of dollars and they're the centre of it all, and there's no mention of any of that. That's the way they are."

The Seaman Family MR Research Centre works closely with the University of Calgary's Hotchkiss Brain Institute, which was generously endowed by Harley and Becky Hotchkiss. Headed by Dr. Sam Weiss, the institute works to bring scientific advances into the treatment, prevention, and care of neurological and mental health disorders. In 2008, Weiss's initial discovery of neural stem cells in the adult brain won him the prestigious Gairdner International Award.

Sutherland points out that the Seamans' initial $2 million donation for the MRI research centre triggered the release of monies from the Alberta government to construct the building.

"Before 1995, and the building of the Seaman Centre, Calgary had no presence in MRI research," says Sutherland. "Now Alberta has international visibility in the application of MRI technology to neurological disease."

Doc felt strongly that any commercial application of the technology should remain in Albertan and Canadian hands. Based on the pioneering work of Sutherland's research group and the National Research Council, Innovative Magnetic Resonance Imaging Systems is a mobile MRI system for imaging during surgery. This landmark technology developed by University of Calgary scientists has achieved international recognition.

"Because of the original contribution from the Seaman family, our technology has benefited the people of Alberta and other provinces and has transferred globally," adds Sutherland. "It has changed how neurosurgery is performed. That's a pretty big accomplishment for an oil guy."

When Sutherland came to Calgary in 1993, he felt the visceral energy of the entrepreneurial city and was delighted to meet up with such go-getters as Bud McCaig, Alvin Libin, Harley Hotchkiss, Dick Haskayne, and the Partners in Health fundraising campaign. "Fortunately we also got connected to Doc Seaman," says Sutherland. "A person can give philanthropically, but he doesn't just do that. It comes with his time and his contacts. Doc gives his heart and is clearly not after anything in return. He doesn't want the front line."

Sutherland sees this attitude going all the way back to Doc's experience as a Second World War pilot and the strong bonds with his aircrew. Doc takes the value of friendship and teamwork to every aspect of his life and work.

"Thank God we got Doc on that robot project. It was a long, winding road, and you need stamina. It was not for the timid. Doc's there for the long haul. For a fellow to be engaged in a very high tech project at his age is remarkable," adds Sutherland. "One of Doc's legacies is that he touches the lives of those who come in contact with him. They come away a bit changed. Because Doc is giving his money, all the people involved in the neuroArm project want to see him happy. They come into alignment — they have too much respect for Doc not to. I saw that before in a very gifted neurosurgeon, Dr. Charles Drake, who has since passed away. In the 1970s and 1980s, Drake was the world's leading neurosurgeon. Because of his presence, none of the surgeons bickered. It was too embarrassing, because everyone held him with such respect and admiration. That brings people together. Doc is like that, and that's one reason why he's so successful."

Doc recalls his early Calgary years, when everyone knew each other and took it as a personal mission to contribute. Sadly, as a city's population stretches beyond a million, the bonds seem to loosen, and many successful people leave the community work to others. "People wait for someone else to do it," Doc says. "It's too bad, because there's such a tremendous feeling of accomplishment when you're building your community and realizing all kinds of goals that didn't seem attainable before.

"I grew up in a small town where community involvement was a fact of life. Everybody had to pitch in to help one another, whatever it was: schools, churches, hockey rinks, ball diamonds. A group of people, including my parents and most other families, did get involved in a very significant way. Quite often there wasn't much money involved, there was just work to be done.

"Calgary was a small community when I first came, and there is still that spirit here. So, we got involved early on. I've forgotten all the projects we were in on. We were the first in the Tom Baker Cancer Centre and the Sports Medicine Centre [which is now the Roger Jackson Centre] and most of the United Way campaigns. At Bow Valley Industries, we always took a percentage of our cash flow each year and made sure it went into various charities around the community."

Doc and Harley Hotchkiss grew up with a sense of social responsibility. Both believe community philanthropy should begin early when time, experience, and energy can jump-start an idea into action. They support projects that are collaborative, innovative, and reach far beyond traditional and geographical boundaries.

"Sometimes those things are more important than money," says Hotchkiss. "I always found that I got back more than I put in. So when Doc came to see me about the neuroArm project, I said, 'Doc, I want to help.' And I did."

Entrepreneur and Calgary Flames co-owner Alvin Libin is another Calgary philanthropist; with his late wife, Mona, he established the Libin Cardiovascular Institute of Alberta.

"Doc's a first-class citizen in community initiatives," says Libin. "He's an outstanding individual, and I've always appreciated his point of view. Doc's a serious thinker and a smart guy. His and his brothers' contribution to the health system and the Partners in Health campaign, where they funded the Seaman Centre, is a huge accomplishment. Together, Doc and I have ridden horses, attended meetings, watched hockey, and played gin rummy. We've had lots of good times. We're lucky to have guys like Doc Seaman in this community."

Investment banker Michael Tims is known for getting directly involved, most recently as chair of the United Way. His relationship with Doc bridges business and community, and he sits on the neuroArm advisory committee.

"Doc loves technological breakthroughs and the potentially great investment to people's health," says Tims. "He is always interested in the application of MRI to medicine, and the neuroArm ties MRI to new surgical techniques. He and his brothers have been the main impetus to this by providing funding and calling others to come up to the plate to donate, and then get government funding. You know very clearly when Doc phones you up if you're willing to contribute to something, he's there in a very meaningful way."

Dr. Bryan Donnelly, staff urologist at the Calgary Regional Health Authority, is also the Chairman of the Prostate Cancer Institute in Calgary. He knows Doc well for his financial support of the Prostate Centre and for a huge donation to the Southern Alberta Urology Centre, which will be a state-of-the-art facility for the entire country. Doc had committed the initial funding for the centre, but even though the cost estimate doubled, he continued his obligation. Brett Wilson, a prostate cancer survivor, stepped in and offered to join Doc.

"They struck their deal right in front of me," says Donnelly. "Brett said to Doc, 'If you give $5 million, I'll match you. Then you can give $2.5 million to a worthy children's charity and I'll match you on that one.' And Doc replied, 'Whatever you're comfortable with, Brett.' That was something."

Wilson, the chairman of FirstEnergy Capital Corp., is one of a growing number of younger Calgary philanthropists who believe in giving while living. The investment banker is also one of the Saskatchewan crew whose commitment to community prods their colleagues to build their city through social responsibility.

"Doc is a man I greatly admire," says Wilson. "This was a wonderful opportunity to have a fifty-year-old try to follow in his footsteps. I'm hoping to do that. Doc walks with a big stride and leaves a huge legacy. When I was a junior investment banker, I had the privilege of sitting in meetings that Doc attended. This was 1985, and he was running Bow Valley Industries. Doc stood alone with his presence and his ability to influence and lead. Doc could dominate a meeting in a powerful and positive way with just a couple of quiet words."

Like Doc and his brothers, Wilson also earned his engineering degree at the University of Saskatchewan. The Seaman brothers were legends to Wilson, and when he first met Doc, Wilson was both excited and nervous. Asked when he stopped being nervous, Wilson quipped, "I don't know that I did. Doc is a true Canadian icon whose actions speak larger than his words."

Wilson's philanthropic efforts have thrust him into the company of such community-minded leaders as Allan Markin. A Flames co-owner, Markin is admired across the province and country for his exceptional social conscience, especially his compassion and devotion to social, cultural, and educational endeavours.

Sometimes, Donnelly was convinced that the Urology Centre would remain only a vision in his mind. "There were times when it was going to falter," he says. "Doc was always there. He guaranteed that it never fell off the radar screen. He phoned people and made sure they kept on it. He has been hugely helpful. Without him, this thing would be dead. Doc is a very sharp cookie. He assesses things, makes up his mind, and when he does, he acts. I suspect very few movers and shakers in this town wouldn't respond positively to a phone call from Doc Seaman. He's a straight shooter and a very honourable man."

Donnelly recalls seeing a painting of Doc and his brothers, B.J. and Don, as youngsters. They're sitting against a big barn, and one of them has holes in his shoes. "The Seaman brothers never forget where they came from, and are more than happy to give a lot back," Donnelly says.

Donnelly also knows Doc well for his medical condition. Like his late dad, Doc contracted prostate cancer. His father's illness was too advanced to save him. To honour Byron's memory, Doc contributed more than $1 million to the Prostate Cancer Institute to fund a five-year research chair. Donnelly was the first research recipient. Some of the donation was made through The Calgary Foundation, where Doc has a charitable fund. Founded over fifty years ago by civic-minded leaders, The Calgary Foundation attracts, invests, and manages donations of funds and endowments totalling over $320 million, distributing $32 million to 650 charities in 2008.

"When I first found out that I had prostate cancer, there was really no place to access information. You had to talk to people who had been around a bit," says Doc. "It took me a few years to get a handle on it, because there are several options. The most common practice at the time was a radical prostatectomy, which removes the prostate and some of the surrounding tissue. I opted for cryo-surgery, which is freezing. Dr. Donnelly has been good to me on that, and I've been following his program and advice. Originally, the urologist said I'd probably have eight years left, and I'm going on seventeen years now, trying to get as much out of it as I can."

Donnelly is the primary researcher at the Prostate Cancer Institute, where Doc has sponsored research for more than ten years. The new facility will house all the urologists and the institute in one building at Calgary's Rockyview Hospital. (Funding for the new institute was also led by Ann McCaig, volunteer chair of the Calgary Health Trust, Sam and Betty Switzer, the Priddis Greens Golf Charity Classic, and the Bill Brooks Gala.)

Phyllis Kane was hired as president of the Calgary Prostate Cancer Institute in 1998 and retired in 2003. She initially met Doc when she was chairing the Calgary Health Trust. One of the motivating factors in accepting the position and building the Prostate Cancer Institute was that Doc was there," says Kane. "Doc is so bright and so organized in his thoughts. He does his own research and is selective in his philanthropic interests. He wants to know what's going on, but he's never invasive."

Kane especially respected Doc's visibility on the board and the fact that he was public about his prostate cancer. She was pleased that he brought his business sensibilities to the philanthropic world.

"Doc comes prepared and asks questions that provoke the kind of thinking that needs to happen around the board table," says Kane. "It doesn't take him long to get it. He's a seasoned businessman; he knows the numbers and what to look for. When you go out to raise money with a Doc Seaman on your board, you have all the credibility in the world." For Kane, Doc's legacy to Calgary is that he hasn't stuck to the glamorous philanthropic interests. He's gone for prostate cancer and focused on community organizations.

Educator and community volunteer Jeanette Nicholls says Doc and people like him established the "culture of giving" in Calgary. "It was a responsibility to the community and a thank you for living in such a successful environment. Over the years Doc and his friends have supported kids and families, athletes and teams, as well as a vast array of other charitable organizations. The Docs of Calgary didn't see philanthropy as an option — they viewed it as an expectation and a debt they owed," says Nicholls. "And they took that seriously. The peer pressure that they exerted on one another resulted in the quality of life that we enjoy today."

Harold Milavsky is another Saskatchewan native who moved west to success, and who always remembers his roots. A former chairman of Trizec Corporation when it was controlled by the Bronfman family, Milavsky was also a fellow board member with

Doc at Nova Corp. "We all just idolize him," says Milavsky. "Doc doesn't want to be in the limelight. He's done a great job at the hospitals. He's intrigued by new things. He phones some of us, and that's how he does his fundraising, with him and his brothers providing a substantial amount. When Doc quietly gives advice, he's right on about what should be done."

Doc believes that participating in community provides an example for the next generation. It also keeps seniors active and engaged. Age should never be a deterrent to getting involved.

"Doc's concept is that we should always continue to stimulate our minds, which in turn hopefully garners better health and lifestyle," says former Bow Valley president Bill Tye. "Being active and volunteering leads to greater longevity and a healthy outlook on life. Doc is the epitome of this."

When Darryl Sutter describes Doc's giving in Canada, he cites his financial support for Hockey Canada, amateur sports, and medical breakthroughs like the neuroArm. "It's overwhelming to think of what he's done," says Sutter. "But he doesn't like talking about it. It's very simple. It doesn't matter what you have, it's important to give what you can."

Charlie Fischer recalls working for mentors like Doc, Gerry Maier, and Dick Haskayne. They felt that because they belonged to the community they should get involved in the community. Fischer worries that people aren't as committed today because they feel their jobs leave less time to participate and contribute.

"When I look at Doc, I think he's an example for many," adds Fischer. "But if people were aware of how many things he's done and the help he's given in so many ways, it might encourage others to get involved earlier and help more."

Doc continued to fund community projects while still building his company. For Doc, success must be shared. Precisely because he loves contributing quietly, his deeds were often known to only close friends and family.

"Doc's made a huge difference to our community, but he's never looked for recognition," Fischer says. "Dick Haskayne believes that you should let your name stand, demonstrate to others, and encourage them to participate." Doc does agree that the Haskayne way has considerable merit, especially if it can prod others to participate. Oilman Jim Gray has spent much of his considerable philanthropic life doing that. Other quiet community-minded benefactors who've gone public include investment manager David Bissett and Engineered Air founder Don Taylor. Bissett has said one of his key goals is to encourage others. It's largely a matter of personal style; Doc has always preferred to stay more in the background.

Not giving was never an option for Doc. Tom McGlade Jr. compares philanathropists like Doc to Warren Buffett. Their joy is the fun and challenge of business, but in the end it's about giving, not acquiring. Buffett, the legendary CEO of Berkshire Hathaway, is donating the bulk of his estimated US$30 billion fortune, in US$1.5 billion annual chunks, to the Bill and Melinda Gates Foundation. "I'm certainly not in Warren Buffet's league," Doc says, laughing. "But that's a pattern of wealth transfer that makes sense here in Canada, too."

After he and his wife established the Gates Foundation, the richest in the world, Bill Gates told reporters on June 16, 2006, "With success, I have been given great wealth. And with great wealth comes great responsibility to give back to society, to see that those resources are put to work in the best possible way to help those in need."[25]

Buffett told Charlie Rose on his eponymous PBS program on June 26, 2006, "I don't believe in dynastic wealth … the idea that many generations should be able to go without doing a thing if they wish, simply because they came from the right womb, I mean that strikes me as flying in the face of really what this country is about." Buffett believes children should be left "enough money so that they would feel they could do anything, but not so much that they could do nothing."[26]

Giving away earned fortunes is a philosophy that Doc fully supports. He looks also to Sir John Templeton, who passed away at age ninety-five, fully engaged in donating his life's earnings. Knighted for his philanthropy, Templeton focused on spiritual over material wealth. He was fond of the words of social reformer Henry Ward Beecher, whom he quoted in his book *The Templeton Plan*.[27] "No man can tell whether he is rich or poor by turning to his ledger. It is the heart that makes a man rich. He is rich according to what he is, not according to what he has," Beecher said.[28]

In 2005, Christopher Ruddy, the publisher of *Financial Intelligence Report*, interviewed Templeton in the Bahamas. Like Doc, Templeton abhorred the notion of retiring. "I have observed in ninety-two years that the people who are most diligent in working do live many years longer than those who are lazy," he told Ruddy.[29]

Dr. Jack Templeton, who left the medical profession to manage his father's philanthropic fund, clearly inherited Sir John's spirit. He told writer Leah McLaren, "The more you have, the more you can give away."[30]

McLaren also quotes Templeton's friend, financier Foster Friess, on Templeton's character: "I don't think he went out of his way to accumulate. It's just something that happens to people who are committed to serving others … His faith dictated that the money wasn't really his anyway but that he was merely a steward of it. So that is probably why he was motivated to spend it in a way he thought would be pleasing to God."

Doc's will to serve and give was born in his humble Saskatchewan roots and honed by the sharp winds of war. As Fischer notes, "Even when you start small, you learn you can make a difference and it makes you feel good."

Gold and real estate entrepreneur Peter Munk made a fortune, and now he, too, is giving it away. As a child, Munk escaped the

Nazis with his father and grandfather. Tragically, his mother was sent to Auschwitz, but survived and later made it to Canada. When Andrew Cave of the *Telegraph* asked Munk, "Is it more enjoyable to make money or to give it away?" he replied, "Both are superb. I feel sorry for those who don't give it away because they only get half the pleasure. Being able to give it away is a big motivating factor for me."[31]

When asked about leaving his fortune to his children, Munk pointed out that they are well educated "in terms of the values that are important in life. You do not start them off with so much money because if you do that, you just take away from their own initiative." Munk feels that leaving large inheritances to children "will only lead to tragedy." Instead, he will establish their own charities so his children can experience the joy of giving.

Doc shares a similar view. He wants his children to be comfortable and respects them for making their own way. He also recognizes how difficult it can be for children of wealthy parents.

"It's hard to be the son or daughter of a successful person," Doc says. "I've tried to be careful about my estate planning. Basically, I've left them ranchlands that are quite valuable, but they can't sell them. They'll still have to make their own, and if they sell the land they have to sell to each other. So it's a concept I hope works, because I've seen so many rich families in difficulty. In business in the past, we'd partner with extremely wealthy families. I noticed that too often the children that inherited great wealth just played tennis, went to parties, and never really fully engaged with life. It seemed a pretty empty existence."

Doc is also concerned that the core value of community giving is eroding in Canada when compared with the United States. "My impression is that Calgary is good," Doc notes. "But when you consider giving across Canada with respect to that in the U.S., we don't compare well. This is shocking, particularly today, where any institution you give to is a direct offset to your taxes."

Doc is completely correct. The Fraser Institute compares charitable donations within Canada and between the two nations. Its scale reveals a generosity gap within Canada, but also between the amount Canadians give versus what Americans donate. "A higher percentage of tax filers donated to charity in the United States (30.6 percent) than in Canada (25.1 percent) in 2005. Similarly, in the same period, Americans gave a higher percentage of their aggregate income (1.77 percent) to charity than did Canadians (0.75 percent)," stated the Fraser Alert.[32]

Americans donated US$182 billion, while Canadians offered C$7.8 billion. There are ten times more Americans than Canadians, but our national giving is clearly much lower per capita. "If Canadians had given, in aggregate, the same percentage of their incomes to charity as Americans did, the Canadian charitable sector would have received an additional $10.4 billion in privately donated revenue," continued the Fraser Alert authors.

Globe and Mail columnist Margaret Wente soundly chastises Canadians for the charity gap. "On the generosity scale, the Americans lead the world," she wrote on January 20, 2007. "They make us look pretty chintzy."

At least Canadians give more than Europeans. Yet the generosity gap isn't about economics but time-honoured virtues found in the kind of small town where Doc grew up. They are places where people still believe in volunteering and helping each other. Perhaps it's time for neglected ideals to kick-start a new age.

"These findings are a little rattling for people who think 'compassionate conservatism' is a joke," Wente points out. She quotes Syracuse University economist Arthur Brooks and his book *Who Really Cares*: "I came into this thinking that people who say they're compassionate, are compassionate. I found that's not the case." Rather than expecting government to do it all, and thus assuaging any guilt over not giving, Wente suggests, "You want to get something back? Try giving."

Judge William Pepler was playing golf with Doc when a massive mansion suddenly jolted their view beyond the fairway. Doc turned away, looked at the judge, and said, "Some guys build monuments to themselves, but I prefer to give my money away." As Warren Buffett says, "It's dumb to let possessions rule you." Pepler says Doc is smart and daring and has carefully developed a network of people he can rely on. "There are a lot of people that are doing well in the oil patch who worked with Doc in the past. Their success, I think, is a reflection of his influence."

Doc has never been motivated by a desire to amass status-laden mansions, jets, and yachts. Some of today's chief executives would do well to follow his example. New York University finance professor David Yermack and Crocker Liu from Arizona State University studied the size of a CEO's home versus the company's stock performance. "When a company's chief buys a big estate, the stock is about to tank," explained columnist Michael Brush at Intelius.com on April 11, 2007.[33] "It gives you some insight into the CEO's mindset," noted Yermack in the Brush article. "An entrenched CEO perceives himself as immune from discipline by his board and is uninterested in maintaining or improving his performance to attract outside offers."

Coincidentally, Warren Buffett still lives in his Omaha, Nebraska, bungalow that he purchased for $31,500 in 1958. Since 1980, the share price of Berkshire Hathaway has soared 34,820 percent. Doc lives in the same Calgary condominium he has owned for three decades and on weekends drives his basic Ford Explorer to his cattle ranch in the foothills of the Rockies.

Yermack also studied the use of corporate jets by CEOs versus the company's stock performance. An Agence France-Presse article of April 13, 2004, quoted Yermack: "The central result of this study is that CEO's personal use of company aircraft is associated with severe and significant under-performance of their employers' stock. Firms' stock prices drop an average of 2 percent around the date of initial disclosure of corporate plane use."[34]

Former press baron and CEO of Hollinger International, Conrad Black, wrote an internal e-mail on August 5, 2002, about corporate jets and the rights of the proprietor. Lord Black of CrossHarbour's attitude couldn't be farther from Doc's: "There has not been an occasion for many months when I got on our plane without wondering whether it was really affordable. But I'm not prepared to re-enact the French Revolutionary renunciation of the rights of nobility. We have to find a balance between an unfair taxation on the company and a reasonable treatment of the founders-builders-managers. We are proprietors, after all, beleaguered though we may be."[35]

Author Peter Newman discussed greed with Black in an interview for his biography of him, *The Establishment Man*, published in 1982. "Greed has been severely underestimated and denigrated — unfairly so, in my opinion," said Black. "There is nothing wrong with avarice as a motive, as long as it doesn't lead to dishonest or anti-social conduct."

Conrad Black was sentenced December 10, 2007, for three counts of mail fraud and one count of obstruction of justice; on March 3 2008, he began serving his six-and-a-half-year term in an American prison.

Today he is prisoner 18330-424 at the Coleman Correction centre near Orlando, Florida. Doc Seaman, to whom Black's views on personal wealth are abhorrent, remains focused on the needs of others and is content with life.

Chapter Eleven

The Rancher

"*The greatest use of life is to spend it for*
something that will outlast it."
— William James

The southern Alberta foothills, with the mountains on guard to the west and prairies opening to the east, are surely as close to paradise as anything on earth. Sadly, the land in those foothills is today worth more as scraped lots for city dwellers than as grazing land for ranchers' cattle. The endless sky and the land that promises boundless possibilities are often blocked and scarred by McMansion retreats. The breathtaking vista, the bounty that once belonged to all, is up for grabs.

Yet there are ranchers whose respect for the land and the pristine wilderness trump the siren scent of cash. Whether it's a grubstake or a spread of fifty thousand acres, many ranchers of Alberta's eastern slopes are committed to the old ways of free-roaming wildlife and livestock on open rangeland. When the buffalo commanded the prairies all the way to the Rocky Mountain foothills, nature offered an abundance of trees, flowers, animals, and birds. Far too much of the native grasslands have gone the way of the buffalo, but the ranchers of the eastern slopes are determined to preserve as much as they can. They know the proud and ancient history of the rolling wonder of foothills and mountains.

The Blackfoot remained a strong and dignified people even as their culture was threatened by the slaughter of the buffalo and the surrender of their lands through the signing of Treaty 7 in 1877. The great ranches of the late nineteenth and early twentieth centuries, and the settler families who created them, relied on the traditions and insight of the Blackfoot who had dominated the land, living amongst the buffalo for thousands of years.

The cowboy way of life hearkens back to the world of wonder that greeted the Europeans who first landed on Canadian shores and moved westward. Far more than is commonly recognized, the settling of the West relied on the traditions and co-operation of the First Nations. The great ranches of the Alberta foothills respected the First Nations' stewardship of the land, and the smart owners were ready to hire Native cowboys who understood everything that walked, swam, ran, flew, and grew.

"While they were quick to fence the prairie, and appropriate its grasses to beef, the early ranchers worked closely with Blackfoot cattlemen, and kept up this relationship well into the 1950s and early 1960s," wrote Mike Robinson, former CEO of Calgary's Glenbow Museum. "Today, the great southern Alberta ranches that stretch out on either side of Highway 22 carry on the tradition of grassland stewardship established by the OH-Rio Alto, the Bar U, the A7, and the EP back in the foundation days of ranching."[36]

When Robinson was at the Glenbow, Doc donated to the acclaimed Maverick's display, inspired by author Aritha Van Herk's superb history of Alberta characters, curmudgeons, and creators. Doc discussed ranching with Robinson and was delighted that the display featured the OH Ranch as a typical ranch of the time.

The OH covers land that instantly inspires both respect and awe. At the primary spread just west of Longview, Mount Kidd and the Holy Cross peak stand like sentries guarding the pine, willows, and aspen. The fescue grasses grow beyond the creeks and ponds that seem to place their bets every spring on the cresting of the Highwood River. On these lands roam a host of four-legged predators, including grizzlies, black bears, cougars, and wolves.

The OH Ranch is actually three separate spreads, with the flagship located west of Longview. The ranch headquarters sit on a nearly square block of 16,500 acres, bounded on the south by the steep banks of the Highwood River for a stretch of more than five miles. South of the river is the Pekisko, four thousand acres of treed land used for winter pasture. Other parcels are Bassano, north of the TransCanada highway, and Dorothy, southeast of Drumheller. Each is crucial to the cattle operation: cows graze on the grass in one area and then are moved to another so that none of the land loses its ability to renew the native grasses. During calving and branding season, the cattle roam land close to the ranch buildings near Longview. "The rotation within the ranchlands takes place over the year, and when it's time to sell the cattle, they end up back at the main ranch," says former OH manager Bud Maynard.

The OH and its fifty thousand acres offer a panorama of glory where cattle roam free and the cowboys seldom interfere. The OH cattle are self-sufficient, existing naturally in a changeable climate that ranges from balmy and beckoning to severe and dangerous. "The cattle are Hereford and Angus breeds," says Doc. "They're hardy and able to find food and shelter even in a thirty-below blizzard."

Bud Maynard calls the operation "cowboy-style," meaning that cows range over the land and hills throughout the year, eating the natural grasses and calving in the fields. Doc's son Bob Seaman, who manages the OH ranching operations, eagerly embraces the legacy of the past with practices honed from his educated background in cattle genetics. "Bob runs the ranch, is a good herdsman, and understands genetics well," notes Doc proudly. Bob feels strongly that the OH must be preserved: "It's a wonderful idea because those ranches are going to become rare," he says.

To truly understand ranching, Bob believes a person must live the life. From sunrise to sunset, the work can be punishing; but the cowboys — and cowgirls — wouldn't trade it in (or for) a New York minute. On some ranches hands are forced to leave because the land no longer sustains the life; but when they do, they forever look back. The songs of rancher-troubadour Ian Tyson, Doc's near neighbour, hauntingly evoke both the joy and melancholy of a fading way of life.

"It isn't always about making money, because the land always drags you through the mud and, generally, will pull you out of the mud," says Bob Seaman. "It's nice to make a profit, operationally, but that's not easy to do in the cattle business. I believe we can do some good genetically. I think we can develop a product that's more predictable."

The Seamans are exceptionally proud of both their cattle and their feed. Doc points out that the ranch delivers hay as far away as the British stables of Queen Elizabeth II, as well as to customers in Abu Dhabi, Japan, and Florida. Its major client is Spruce Meadows, the world-ranked equestrian facility south of Calgary, founded by Ron and Marg Southern.

"We do have arguably the best winter range anywhere at Pekisko where you can run cows all year round," notes Bob Seaman. "The land has that natural ability to winter cattle. In April, we bring the cow herd back across the river and they glow with such wonderful health and condition."

Spring snowstorms can abruptly transform a warm, clear field into a white danger zone, with disastrous results for cattle. In the past, the OH has lost up to one hundred calves in May, mainly to predators like wolves and grizzlies. "One spring we had a grizzly that tore us up," recalls Doc. "Our pasture must have looked like a buffet where he helped himself to a calf a day."

The OH has since moved its calving season to June to get away from such stormy risks.

"Our cattle operation does very well with little input," Bob says. "Our advantage is our natural capital. Normally we don't offer our cows winter feed because they're able to forage for themselves."

The foothills climate can be cruel to even the most seasoned ranchers. The OH cattle are bred to be self-sufficient so even a late spring storm doesn't leave them in distress. The OH Web site explains: "The Range Tested® Program ensures OH cattle can excel under any conditions with minimal inputs."[37]

As a rancher, Doc's mission for the OH is simple: cultivate a world-class cattle operation, protect the environment, and preserve the history of ranching. Doc intends to leave the ranch to the people of Canada as a legacy honouring our Western ranching heritage. Jim Smith, an agrologist who farms near Olds, Alberta, says, "Doc wants to find a way he can maintain that good stewardship and environmental land ethic in perpetuity. In addition, he wants to help build some bridges between rural and urban communities."

Too often, ignorance obscures the mutual connection between the city and the country. Politicians sometimes exploit the divide, although they'd do much better to focus on the cultural, social, ecological, and economic interdependency between the urban and rural ways of life. Misplaced stereotypes of city slickers and country bumpkins belie the intelligence and sophistication it takes to farm and ranch in the twenty-first century. They ignore the reliance of the city resident on the country dweller's stewardship of the environment. No one is more dependent on, or more knowledgeable about, the environment than a rancher or farmer. The stereotypes need to be dismantled to foster mutual understanding and respect. Doc's OH legacy to future Canadians is a giant leap in that direction.

By placing a conservation easement on the OH Ranch, Doc hopes to protect airsheds, watersheds, wildlife, and the magnificent vistas. The OH will continue to sequester carbon dioxide as part of nature's cycle and maintain the ecological integrity of the land.

Indeed, the OH is a working example of sustainable landscapes, covering four of southern Alberta's significant ecological zones.

"By donating the ranch, Doc is making an absolutely huge financial commitment," notes Smith. "It will be a very large gift to Albertans and Canadians, and Doc feels strongly that this is the right thing to do. Doc Seaman is one of my heroes; he should be one of yours."

As an environmentalist, Smith has chaired the Canadian Land Trust Alliance. He got to know Doc well through his conservation easement plans and was immediately impressed with Doc's land ethic.

"Right from the start, Doc had preservation in mind," says Bud Maynard, who managed the OH Ranch from 1988 to 2005. "Keep it a working ranch as opposed to breaking up a bunch of land. I wanted open-range style, and Doc backed me all the way. He wanted to preserve the cowboy image of the ranch. We set out to do all our cattle work by horseback."

It wasn't only the romance of the range that compelled Doc and Maynard to do everything on horseback, although that was part of the appeal. It was also respect for the environment, the grasslands and the animals. When people visit the OH, they know it's a working ranch, reminiscent of the heritage ranches of the late nineteenth and twentieth centuries. Solid maintenance and damage control preserve the OH Ranch and its land while protecting and promoting at least one chunk of our country's ranching heritage.

"Sustaining and not damaging anything, especially maintaining the grass, is very hard with drought and conditions in the country," notes Maynard. "It's so easy to damage the grass, and it takes such a long time to come back."

Doc encouraged Maynard and his successor, Todd Snodgrass, to take courses in ranch and grass maintenance. What they learned, they passed on to the other cowboys and to Doc.

"We didn't seed much and managed our grass, so we had winter grass," says Maynard. "We let the cattle range and help themselves.

They've done this for thousands of years. If you do a few things right for them, the cattle do things for themselves. We're using as little machinery as possible, although we do need a tractor. It cut our costs down quite a bit. When you do everything on horseback, you do it properly. There are lots of guys who ride and wear the boots and the hat but don't know what's going on."

Maynard recalls his early years at the OH when the large crew of cowboys didn't necessarily know the job as well as they could have. From a high of fifteen, the operation ended up with a crew of four or five highly skilled ranchmen.

"We were pros and knew what we were doing," he says. "We prided ourselves on the amount of work we did and on the small number of cowboys we did it with."

The crucial thing for Maynard was to reduce or even eliminate stress on the cattle. That meant a ban on whooping and hollering and running the animals: no Western movie theatrics for these professional cowboys.

"We don't overwork the cattle," he says. "If you're running your cattle, you're stressing them and they're losing weight from all of that. Through Doc, we were given leave to run the ranch in a traditional way, which was just wonderful. Some owners are always telling you what to do; not Doc."

Doc's approach is one he's used from youth, through the war and into business, sports, philanthropy, and ranching. It's all about creating a working team, choosing knowledgeable people, leaving them with the job, and allowing them to do it well.

"Doc doesn't micromanage," says Stan Grad, one of Doc's most avid pheasant hunting partners. An oilman and founder of Soderglen Ranches, Grad supplies purebred bulls to the OH. Borrowing from business author Tom Peters, Grad describes Doc's approach as: "trying to get the herd moving roughly west."

"Doc would hire somebody who understood the business and then guide them," says Maynard. "He helped guide me a lot, and

I also understood a lot that he didn't. But I learned solid business practices, and between the two of us we taught each other."

The Seaman family had always ranched, but the OH was ten times larger than the family ranch at Millarville, near Turner Valley, where they grew some hay and bred a few cattle. The OH was a huge historic ranch with an inventory of two thousand cows that would produce up to two thousand calves. The number increased or decreased depending on the amount of moisture through snowfall and rain.

"All calves not kept for replacements go to Bassano for finishing," says Doc. "Once they reach between nine hundred and one thousand pounds in the fall, we sell them as yearlings." Throughout the OH operation, there's also a big battery of bulls, especially at Longview.

"Doc's whole approach to success is choosing the right team," says Maynard. "Ken Stiles [Doc's great friend and business associate] really told me a lot about Doc and how he operated. Doc would have an idea, put a team together, and then move off. Doc's a real forward thinker. He was smart enough to get the right people so the business didn't tie him down. One of the real treats of my life has been getting to know Doc."

Brenda Maynard, Bud's wife, kept the accounting books for the ranch and worked closely with Stiles on the business side of the OH. After Stiles passed away in 2006, the respect for him in cowboy country for his business advice and general kindness was warmly expressed in a eulogy by the webmasters at COWS (Cowboy Oriented Web Sites): "Ken, we are so grateful … Your words to us will continue to guide us on our journey … and every future endeavor. Thank you so much — and we'll see you again when our time comes."[38]

Doc respects simplicity. A tidy desk reflects a tidy operation, and Maynard liked that approach to ranching. The buildings on the OH Ranch are neat, clean, and simple. It's plain respect for the cowboys and the work they do.

"Doc's not a fancy person, and we worked to keep it orderly," adds Maynard. He chuckles as he recalls the tours of the OH Ranch that Doc took with his friends and old buddies. "We'd go for a ride in the back country. Doc could outride his friends and they were always a little sore when they returned. We'd say maybe we should cut it back a bit."

When Maynard and his tight crew were working, Doc would often tag along. He'd ask for a task, follow orders, and remain in place working. They used to kid Doc about being a fair-weather cowboy because he doesn't like to ride in the winter when the temperature becomes brutal or there's a harsh blizzard. Yet when the foothills beckon even on a sun-filled day, many men half Doc's age retreat to the comforts of the ranch house rather than face the thought of saddle sores. "Doc rides a lot, and rides very well," says Maynard. "He's still fantastic." On the range, Doc wears his dad, Byron's, battered beige hat, a totem marking the tenacity and simplicity that Byron passed on to his son.

Doc bought the historic OH Ranch in 1987, 106 years after a buffalo hunter and a mule-skinner decided to set up camp on the banks of the Highwood River. The North West Mounted Police had already kicked the pair out of Blackfoot Crossing for whiskey trading and price-gouging the locals. The dubious duo acquired a few cattle and squatted on land that now houses the OH headquarters. LaFayette French and Orville Hawkins Smith took Smith's first initials and formed the OH brand, creating the twenty-fifth cattle brand in the entire North West Territories. (At the time, the vast area included Alberta and Saskatchewan before they became provinces, as well as part of Manitoba.)

In 1883, the two rascals sold both the brand and the cattle to Frederick Ings, whose brother Walter joined him from Prince Edward Island the following year. They called their cattle operation Rio Alto, Spanish for "High River." At the gravelled road entrance to the OH Ranch headquarters rests a simple front gate with the faint metal engraving "OH Rio Alto Ranch."

In his 1936 autobiography, *Before The Fences*, Ings related how a young American cowboy named Harry Longabaugh had saved his life during a blinding blizzard. In the U.S., that cowboy was called "The Sundance Kid," after a stint in a Sundance, Wyoming jail for horse theft. A botched bank raid pushed the Kid to Canada where the Bar U ranch, just south of the OH, was as good a place as any to hide out in 1890. No one would ever convince Ings that the outlaw wasn't a "thoroughly likeable fellow . . . a general favorite with everyone, a splendid rider and a top notch cow hand."

"One night . . . on Mosquito Creek was one of the worst times I ever went through. A blizzard was coming from the north with blinding snow. I was given the ten o'clock shift, and with me was Harry Longdebough [sic], a good-looking young American cow puncher who feared neither man nor devil . . . I was riding a sure-footed, thick-set, little grey horse, but I had a dozen falls that stormy night. In spite of being warmly dressed, we found it desperately cold and in the thickly falling snow lost all sense of locality." The Sundance Kid went back to find Ings and led him safely to camp.

Others weren't so sure about Longabaugh, especially a cowboy at the Bar U who spotted a hacksaw blade hidden between his saddle and horse blanket. Such tools were often used to modify branding irons. Back in the U.S. by 1892, Longabaugh began his notorious string of train robberies with the Wild Bunch. In the 1969 film *Butch Cassidy and the Sundance Kid*, Robert Redford played the Kid opposite Paul Newman.

The North West Mounted Police built a tiny post next to the OH cottage in 1890. A fire razed the original log cabin in 1962, but Doc meticulously recreated it in 1989. Today the cabin offers a fascinating glimpse of a Mountie's life on the Canadian frontier, where rogues, renegades, isolation, and a cruel climate tested the resolve of all who lived at the edge of settlement.

"I've done a lot of work with the history of the ranches, and

I've got a good collection of Northwest Mounted Police artifacts. I've also got an etching of John Ware at the house," he points out. Doc restored the OH ranch house and placed on the original wall a framed drawing of the legendary Canadian cowboy. A former American slave, John Ware joined a cattle drive in Texas after the Civil War and made his way to Alberta. Ware wound up with his own ranch near Millarville. In the ferocious winter of 1886–87, a blizzard pushed Ware's cattle south as far as the OH. Ware followed and remained at the OH until spring, tending his herd and leaving the other cowboys in awe of his strength and ranching skills.

In 1918, Pat Burns bought the OH Ranch at Longview. Burns, who died in 1937, was one of the "Big Four" who started the Calgary Stampede in 1912, along with George Lane, A.J. MacLean, and A.E. Cross. Burns Limited sold the OH in 1950 to Kink Roenisch and Bill Ardern, who legally changed the name from Rio Alto to OH Ranch Ltd. Then Ardern sold the OH to his son-in-law, Doug Kingsford, and to the OH manager, Bert Sheppard, who added the sign on top of the log gate that remains today.[39]

By 1987, however, the historic OH Ranch suddenly faced an invasion. The department of National Defence announced plans to buy the OH as a military training ground, similar to the range near Suffield in southeastern Alberta. The magnificent lands were about to be chewed up by tanks, troops, and shellfire. A cheque for $6 million was cut in Ottawa and readied for delivery to the owners. But the plan provoked instant resistance, with support from local families, staff of Bow Valley Industries, and Doc himself. He quickly resolved to make the owners a better offer. Meanwhile the Tsuu T'ina First Nation helped considerably by offering an extension of a lease for army use of reserve lands closer to Calgary. The military had a graceful and inexpensive exit, and Doc had the ranch.

No one understands more than Doc the need for military training, but the Second World War veteran was distraught that such a historic and ecological wonderland could face ruin.

"A number of the ranchers in the area, like Tom Bews, Ian Tyson, and Ken Stiles, banded together to dissuade the government," says Maynard. "Then when we heard an oilman was buying the OH, we were worried and wondered if he was going to subdivide the land and sell it for building lots. When we met Doc and realized his philosophy, we knew there couldn't have been a better person to buy it."

Tom Bews, a former rodeo champion who was twice named the top Canadian all-around cowboy, ranches next door to Doc. Bews and his sons look after the horse work for many Hollywood movies that film in the foothills along the Cowboy Trail between Millarville and Longview, including Clint Eastwood's *Unforgiven* and Kevin Costner's *Open Range*.

"Clint Eastwood, Morgan Freeman, Robert Duvall — who does ride — they love it here," says Bews. "The actors are overwhelmed with the beauty of the land."

Bews and his sons would ride with some of the actors and supply the horses and gear. "The actors would sit there in awe of the beauty. Then they'd wonder about winter. I'd say, 'This is kind of the banana belt of Alberta. The winters are not that bad, and we do have chinooks.'"

The Emmy Award–winning miniseries *Broken Trail* with Duvall was filmed on the OH Ranch. "Robert Duvall is not a bad rider," adds Bud Maynard. "Doc and I took him out riding a couple of times."

To this day, many local people see Doc Seaman as the saviour of some of the nation's most beautiful countryside. Bews, who competed globally, says every Canadian should know the thrill of driving south to Longview, topping the ridge just before the town, and suddenly seeing the vast sweep of mountains, foothills, and prairie stretching out to the south and west. It is truly a breathtaking sight that stuns tourists every day in summer. Doc Seaman rescued the most precious portion of this vista, a huge chunk of land between Longview and Kananaskis Country to the west. The very thought of tanks rolling and shells bursting in that countryside, even to train our own soldiers, is almost sacrilege.

"Not in cowboy country," says Bews. "Doc has his heart in the ranch. He believes in it, and he didn't try and come up with fandangle wild ideas. We went through a lot of pressure with the army, so it was a great thing when Doc bought the OH. It tickled us all because we wanted the valley to stay as ranching country. It's the last of the big frontier. Doc said he didn't start out as a cowboy, but he does have a lot of it in his system and he rides a horse well. His OH operation stayed with the old ranching way, and it's paid off for him. It can take the ups and downs."

Doc, Bews, and rancher Paul Fuller ride together on the OH on free weekends. Fuller is also a pilot who flew Bow Valley's Lear Jet when the company built drilling rigs in Norway. Today, Bews and Fuller travel the team-roping circuit in the southern United States.

From the start, Doc wanted to revive cowboy tradition on the ranch. He felt it was important for Canadians to understand their heritage and the time-honoured methods that have characterized the OH from its birth on the banks of the Highwood River. "The OH is a piece of the old West, and I want to make sure it remains so," says Doc.

Even his brothers, with whom he's exceptionally close, don't always fully grasp Doc's fondness for the wilderness. As Don Seaman quipped to journalist Gordon Jaremko, "When he sees a cow, he sees something different than I do."[40]

Doc shares the green gene with his daughter, Diane Lefroy, a staunch environmentalist who believes all people can lessen their footprint on the earth. Rather than being daunted by the enormity of environmental worry, she says, each person should consider his or her own role, no matter how huge or tiny. "If everyone did something small, it would make a difference."

There was another crucial element to owning the OH Ranch — community. Before Doc, the relationship with the OH and the surrounding ranchers and townsfolk was tested during the military troop talk. "I wanted the OH to be part of the community," says Doc. He set about rebuilding relationships.

Maynard notes that Doc made a point of knowing the names of all the neighbours, ranch hands, and townspeople he met. "Doc can get along with everyone, from kings to cowboys," says Maynard. "When Doc came out to the ranch, the young kid who was cowboying was given as much of his time as anybody."

Doc encourages his friends to join him on horseback in the wondrous wilderness of the past, if just for the day. Two who relish the opportunity are Darryl Sutter and Ken King.

Sutter, who was raised on a farm near Viking, Alberta, and who is as fond of horses as Doc, first visited the OH Ranch in December 2003. Early the next spring he went riding with Doc and the cowboys. "We went far into the hills to the site of the Indian graves," says Sutter. "The higher you were in that First Nations culture, the higher you got to be buried. There's so much rich history about the land and its people. Doc strongly feels we must preserve this."

King is a cowboy culture buff whose rapport with horses has often left Doc in stitches — especially when King, a very large man even when slender, at one point nearly matched the heft of a horse. "I've ridden horses for a long time," says King, who owns quite a few. "It cracks Doc up seeing me getting piled up off a horse — he teases me about that. You can see his whole heart and soul when he laughs."

When life smacks King with a slapshot, he likes to saddle up for a long ride of reflection. Doc took Sutter and King to the Pekisko Ranch, where they rode to the dream chair on the Indian gravesite. The dream chair was important to First Nations people living in the foothills. The braves would ride alone to the dream chair, sit in it, and remain there until a vision appeared. Enlightened, they would return home.

"It's a rock chair that faces due east," says King. "The idea is that you sit in it and look eastward until you have a vision. It's a place where very few have been, and it was an amazing experience. Doc has a great relationship with the land. He once said to me, 'I'd have bought more land if I had more money.' The beauty of it is that he didn't buy the land to own it — he bought the land to protect it. Doc looks like he belongs there. He loves to be there."

Doc calls himself a "cowboy addict" who admires the cowboy way of life. He allows modestly that he's "not a cowboy — although I've ridden a lot." Tom McGlade Jr. calls Doc an environmentalist and historical preservationist: "Doc's attempting to make the OH Ranch a living museum of western Canadian ranching."

One day Doc called Dr. Brad Stelfox, an environmentalist, to discuss the grasslands on the eastern slopes of the Rockies. Doc was concerned about conserving the fescue and confronting the challenges of urban encroachment.

"Once the oil field roads break up the soil gophers come in, and it's tough getting the land back," notes Doc. "Then the weeds like Canadian thistle invade. We need to protect the native fescue because it acts like a sponge that retains the mountain snowmelt and feeds small streams and creeks that run through the land. The fescue root system descends ten to fifteen feet below the ground. That's why it's so precious out there, and we don't want it disturbed."

Stelfox has also examined the landscape, water, and grasses of the southern foothills. The OH Ranch has been an important partner in his study, and he strongly endorses Doc's plan to forever protect the OH's legacy and its unique ecology.

"Doc's appreciative of the story I've been telling," says Stelfox. "It's consistent with his philosophy. When he speaks, he has something to say, and people listen attentively. I rode with Doc and his son Bob on the OH and listened to their key concerns about the transformation of the landscape, the expanding city, and ranchland becoming acreages for houses. It's interesting for Doc, as he understands the benefits of hydrocarbons, but also the liabilities and their effects. He is concerned about water, soils, erosion, and simply treating the land well. If it's not treated well, the cattle operation won't work well."

In his work with the ranchers in the area, including Doc, Stelfox has been impressed with their understanding of the land and space. As a landscape ecologist, Stelfox appreciates the constraints of the overheated economy and the potential degradation of the natural capital. His goal for the forestry, energy, and agricultural sectors is an environmental plan that focuses on best practices.

"We're paying a price," explains Stelfox. "The energy industry represents a spectrum, and many are responsible players. Companies need to make a profit and please shareholders, and most see the writing on the wall. They try to conduct business in a way that positively affects the environment. But there are cut-and-run players for whom the environment is not the most pressing concern on their file. For some companies, environmentalism is just rhetoric. Thankfully, there are those who want to be more open and transparent and want to talk about limits."

Doc's love of the ranch is so powerful that at one point, he considered retiring there in order to help bring the ranch back to its original condition by fixing the buildings, reviving water sources, and protecting the delicate balance between the cattle operation and the land. His many other interests always kept him from moving permanently to Longview, but there has still been plenty of time for enjoyment — and, sometimes, for danger.

On one occasion, Doc and his son Bob went into the wilderness for a week-long trek. Their companions were outfitter and adventurer Chuck Hayward and Calgary Flames players Jim Peplinski, Paul Reinhart, and Doug Risebrough. They trailered their horses to Rickert's Pass, a popular hiking trail that begins near the stunningly beautiful Kananaskis Country golf courses. High above the timberline, near the crest of the mountains, the scenery was spectacular. As the riders soaked up the glorious views, the narrow track abruptly stopped at a sharp drop.

"It was a hot day, and our horses were sweating heavily," Doc recalls. "We got off, had a drink of water, and Chuck tightened up the cinch on the pack horse. We were nearly three thousand feet above the timberline. The way down to Burn's cabin in the Sheep River Valley was on a narrow goat trail traversing the upper part of the mountain. Chuck told us to lead our horses down — the top section was really steep, and rock scree made the footing treacherous."

All the others were ahead of Doc, except Hayward, who was guiding his horse along with the pack horse. Suddenly, the pack horse stumbled, shifting his load. The pack slipped to one side, under his belly and against his flank.

"The pack horse spooked and came barrelling down the inside of the trail," says Doc. "He broadsided my horse and knocked him off the trail ledge. I was knocked flat on my stomach, but Smoke had taken the brunt of the collision and thankfully I stayed on the trail — it was only about two feet wide.

"Smoke ended up just below the outside edge of the trail where the rock slope declined more steeply. His body was twisted around almost 180 degrees and his front legs were splayed out, but incredibly, he was still on his feet. Had he lost his footing, he would have tumbled all the way to the timberline.

"I was a bit winded but not hurt and got back on my feet. 'What should I do, Chuck?' I asked. 'You've got to try to get him back on the ledge,' he replied. I put my hand on Smoke's rump and spoke softly, to reassure him: 'You've got to get up here, boy.' Smoke gathered himself, took two jumps in rapid succession, torquing his body uphill. On the second jump, he landed back on the trail, facing in the right direction. A mountain goat couldn't have done any better. Chuck said he'd never seen anything like it."

Meanwhile, Bob, who was farther down the trail, stopped the pack horse. His pack had broken when he collided with Smoke, and the supplies bounced down the rock face to the trees below. Peplinski, Reinhart, and Risebrough scrambled down the harsh slope to see what they could salvage.

"The boys were training for the upcoming hockey season and were in great shape," says Doc. "Still, all they could find were two eggs, a can of corn, plus a bottle of whiskey which I'd put in a plastic container for safety. We were three days by horseback from Turner Valley, with our supplies gone. For everyone's breakfast the next morning, I whipped up the canned corn and the two eggs and called it a soufflé. For the rest of the trip, we had to catch our own fish. And I think we sometimes had a nip of whiskey for dessert."

Peter Lougheed, former Alberta premier and Canadian statesman, loves to backpack into the Kananaskis mountains with his wife, Jeannie. But the vistas never look more expansive than when he saddles up and rides the OH with Doc. "We go out annually," he says. "Doc gives me the quietest and most gentle horse he can find. Doc's own horse is a real lively one, and he's up at the front of the group. It sure is great. We have a wonderful day every summer."

The group has ventured into the Kananaskis for twenty years and combines trail riding with a fishing trek. It usually includes Doc and his brothers, B.J. and Don, as well as Harold Milavsky, Fred Mannix, Don Taylor, Peter Lougheed, and the three cowboys, Tom Bews, Paul Fuller, and Todd Snodgrass, who took over from Bud Maynard as OH manager.

"Oh, we need the cowboys so the others don't get into any trouble," says Doc with a smile. "A couple of our regulars are very good riders, though." The 125th anniversary of the OH was marked by a celebratory ride in the summer of 2008.

To Doc Seaman, ranching represents everything he's always valued — independence, hard work, co-operation, generosity, and friendship, all harnessed to the achievement of a worthwhile larger goal. On a big ranch that is still but a tiny part of Canada, he strives to preserve not just the land but also the very values that make the country great. And that's pretty much the story of Doc Seaman's remarkable life.

CONCLUSION

A Handshake Seals a Deal

Today, Doc Seaman still rides the range with the same vigour, plays gin rummy with the same enjoyment, and goes to the office most working days, secure in the knowledge that old ways are usually the best ways. They seem archaic only because they've fallen out of use in a country growing more selfish and materialistic. Whatever the fashion of the day, some attitudes are just right and others wrong, and Doc Seaman knows the difference.

Doc's is a purposeful life. His mind brims with plans to benefit the community. He loves helping talented young people get started. Material "toys" — whether luxury cars, mansions, or yachts — are inconsequential. Men like Doc are quietly appalled by the conspicuous wealth so vividly flaunted in the newly prosperous West. They helped create that wealth, and they don't like seeing it used frivolously and selfishly, without any social or community purpose.

Doc grew up in a harsh time where financial depression and world war could have corroded character with vanity, greed, and brutality. That happened to some. Others had their health and sanity shattered. But Doc retained the values of hard work and a pioneering spirit that defined small-town Canada in the early twentieth century. He was able somehow to set the horror of war respectfully aside while using its skills and lessons. The military taught teamwork and the need to make decisions quickly but intelligently: if they weren't right, you might not get a second chance, and others would go down with you.

Doc's aptitude and attitude helped build a Canadian oil and gas industry and wrest it from complete foreign control. He took risks that were breathtaking but never irresponsible. Some failed, but the big ones paid off. As in any life, there were sacrifices and tragedy. He tries not to dwell on these, but the pull between family and work still grates. "I was working with the seismic crew and had to keep at it. It was July 1949, and I wasn't there at the birth of my first child, Diane," he recalls.

Doc's purpose is still to create more jobs, invest in more companies, and do more in the community. It's remarkable how one person can have so many things going on at age eighty-six yet also make time to enjoy himself.

One message in Doc's life is that there is a way to find success and achieve a great many things while creating and preserving a flawless reputation. He did this by simply hewing to the principles that built modern Canada: honour, respect, integrity, fair play, and social justice. These principles are very much at risk in twenty-first-century society.

Doc has a great deal of talent too, of course. Some see a kind of genius in his ability to spot an opportunity and move quickly. His business life demonstrates this many times over, but his community abilities are even more striking. Nothing shows this more clearly than his insight into the potential of linking an NHL hockey team, a coliseum, the Olympics, and amateur sport. There was only a brief moment when all that was possible. If any part of the plan hadn't worked, the whole project might have collapsed. But the only thing this huge success did for his bank account was shrink it, because it became just another way to give away money. People like Doc have a way of making the improbable possible. Almost always, they do it by thinking far beyond themselves and their own interests.

Doc could have retired at sixty-five after he sold his stake in Bow Valley Industries. But Doc and deals are synonymous, so he became busier. Even after he got prostate cancer, he didn't stop. He eats smart, exercises regularly, and still golfs his age.

"Most nights, if it isn't too miserable out, I walk three or four miles," he says. "A brisk walk is relaxing. I don't mind going out when it's cold. I get dressed up and away I go. In the morning, I do a half hour of stretches, push-ups, and a variety of things. I believe in a lot of exercise, and on the weekends I ride horses quite a bit."

In the long preparation of this book, over scores of hours of conversation, the author never once heard Doc complain. Well, there was one thing, although it wouldn't even classify as a complaint for most people. "I haven't done enough yet," he said once, just before he left to advise another friend to keep on working and achieving. One of his current missions in life is to encourage boomers waiting for an arbitrary age of sixty-five to ignore it.

Instead, he says, take control, keep moving, and, most of all, stay in the game.

Endnotes

1   Peter Newman, *Titans* (Toronto: Viking, 1998).

2   Daryl Seaman, *Oilweek Magazine* (November 6, 2000): 19.

3   Tom MacGregor, "New Brunswick Convention," *Legion Magazine* (November/December, 2005).

4   Peter Foster, *From Rigs to Riches,* (Calgary: Bow Valley Industries, 1985), 22.

5   Foster, 32.

6   Foster, 37.

7   Foster, 39.

8   Foster, 64.

9   Foster, 90.

10   Foster, 95.

11   Foster, 75.

12   *Time* Magazine (June 19, 1989): www.time.com/time/magazine/article/0,9171,957941,00.html.

13   Foster, 142.

14   Jack Gorman, *Père Murray and the Hounds* (Hanna: Gorman, 1977), 108.

15 Their findings are published in the National Bureau of Economic Research Working Paper No. 12123, March 2006.

16 Chris Vander Doelen (Windsor, Ontario: CanWest News Service, October 9, 2007).

17 Isaac Mangena, Agence France-Presse, *Calgary Herald* (July 19, 2007).

18 Dawn Walton, *Globe and Mail* (June 30, 2007).

19 *Globe and Mail* (September 28, 2006).

20 *Globe and Mail* (June 14, 2006).

21 See Katherine Dedyna's "Loneliness Can Take Toll on Health," *Victoria Times Colonist* (August 30, 2007).

22 "Loneliness Linked to Alzheimer's," quoted in the *Calgary Herald* (February 8, 2007).

23 Quoted by Luke Layfield and Tamara McLean of the *Daily Telegraph* (May 8, 2007).

24 *Ibid.*

25 www.washingtonpost.com/wp-dyn/content/article/2006/06/15/AR2006061501300.html.

26 http://money.cnn.com/magazines/fortune/fortune_archive/198 6/09/29/68098/index.htm.

27 Alexander Green, "How to Find the Roadmap to Spiritual Wealth," special publication (Oxford Club Investment, April 4, 2008).

28 www.investmentu.com/IUEL/2008/February/sir-john-templeton.html.

29 www.newsmaxstore.com/newsletters/fir/reports/FIR_16_Templeton.htm.

30 *Globe and Mail* (March 22, 2008).

31 *Calgary Herald* (March 2, 2008).

32 www.fraserinstitute.org/COMMERCE.WEB/product_files/Generosity.pdf.

33 www.intelius.com/corp/news.html?ShowID=04-11-07.

34 www.corporateturnaroundcentre.com/business_blog/.

35 David Olive, *Toronto Star* (May 11, 2007): www.thestar.com/News/article/190677.

36 *Calgary Herald* (July 6, 2007).

37 www.ohranch.com/cattle.html.

38 www.thecattle.net/ken-stiles-memorial.htm.

39 www.rootsweb.ancestry.com/~abarchiv/foothills/pubspitz.txt.

40 *Calgary Herald* (September 14, 1990).

ACKNOWLEDGEMENTS

Acknowledgements usually begin with a list of helpful people. These must start by giving full credit to one remarkable man: Calgary businessman Rod Blair, who has contributed enormously to every aspect of the book by providing extra research, interviewing and re-interviewing friends and colleagues of Doc Seaman, editing the text with a sharp eye, and, on many occasions, providing fascinating new content. Rod, who did nothing less than voluntarily assume the multiple roles of copy editor, content editor, researcher, and, in the end, collaborator in the preparation of the manuscript. After writing or co-writing seven books, I have never encountered anyone remotely as devoted to a project as Rod has been to this one, simply because he believes the story of his friend Doc Seaman has continuing social and community value and must be told. He is correct; it is a fascinating, inspirational chronicle of achievement and generosity. Rod has also collaborated with Calgary photographer and graphic artist, Russell Moore, on the cover and photos pages that add to the book's visual appeal. So thank you, Rod Blair, for caring so deeply about the whole story, and every detail.

Many others need to be mentioned: the Honourable Peter Lougheed for writing the foreword and agreeing to be interviewed; Calgary Centre MP Lee Richardson, who helped me obtain other key interviews; Journalist Gord Jaremko for his notes and insights; Dr. David Bercuson, who met with Doc to discuss his war years; Jean Brown, Doc's executive assistant, for her cheery professionalism.

Also enormously helpful were hockey great Bill Hay, president and CEO of the Hockey Hall of Fame; Calgary Flames CEO Ken King; and many others from Canada's vigorous hockey world.

Clare McKeon in Toronto was a great help in the publication of the book as were the editorial and marketing people at Dundurn Group, especially Barry Jowett, Michael Carroll, and Beth Bruder. My heartfelt thanks, too, to Don Braid for his support of my manuscript and his awareness of all the trials along the way.

The book would be much less complete had I not enjoyed the full co-operation of Doc's family — including his brothers B.J. and Don Seaman, and his son Bob Seaman and daughter Diane Lefroy.

More than fifty people were interviewed at length for the book, including Doc Seaman, who made endless time available for conversations and interviews. My admiration for him, strong at the beginning, grew deeper over time. Some people are born to be models to others; he is one of them.

Index